ADVERTISING TO CHILDREN ON TV

CONTENT, IMPACT, AND REGULATION

ADVERTISING
TO CHILDREN ON TV

CONTENT, IMPACT, AND REGULATION

Barrie Gunter
Caroline Oates
and
Mark Blades
University of Sheffield, United Kingdom

LEA
2005

LAWRENCE ERLBAUM ASSOCIATES, PUBLISHERS
Mahwah, New Jersey   London

Lawrence Erlbaum Associates, Inc., Publishers
10 Industrial Avenue
Mahwah, New Jersey 07430

Cover design by Kathryn Houghtaling Lacey

Library of Congress Cataloging-in-Publication Data

Gunter, Barrie.
    Advertising to children on tv : content, impact, and regulation /
    Barrie Gunter, Caroline Oates, and Mark Blades.
        p. cm.
    Includes bibliographical references and index.
ISBN 0-8058-4488-0 (cloth : alk. paper)
1. Television advertising and children. 2. Advertising and children.
    I. Oates, Caroline.   II. Blades, Mark.   III. Title.
HQ784.T4G858   2004
302.23'45'083—dc22   2004043266
                                                           CIP

Books published by Lawrence Erlbaum Associates are printed on acid-
free paper, and their bindings are chosen for strength and durability.

Printed in the United States of America
10 9 8 7 6 5 4 3 2 1

Contents

Preface

This book examines research concerned with advertising to children on television. Its purpose is to establish the status of our knowledge about how children respond to advertising on television, how much the research evidence can be taken at face value, and the degree to which research can usefully inform regulation of advertising aimed at young viewers. It comes at a time when concern is growing about the effectiveness of television advertising regulation in light of technological developments in media. Such developments include the rapid growth of television channels that are available via a number of platforms—terrestrial, satellite, and cable—and that are being further facilitated through the transition of broadcasting from analogue to digital transmission.

Digitalization means not only more television channels for viewers to choose from but also greater scope for interactivity. This, in turn, may mean more power to consumers to select what to watch, when to watch, and how to watch. Concerns about increased volumes of advertising on burgeoning television channels and the use of more subtle forms of advertising that accompany greater commercialization of the television system (e.g., program sponsorship, product placement, program-related merchandising) have led to calls for tighter regulations governing televised advertising. This development is regarded as being especially necessary where children are concerned because their psychological immaturity as viewers and consumers leaves them more vulnerable to advertising influences.

Any move toward tightening restrictions upon advertising will create a tension with freedom of speech rights in democratic societies. To overrule freedom of speech (which includes freedom to advertise) rights, a legislator, regulator, or complainant will need to prove that harm is being done by commercial messages. Discussion of this issue has become particularly acute in debates surrounding moves to harmonize or even to standardize advertising-related regulations across national boundaries—such as in Europe. Some countries operate much tighter regulations than others over advertising to children on television, and finding common ground that satisfies all national partners' concerns about children and about the freedom for advertisers to reach consumers with promotional messages can be difficult.

Concern about advertising aimed at children on television represents part of a wider public debate about how much protection children need in a society where sources of information and entertainment are expanding and new communications technologies have facilitated greater access to content through a variety of platforms. In this environment, parents may find it increasingly difficult to control their children's media consumption, despite their willingness to assume such a responsibility. Hence, there may remain a need for centralized regulation and control over media content of all kinds. But what degree of regulation is needed to offer effective protection of children against misleading commercial messages and advertising treatments that may encourage potentially harmful behavior among young viewers? Within this context, how useful is research into children and advertising? Has it yielded findings that can be helpful in informing policy, regulation, codes of practice, and control implementation strategies?

The research reviewed in this book examines the content of advertising on television aimed at children, children's understanding of advertising, and the influence of advertising on young viewers. Research into children's comprehension of small-screen advertising has considered initial identification of advertisements as features of television separate from programs and has investigated more advanced understanding of the concept of persuasive intent. Researchers have used measures of attention to the screen, memory for content, and direct verbal comments on the nature of advertisements in the process of understanding more about children's and teenagers' abilities to comprehend advertising.

The influence of advertising can be differentiated into effects on knowledge and attitudes and effects on actual purchase choices and consumption behavior. Influence can also be divided into intended and unintended effects of advertising. As well as having an effect on product purchase and consumption, some advertising may have spin-off effects, shaping social values or influencing behavior beyond immediate purchase and use of the advertised product. Concerns have been voiced about advertising side effects on diet, alcohol, and tobacco consumption; drug taking; sexual behavior; and the wider health of children.

The authors have conducted their own research into children's understanding of television advertising that is continuing and will examine in particular the efficacy of certain regulations and codes of practice concerning advertising aimed at children. Hence, the book is informed by the latest research in the field.

In addition to providing a review of research into key areas such as understanding and influence, the book turns a critical eye on the nature of the methodologies used to investigate children and television advertising. Researchers have used a range of qualitative (e.g., focused interviews) and quantitative techniques (e.g., surveys and experiments). Each methodology has idiosyncratic advantages and limitations that need to be borne in mind when interpreting research findings. This level of analysis is necessary in the context of judging the value of research evidence in informing advertising regulation.

Finally, the book considers what research completed so far has revealed in terms of the sum total of our knowledge about television advertising and children. In looking to the future, it is important not just to consider how effective advertising regulations and codes of practice have been in the light of what is known from research. It is also essential to be mindful of the technological developments in television broadcasting and advertising. Will these developments engage young consumers differently and require a different form of advertising regulation? Can consumers be expected to have the ability to self-regulate? Will young consumers need help in understanding the nature and intent of advertising in a more dynamic and varied media and marketing environment?

—B.G., C.O., *and* M.B.
September 2003

1

The Issues About Television Advertising to Children

This chapter introduces the issues related to advertising aimed at children and describes the concerns that it generates. In particular, the debate about television advertising is discussed. This debate has raised many questions about the nature of advertising. Is it fair to advertise to children unless they fully understand the intent of the advertisers? If young children do not understand that intent, then when do they develop that ability? Is television an effective way to market products to children? Are the products (such as food and toys) typically aimed at children, the type of products that children should be encouraged to buy? Are children encouraged to buy or try unsuitable products (such as alcohol or tobacco) from viewing advertisements even when those advertisements are not aimed at them? Does advertising encourage a more materialistic attitude in children? Or is it appropriate that children learn to be effective consumers from an early age? Does encouraging children to buy products lead them to pester their parents and cause family disputes? Does television advertising present an accurate or misleading image of the world to children? Should advertising aimed at children be regulated? If so, how strict should that regulation be and, in a global market place, should regulators draw up common guidelines across different countries and cultures? Should we educate children about advertising, and if so, who should take on the role of educator?

All these questions have generated debate and research and will be discussed in this book. Given the controversial nature of television advertising aimed at children, this chapter discusses issues relating to television advertising and explains why they have become matters of concern. This book touches on the different concerns by way of introduction to the controversies that have been generated, and in doing so, it mentions the different points of view that have been put forward. None of the issues are straightforward because most involve a debate between those who accept or argue the economic importance of reaching the large children's market and those who believe that children need protecting from the effects of advertising in general or from the advertising of particular products. Nonetheless, most of the issues that have generated debate are open to empirical research, and the results from this research will be examined in more detail in the following chapters.

Children have spending power. Children 12 years or younger in the United States controlled the spending of $28 billion in 2000. This was spending from their own allowances and earnings. In addition, they influenced $250 billion of family spending. In the United States, the amount that children have to spend doubled between 1990 and 2000, and similar trends are found in European countries (Lawlor & Prothero, 2002). The figures for other countries are equally impressive. For instance, McNeal and Zhang (2000) estimated that only one fourth of Chinese children live in the main cities of China, but these children alone spend more than $6 billion of their own money and influence more than $60 billion of family spending.

Given these figures, the market for selling products to children is potentially immense, and it is not surprising that in those countries that have established traditions of advertising, much of that advertising is aimed at children, often via television and other media. Children and teenagers in the United Kingdom and in the United States may, on average, spend between four and five hours a day, outside school time, watching some form of electronic media (Cooke, 2002). In the course of that time, they will be exposed to a very large number of advertisements. Estimates of how many advertisements vary depending on the age of the child, the country in which they live, and the particular channels they watch. Kunkel (2001) suggested that contemporary children in the United States may view more than 40,000 advertisements every year, and Kunkel and Gantz (1992) found that more than 10 minutes of every hour of network U.S. television programs were given over to advertising material. The sheer number of advertisements means that many children spend a significant proportion of their lives watching advertising.

Marketers are particularly interested in how effective their advertising is in selling more products and establishing new markets. This includes finding ways to make existing media campaigns more effective within existing regulations or by campaigning to relax regulations (Curran & Richards, 2000). It might mean reaching children in different age groups—for example, reaching children younger than advertisers targeted in the past. The increase in popular programs (e.g., the BBC's *Teletubbies* in the U.K.) designed for very young children has opened up new opportunities for selling toys and associated material to ever younger age groups (Hind, 2003). The markets for such commodities can be global. Marketers may also exploit opening markets where advertising and marketing has been limited previously because as pointed out above, countries such as China have vast potential children's markets (O'Hanlon, 2000).

Advertising to children is, therefore, increasing, and despite new marketing approaches aimed at children, such as the Internet (Thomas & Dillenbeck, 2002; Thomson & Laing, 2003), the predominant way of advertising to children is via television. Television is an invasive medium because it reaches children in their own homes, and there is only limited control over the advertisements that are seen. Of course, children (and adults) may not always give their full attention to the screen during advertisement breaks because they can turn away or leave the room, but in practice, the viewer has the opportunity to see all the advertisements associated with any program they watch. Parents may restrict the channels that children view or the times that children watch television. But parental control is obviously weaker if children have access to television independent of their parents, and in the United Kingdom, two-thirds of children aged seven to 10 years have a television in their bedrooms. Three-quarters of children aged 11 to 14 years not only have a television in their own room but a third of that age group also have a video recorder that in effect allows them access to programs at any time (Smith, 2001).

The underlying concern about television advertising is whether it exploits children, and this exploitation is sometimes described in emotive terms with references to "seducers" (the marketers) and "innocents" (the children, particularly young children). In this context, advertising is seen negatively with the criticism that advertising persuades children to buy products they do not need and spend money they may not have (Young, 1990). Product advertising places an emphasis on possessions and on aspiring to a certain lifestyle (Hahlo, 1999). This is especially the case for branded products where the emphasis of the advertising is on purchasing not just a product but a product with a particular label, and as Weller (2002) found, children can recognize brands and logos before they can read.

Children's desire to possess products they have seen on television is said to lead to "pester power," which means that children pester their parents or other adults to buy things for them (Proctor & Richards, 2002). This can be at the level of children negotiating products during family shopping trips—often successfully from the child's perspective; Parker (2001) pointed out that U.K. parents spend, on average, £7 ($10) more when supermarket shopping with children than without them. Pester power can also be long term when children wage a campaign of requests and demands in advance of birthdays and Christmases. For instance, Crouch (1999) found that three quarters of children had started asking for Christmas presents before October. Children's pestering can lead to family conflicts when parents refuse to buy products either because they cannot afford to buy them, or because they believe them to be inappropriate for their children (e.g., snack foods), and this may lead to anger, frustration, and disappointment (Atkin, 1978). Such is the significance of children's influence in commodity purchasing, whether they purchase for themselves or through their parents, that marketers have increased the volume of research they conduct among young consumers. Specialist agencies conduct research even among preschool children (Swain, 2002).

Given the large number of television advertisements that children experience, children inevitably are aware of far more products than parents are able or willing to buy. But some marketers have argued that pester power is not a source of conflict but more the basis for child–parent negotiation about what to buy (Pilgrim & Lawrence, 2001). Others have pointed out that advertising may not always be the reason for children pestering parents. Proctor and Richards (2002) suggested that many toys sell well with little or no advertising at all because they become part of a popular "craze." For example, the Harry Potter range of toys, games, and foods were marketed following the success of the Harry Potter novels, but the books themselves became a success mainly because of word-of-mouth between children. Other marketing phenomena like Pokémon take on an existence of their own that goes well beyond any initial advertising (Proctor & Richards, 2002). According to this argument, therefore, children may well pester adults but not all such pestering is the direct result of advertising. We discuss the issue of pester power in chapter seven.

Critics have argued that advertising encourages children to view important social and religious events (such as Christmas) in purely commercial terms. For example, Pine and Nash (in press) asked children to write letters to Santa Claus listing what they wanted for Christmas. They found that the children who watched more television advertisements asked for more presents and that they asked for more presents by brand name. The pressure to buy particular brands leads to a conformity across different cultures (Byfield, 2002), and more generally, the international market for children's products detracts from local products and traditions.

An alternative way of considering these issues is to point out that the globalization of children's markets and the use of advertising means that children in different countries now have a greater choice of products. They are no longer limited to locally produced goods, and aspiring to the same brands implies a desire for certain standards and a conformity that is actually positive in a world that, in both the past and the present, has been divided by national, cultural, and religious conflicts. Eden (2000) suggested that selling the same products to children in different countries does not necessarily damage local traditions and practices. Eden pointed out that European countries have many different traditions relating to events such as Christmas, Easter, or Halloween, which all generate a market for selling to children. But the different traditions all overlie themes and beliefs that are held in common, and marketers address these common themes rather than the expression of them in a particular culture.

There are concerns about the advertising of particular products, particularly the promotion of food products (see, e.g., chaps. 2 and 8, this volume). A large proportion of advertisements aimed at children promote food or drinks. For instance, Lewis and Hill (1998) found that half the advertisements aimed at children on U.K. television concerned food. A third of these advertisements were for cereals, a third were for sweets and snacks, and most of the rest were for ready-made meals and other convenience foods. These are all products that have been criticized as being the less healthy food choices (Dalmeny, Hanna, & Lobstein, 2003). Such food advertising is one-sided because little television advertising aimed at children emphasizes healthy eating. This is because of the relative wealth of the advertisers who market food products and who can afford extensive advertising campaigns and those who advocate healthy eating but do not have the same resources available to convey their message (Conner & Armitage 2002). Few health campaigns could match the size and extent of the marketing that might go into selling a product such as a chocolate bar (see, e.g., Ellyatt, 1999b). The result is that children are exposed to a large number of television advertisements trying to persuade them to choose sweetened drinks and snack foods, with little emphasis on alternative, more healthy foods.

Children in some countries do not eat a balanced diet. For example, hardly any children in the United States meet recommended dietary requirements (Munoz, Krebs-Smith, Ballard-Barbash, & Cleveland, 1997). But it is not clear how far the failure to eat a well-balanced diet can be attributed to the effects of advertising. Children's recall of food advertisements correlates with what they ask for during shopping trips (Galst & White, 1976) and with what they eat (Hitchings & Moynihan, 1998), and so there is a relationship between advertising and eating choices, but the nature of that relationship is not always clear (Lewis & Hill 1998).

The number of children with obesity in the United States has dramatically increased in recent years, and this may in part be due to the persuasive nature of food advertising (Strasburger & Wilson, 2002). However, since the start of television advertising, the largest proportion of advertisements aimed at children has always been for food products (Young, 1990, 2003). For this reason, marketers have pointed out that the proportion of food advertising is unlikely to be the only or the main factor in the recent growth in obesity. Other changes in lifestyle, such as lack of exercise, increased use of cars, sedentary occupations (including more time spent watching television and playing computer games), and different family eating habits (such as a dependency on convenience foods), may all be factors in the increase in children's weight (Lvovich, 2003).

Advertisers could also point to the fact that children receive information about nutrition through other sources (such as school) and should be aware of healthy eating practices. Some have argued that the best way to market food to children is by stressing healthy eating and by including nutritional information that complements other sources of that information (Strong, 1999). Indeed, Reece, Rifon, and Rodriguez (1999) found that most cereal advertisements included nutritional information, but this usually consisted only of statements that the food was part of a balanced breakfast or brief details of a specific nutrient such as vitamin C. Other food advertisements were less likely to include nutritional information. The use of nutritional information can be viewed as either a positive addition to food advertisements or just a marketing strategy; it also raises the issue of how well children understand and interpret such information.

Other television advertisements such as advertisements for toys may be less controversial than food advertising because toys do not have the same sort of health implications. Nonetheless, specific issues are associated with toy advertisements. For instance, parents may be concerned that toys are presented in an unrealistic or inaccurate way. In many countries, regulations or guidelines prohibit advertisers from making exaggerated claims about the properties of the toys being advertised (see chap. 9). Such rules might include presenting the toy in a context that shows its true size or making it clear how the toy is operated (e.g., by hand or by a power source). Advertisers may also be encouraged to say whether a toy needs to be assembled and, if so, whether an adult's help is required. The issues here relate to how conscientiously advertisers adhere to any guidelines and, even if they do, whether children understand the disclosures associated with advertisements. For example, Muehling and Kolbe (1999) found that although many advertisements aimed at children included visual statements (usually in small print) disclosing information about a product, such statements were presented so briefly that they required, on average, a reading speed of 160 words per minute. But even if children can read such statements, whether they can understand them is not clear (Liebert, Sprafkin, Liebert, & Rubinstein, 1977).

As well as seeing advertisements for products that are aimed specifically at them, children may also see advertisements for other products—ones that cause concern, such as alcohol, tobacco, and medicines (Strasburger, 2001). The frequency of advertisements for such products depends on national regulations. For instance, tobacco advertising on television is not permitted in several countries, but children may well see brand names in programs that include sports sponsored by tobacco companies (Sparks, 1999). The effects of advertising such products might vary. Kunkel (2001) referred to the research into the influence of U.S. advertisements for medicine and concluded that such advertising had little effect on children's beliefs about the effectiveness of different brands.

However, advertising other products might affect children and adolescents. This may be particularly the case when advertising associates products with lifestyles that are attractive to young people (Gunter & McAleer, 1997). Evidence shows that alcohol advertising does effect young people's brand preference (even before they are regular drinkers) and that young people's expectancies about alcohol are partly influenced by alcohol advertising (Grube & Wallack 1994). Not only might children see alcohol advertising that is aimed at adults, but some alcohol campaigns, using animated characters and catchphrases, often seem to be aimed at the youth market. In the same way, researchers have shown that tobacco sponsorship on television affects adolescents' recall of cigarette brands (Hoek, Gendall, & Stockdale, 1993) and some cigarette advertisers have been accused of deliberately targeting young people in their advertising campaigns (Fox, Krugman, Fletcher, & Fischer, 1999). But despite the influence of tobacco and alcohol advertising on young people, it is difficult to separate the effects of specific advertising and the effects of portraying these products positively in most television broadcasting. As Gunter and McAleer (1997) pointed out, alcohol drinking is frequently shown in positive contexts including celebrations, parties, and eating out. In contrast, the negative effects of drinking, such as drunkenness or ill health, are depicted much less often. Even though several countries now limit the portrayal of cigarette smoking on television, older programs and films often show smoking as a common and acceptable social habit, and few programs refer to the negative effects of tobacco. In these ways, alcohol and tobacco are more often than not shown in a positive and attractive light even when they are not being specifically advertised.

There are also concerns about the way that products are presented to children. Advertisers naturally want to present their products in the most appealing way, and this might mean, for example, using celebrities to endorse a product. This can increase children's liking for a product (Ross et al., 1984), but inevitably raises issues about children's ability to realize that the celebrity is being paid for the endorsement and may, therefore, not be providing an objective recommendation. More generally, the use of popular characters (whether real or fictional) from children's programs may make it difficult for children to distinguish between advertisements and programs (Wilson & Weiss, 1992). The blurring of the program/advertisement distinction might be to the advantage of advertisers, especially in an age when some programs are so closely linked to products that the program itself becomes a vehicle for merchandising. For example, in the United Kingdom the BBC is a "noncommercial" channel but derives a large income from the sale of children's toys and games based on BBC programs that have been specifically designed to include products aimed at children (Hind, 2003). But if blurring the distinction between programs and advertisements makes it harder for children to recognize when they are being targeted by marketers, this could be seen as a negative change in children's television.

Marketers reinforce stereotypes when they use idealized images to promote products. For example, the family structure in many western countries has changed, and many contemporary children have very different family lifestyles from children of a generation ago (Hahlo, 1999). But this change is hardly reflected in advertising to children. De Chenecey (1999) argued that although a few television advertisements include atypical families and single parents, most portray happy nuclear families in which "mums use washing powder and dads use power tools" (p. 336). More generally, women in advertisements tend to be shown in the home and in family roles, and men are more often shown outside the home and have a wider variety of roles, especially more authoritative ones (Fox 1996). Though such families do not represent the experience of all children, there remains a lack of nontraditional families and ethnic minority families in advertising (De Chenecey, 1999).

Stereotyping can be harmful. To give one example, marketers use physically attractive people to advertise products (Downs & Harrison, 1985). According to Martin, Gentry, and Hill (1999), the use of attractive models may be based on the idea that people who are physically attractive are often believed to have other positive qualities, including intelligence, competence, integrity, potency, and concern for other people (Eagly, Ashmore, Makhaijani, & Longo, 1991). Therefore advertising a product using physically attractive models may help it to become linked to the other qualities that the viewer associates with physical beauty. However, using beautiful models in advertising can generate unachievable stereotypes.

Martin et al. (1999) found that magazine advertisements that included attractive models had the most influence on girls who had a poor body image themselves. On one hand, this means that such advertisements are effective vehicles for selling products, particularly to a group who may see some of those products as a way to improve their self-image. On the other hand, girls with poor body image may be especially vulnerable to images of physical beauty they view in advertisements. Such advertising may reinforce the pressures on young people to conform to ideals of beauty that are hard or impossible to achieve. As Connor and Armitage (2002) pointed out, there has been an "epidemic" of dieting over the last few decades and includes primary school children (Hill, Oliver, & Rogers, 1992). This, in turn, leads to the marketing of diet products, which although usually aimed at an older market, may also appeal to young children if they aspire to a particular body image. Though these aspirations may not be derived originally from images in advertisements, (because stereotypical images exist across all aspects of the media), advertisements can reinforce those stereotypes in some children and young people (Martin et al., 1999). The issue of stereotyping is discussed in more detail in chapters 2 and 7.

Young children are thought to be particularly vulnerable to advertising because they know less about the intent of advertisers and the process of creating an advertisement (Oates, Blades, Gunter, & Don, 2003). The assumption is that adults are less likely to be vulnerable to advertisements because they are aware that the purpose of advertising is to persuade people to buy products. Adults appreciate that advertisements are deliberately created to present products as attractively as possible and that the advertising message will be biased. Adults also understand who pays for and produces advertisements and that advertising is part of an economic system that depends on selling products. If adults have this level of understanding, we can assume that they are not likely to be unfairly influenced by television advertising. Advertising does influence adults (otherwise marketers would not spend money on it), but adults are well able to interpret the messages in the context of the advertisers' intentions. If adults are persuaded to buy products, their awareness of advertising prevents them from being unfairly exploited. Obviously, children are not born with any knowledge of economic systems; their awareness of advertising and marketing develops only gradually (Gunter & Furnham, 1998). An important issue therefore is establishing the age when children achieve a mature understanding of advertisements. There has been little agreement about this age, and the research into this issue is addressed in chapters three and four.

The age of understanding has been much debated because it has many implications (Oates, Blades, & Gunter, 2002). If children do not fully understand the intent of television advertising, they may need "protecting" from those advertisements. Such protection may take the form of restricting the number, type, or content of advertisements, or it might mean banning advertisements altogether (see chap. 9). In some countries, there may be selective bans on particular products; for example, in Greece, toy advertising is banned at certain times. Countries such as Belgium and Australia limit advertising within children's programs or within a few minutes of those programs, and Sweden bans all terrestrial television advertising aimed at children younger than 12 years of age. Countries such as the United Kingdom have a detailed code of practice to regulate advertisements aimed at children (ITC, 1991a). The range of regulations in different countries reflects different beliefs about children's understanding. This divergence of views has serious implications for any attempt to standardize regulations across countries. For example, in 2001, Sweden proposed a Europe-wide ban on television advertising to children. Not surprising, this provoked much debate, and opposition, especially from marketers in countries that have less restrictive regulations than Sweden.

Parents usually express concern about television advertising. Young, de Bruin, and Eagle (2003) asked parents in the United Kingdom, Sweden, and New Zealand about their attitudes toward advertising. Young et al. found that many parents were concerned about the number of advertisements that children see, especially as they believed that children might be encouraged to want products they did not really need. Parents also felt that advertising led children to pester their parents to buy things for them and that young children might not fully understand the intent of advertising. Although there were some variations in responses between the different countries, many concerns were similar. Young et al. also asked parents in the United Kingdom and Sweden whether they would like stronger or weaker regulations about television advertising, and a large majority in both countries said they would prefer stronger regulations. Though Sweden regulates advertising more strictly than the United Kingdom, parents in Sweden wanted even stronger regulations. As Eagle and de Bruin (2001) pointed out, such findings pressure governments to increase the regulation of advertising aimed at children.

Advertisers usually argue against any extension of regulations for a combination of reasons. Some marketers just claim that very young children, even from the age of three years, have some understanding of advertising (Bowen, 2000). Others emphasize studies that have shown that young children can recognize particular aspects of marketing. For example, preschoolers can recognize some brand logos (Dammler & Middelmann-Motz, 2002), and they can distinguish between television advertisements and programs (Bijmolt, Claassen, & Brus, 1998). These studies are sometimes quoted as evidence of young children's awareness. However, as chapter three explains, children's recognition of advertisements is not the same as children understanding their persuasive intent—a realization that may develop much later. Given the gradual development of children's awareness of advertising, much debate about regulation hinges on what is meant by "understanding" (Goldstein, 1999). Marketers naturally put more emphasis on early recognition as evidence that children are aware of advertisements, and critics place more emphasis on children achieving a full understanding of advertisers' intentions at a later age. How advertising is defined and which studies are quoted have resulted in a variety of conclusions about at what age regulation is necessary to protect children.

Some authors have argued that advertising has little effect on children and have suggested that current regulations (for example in the U.K.) are more than sufficient (Furnham, 2000). As pointed out earlier, many children's products do sell well without being advertised, and therefore marketers have argued that social fashions and peer pressure may be the most important factors in creating the desire to buy products (Proctor & Richards, 2002). Advertising is only one factor in creating demand (Goldstein, 1999), but it is disingenuous to imply that advertising is ineffective. Advertisers do spend large sums of money on television advertising, and marketing communications aimed at children such as marketing via the Internet (Clarke, 2002), text messaging (Jones, 2002), and marketing via schools (Geuens, De Pelsmacker, & Mast, 2002) is rapidly expanding. Such initiatives demonstrate marketers' desire to reach as many children as possible.

Marketers sometimes use the phrase "getting older younger" (Cohen & Cahill, 1999), which refers to the idea that toys and other products traditionally associated with a particular age group are now being bought by or for younger children. There is little doubt that children and young people are adopting fashions, activities, and lifestyles at an earlier age than in the past (Smith, 2001), and therefore the concept of "getting older younger" has validity in terms of marketing the same products to younger children. This phrase, however, has sometimes been confused with the idea that children themselves are developing more quickly. For instance, Cohen and Cahill (1999) argued that children's cognitive development is now more rapid than in previous generations. If young children now have more developed cognitive abilities, the implication is that their understanding of advertising intent might be more sophisticated at an earlier age and therefore regulation is less necessary. As Hastings (2000) pointed out, there is no evidence that children's cognitive development is any more rapid now than it ever was. There is therefore no reason to believe that contemporary young children have greater insights into the nature of advertising than their predecessors had.

Furnham (2000) argued that rather than extend regulations, the most effective way to help children understand advertising is through their parents. He suggested that by discussing products, parents can inform children about the nature of advertising, and he gave examples of games and strategies that parents could use to help their children understand more about advertisements. Furnham said that further regulation and "banning advertising of any sort shelters or at least delays a child's understanding and decision making. It can be no substitute for parental guidance. The responsibility for educating children into the economic world cannot and indeed should not be removed from their parents" (p. 51).

Although Furnham (2000) may be correct to stress the role of parents in teaching their children about advertisements, relying on parents alone can be limited. As children become more independent viewers with access to their own televisions and videos (see earlier discussion), parents have less control over what children watch and less opportunity to discuss advertisements that might have been seen during family viewing. Parents can still explain the nature of marketing and purchasing when children request products or during shopping trips, but this assumes that parents have the appropriate skills for doing so and that they can judge their children's level of understanding. When we discussed advertising with parents of young children, we found that some parents overestimate children's understanding, and therefore they may not always realize the need for intervention. Indeed, parents themselves often lack sufficient knowledge of regulators and their regulatory responsibilities. For instance, more people in the United Kingdom believed that the Advertising Standards Authority (responsible for nonbroadcast advertising) was responsible for broadcast advertising on television than the Independent Television Commission (23% vs. 9%), despite the fact that the latter had had jurisdiction over television advertising for the previous 10 years (Towler, 2003).

Another way to increase children's understanding of advertising is through school education, and media courses designed for young children often include activities to increase advertising awareness (Craggs, 1992). These activities can be effective ways to encourage children to learn about the nature of marketing, but in the United Kingdom, pressures on primary school curriculum mean that time spent on topics such as advertising might be limited, and courses on advertising require resources and time to prepare. However, a group of U.K. companies that advertise to children have produced a teaching resource for teachers of children up to 10 years of age (Media Smart, 2003), which provides video and paper resources for teachers to use in the classroom to introduce young children to different issues related to advertising. These include issues such as comparing similar products, thinking about product information, discussing slogans, designing advertisements, and planning an advertising campaign. The Media Smart package is designed with reference to different age groups and is linked to the U.K. national curriculum. As such, it offers teachers a useful resource, but its effectiveness for helping children to understand advertising has yet to be independently assessed.

None of the issues discussed in this chapter are independent of each other. Only some companies can afford the cost of television advertising, and they have to decide which products to advertise and how those products should be presented. These decisions depend on marketing and economic considerations. These considerations, in turn, depend on reaching an audience of children who might see, remember, and be encouraged to buy (or ask someone else to buy) a product that they have seen advertised. For this reason, marketers need to understand the psychological development of children and the research into that development to know the most effective ways to address their customers. What children are allowed to watch, however, depends on national regulations about what it is reasonable to advertise to children and what might be harmful to them. These regulations are based on cultural assumptions about the nature of childhood (Young et al., 2003) and cultural beliefs about at what age children can understand the purpose of advertising (see chaps. 3 and 4). Such assumptions will themselves be influenced by the results from research into children's development in general, and the research into advertising in particular.

Thus, in any decision making about marketing to children or regarding suggestions made about limiting that marketing, one of the most influential factors is research that has been carried out with children. The remainder of this book summarizes that research, discusses interpretations of the research, and considers its implications for marketing and its implications for policy and regulation.

2

The Nature of Advertising to Children

A large amount of children's television viewing consists of programs aimed at an adult audience, and therefore much of the advertising children see is intended for adults. However, because children are not so interested in products for adults, they are less likely to pay attention to them. Thus, research on advertising and children has focused on commercials designed specifically for the child audience. These advertisements are most likely to attract children's interest and affect their behavior (Kunkel, 2001).

Many common assumptions are made about advertising to children, particularly in terms of the products most frequently advertised and in relation to issues of food, stereotyping, and the possibly misleading techniques advertisers use. Recently, other forms of promotion such as sponsorship and merchandising have become increasingly frequent, although there is as yet less research on these from the perspective of children's understanding compared with traditional television advertising. In this chapter, the nature of advertising to children is explored, looking at these new developments but also investigating more traditional concerns. Important issues such as food and stereotyping in advertising are introduced here, and their implications for children are addressed in more detail in chapter eight. First, the general nature of advertising to children is explored, focusing on the product ranges most frequently advertised.

FOCUS ON A NARROW PRODUCT RANGE

One of the main areas of research in children's television advertising is the actual nature of that advertising, that is, the products that feature in the commercials and whether there is a bias toward particular categories or ranges of products. Parents, for example, might stress the number of toy advertisements on television, especially in the run up to Christmas (Piachaud, 1998). Organizations such as the Food Standards Agency in Britain are more concerned with the quantity of advertising that features sugary or fatty foods that might conceivably affect children's dietary habits. Some research has been undertaken to determine exactly what is being advertised and to what extent advertising is weighted to certain products. Much of this research has focused on food, which will be discussed later, but in general, researchers appear to agree on the broad categories of products advertised.

In the early 1990s, Pecora found that toy advertisements accounted for almost 30% of Saturday morning commercials on U.S. television (Pecora, 1998). Barcus (1980), in a series of content analyses of American television, found that the staples of children's advertising consisted of four product categories: toys, cereals, candies, and fast-food restaurants. Food advertisements overall accounted for 60% of commercials, and of these, 70% were for highly sugared and fatty foods such as cereals, confectionery, cake, and cookies. Barcus's findings are corroborated by other researchers who have identified similar product categories (Alexander, Benjamin, Hoerrner, & Roe, 1999; Gamble & Cotugna, 1999; Kunkel & Gantz, 1992; Lewis & Hill, 1998).

Many of the studies on the nature of children's advertising have been undertaken in the United States. Young (1990), however, carried out a British study in the 1980s funded by the Health Education Council and prompted by concern over children's dental health. The nature of food advertising, in particular sugary foods, was investigated to discover the kind of advertising shown to children and the rhetorical devices used to promote products. Young recorded commercials on a terrestrial channel, focusing on the times when children were the main audience and programs specifically directed at children. From a total of 1,750 commercials, a third were for food products, and of these, a third were for sugared foods. Additional qualitative analysis of 58 of the commercials aimed at children was carried out to define them according to 28 specific features, for example, product, duration, animation, action, humor, metaphor, and fantasy. Using factor analysis, Young then investigated the pattern of relationships between the variables that contributed to the style or rhetoric of the advertisements, concluding that it was possible to separate out certain rhetorical variables from product or brand information and thus identify particular clusters of elements common in children's advertising.

Kunkel and Gantz (1992) pointed out that since the 1970s and 1980s, when much of the research on the nature of advertising to children was carried out, the television environment has changed. No longer restricted to terrestrial television, children now have access to cable and satellite channels, all of which have different profiles for advertisers. Kunkel and Gantz content analyzed 600 hours of children's programming over three channel types—broadcast networks, independent stations, and cable channels. Products advertised were grouped into six categories that included toys, cereals/breakfast foods, sugared snacks/drinks, fast foods, healthy foods/drinks, and other. They found different patterns for each channel, as toy advertisements were more numerous on independent stations; snacks and drinks featured heavily on broadcast networks; and the cable channels had more advertisements in other categories, reflecting the widest range of products/services (e.g., recreation, amusement parks, videotapes). Broadcast networks had the most advertising, with an average of ten minutes per hour. Overall, two of the six product groups (toys and cereals/breakfast foods) accounted for more than half of the advertisements observed in Kunkel and Gantz's study. Adding a third group (sugared snacks/drinks) accounted for nearly three-fourths of all commercials during children's programs.

The time before Christmas has been subject to particular critical scrutiny by commentators who argue that children and parents are exposed to more and more pressure from advertisers competing to be the next big toy or brand in children's Christmas stockings (Piachaud, 1998). With an average of £250 spent in the United Kingdom on Christmas presents for each child, the potential rewards for marketers are huge (Piachaud, 1998). In a content analysis of British television, Young (1990) found that advertisements for toys dominated Saturday morning television and their share increased to 75% during the pre-Christmas period. According to Barcus (1980), toy commercials comprised more than half of the advertisements directed at children in the October-November pre-Christmas season. At this time, toy advertising uses different appeals to those evident during other months—the "newness" of products is emphasized compared with the usual focus on appearance, action, or the fun nature of the product. The success of this appeal is evident in children's letters to Father Christmas, where children specifically name brands in their requests for particular presents (O'Cass & Clarke, 2002).

Overall, children's advertisements focus on a narrow product range, with toys, breakfast cereals, and confectionery being the most frequently advertised. However, much of the research in this area is rather dated, and most of it originates in one country (the U.S.). It would be useful to investigate the nature of children's advertising in today's media-rich environment to compare with the older studies. With reference to the content of advertising, however, a wealth of recent studies from several countries on advertisements for food is available and these will be discussed next.

THE NATURE OF FOOD ADVERTISING

Food advertising aimed at children has been studied in the United States for more than 30 years (Gamble & Cotugna, 1999). In the 1970s, there was concern over food advertisements, with calls to ban advertising for products that contained over a certain amount of sugar and at the same time to encourage advertisers to sponsor advertisements for healthy messages (Ward, 1978). The consistent finding has been that food advertisements are for products containing high amounts of sugar and fat. Gamble and Cotugna also claim that a link between television viewing and obesity has been documented as a correlation exists between number of hours viewed and the consumption of advertised foods. In a content analysis of children's Saturday morning television, Gamble and Cotugna (1999) examined 350 commercials and found that two thirds were for food products. The most frequently advertised product on Saturday morning television was sugary cereal, accounting for 34.5% of total food advertisements. The proportion of advertisements for sugary cereals compared with low-sugar cereal products was nearly 20 to 1. A typical children's meal in the advertisements consisted of a cheeseburger, french fries, a fizzy drink, and a toy. Overall, the majority of food advertising aimed at children promoted a high-fat, low-fiber diet (see chap. 8).

The focus of research on health and advertising rests on the perceived imbalance between the foods advertised to children and the nutritional intake recommendations in dietary guidelines (de Bruin & Eagle, 2002). It is known that food advertising is weighted toward particular categories and that healthy options are by comparison rarely advertised. According to Kunkel and Gantz (1992), healthy foods represent only 2.8% of all advertising to children. In monetary terms, the National Heart Forum (1996) suggested that about £3 million is spent on advertising fresh fruits, vegetables, and nuts in the United Kingdom, compared with more than £70 million on advertising chocolate confectionery.

Lewis and Hill (1998) found a clear bias toward unhealthy food in children's advertisements in the United Kingdom. A content analysis of 800 advertisements showed that half of the advertisements were for food products and that three product categories together (food, toys, and entertainment) accounted for two thirds of all advertisements. Food advertising made up about two thirds of all advertisements during peak children's viewing time, and the majority of these advertisements were for foods high in fat, sugar, or

salt. Such foods, which should contribute very little to the average diet, actually account for most of all food advertising on children's television.
Hitchings and Moynihan (1998) also found a particular bias toward certain
products, namely breakfast cereals, and reported that such cereals are the
advertisements that children most frequently remember.

Lewis and Hill (1998) also explored the influence of food advertising on
the self-perception of overweight children. One hundred and three children
aged nine years were shown specially prepared videos featuring advertisements inserted into a Rugrats cartoon. Half the children saw advertisements
for food, while the other children watched advertisements for nonfood
products. Prior to viewing the cartoon, all the children completed a self-report measure designed to evaluate self-perception and had their weight and
height measured. After watching the video featuring food advertisements,
the overweight children felt healthier in comparison with the other children
and in comparison with their own response to the nonfood advertisements.
These effects were opposite to those the experimenters expected. They
pointed out, however, that the study demonstrated an interaction between
the type of advertisement shown and some feature of the viewer, a finding
worthy of further investigation. Atkin (1980) also found a relation between
children and food advertisements, as heavy viewers of such advertisements
were twice as likely as light viewers to consider sugared cereals and candies
as highly nutritious.

In addition to food advertisements promoting certain products and
brands, advertising also performs another function—it provides information about product use. Connor and Armitage (2002) noted that advertising
communicates certain messages about when, where, and with whom particular food items should be consumed. For children's advertising, this often
takes the form of making mealtimes fun to induce a positive shift in attitude
and mood. Connor and Armitage suggested that to achieve this, marketers
use techniques that focus on the peripheral route to persuasion, that is,
branding, exposure, role models, repetition, and reinforcement, all tools
that suit the medium of television. In contrast, health promotion messages
from government departments take the central route to persuasion, which
relies on a rational, cognitive approach using evidence and strong arguments, often communicated via printed material rather than broadcast media. The use of certain techniques to appeal to and possibly mislead children
about products is discussed in more detail later in this chapter.

De Bruin and Eagle (2002) questioned parents in New Zealand about
children's advertising and found high levels of agreement to sentences that
stated there is too much fat and sugar in food products advertised during
television programs aimed at children. According to a British survey, over
half the advertisements on children's television are for food (National Heart

Forum, 1996). Children in the United Kingdom and United States are exposed to about 10 food commercials for every hour of television, and the majority of these advertisements are for sweets, fast food, sugary drinks, and sweetened breakfast cereals (Revill, 2002).

In contrast to the above negative implications for children's advertising, a study by Dickinson (2000) considered food advertising in a slightly different context. He investigated the food choices of 11- to 18-year-olds, with reference to the role of television. He suggested that the narrow focus on advertising is rather misleading. In a content analysis of a composite two-week block of television output recorded over six weeks, Dickinson found that more than half the references to food appear in programs. There is undoubtedly a large amount of food on television, with an average of 10 references to food in every broadcast hour that includes four food advertisements. The balance of food types featured in programs and advertisements is the interesting result: In programs, the most common food group is fruit and vegetables; in advertising, it is fatty and sugary foods. Dickinson suggested that there is good reason to suppose that television programs, as well as advertisements, have a key role to play in food choices.

The media coverage of food advertising to children and possible health implications is usually critical of the marketing tactics that advertisers employ. Childhood obesity is increasing—in the United Kingdom, one in five of all nine-year-olds is overweight and one in 10 is obese, figures that have doubled in the last 20 years (Revill, 2002). The United Kingdom's Food Standards Agency investigates the promotional activities carried out by the food industry and how these are linked to children's eating habits. In the meantime, aggressive marketing tactics used to sell junk food have been singled out as unfairly exploiting children's desires, with particular attention paid to advertisements in the United States for Pepsi, McDonald's Happy Meals, and Spiderman cereal.

Other analyses of the nature of children's food advertising have focused on the patterns of thematic content. An advertisement, in as little as 30 seconds or less, can construct a complex story, often around quite sophisticated themes. Rajecki et al. (1994) analyzed nearly 100 food advertisements aimed at children and reported that the most common theme to emerge was that of violence, followed by conflict, achievement, mood alteration, enablement, trickery, and product dependence. A cluster analysis revealed groupings of themes, with two thirds of the advertisements characterized by some combination of violence, conflict, and trickery. Rajecki et al. defined these themes as antisocial, compared with the remaining themes that might conceivably be viewed more positively. Their explanation for the presence of the three antisocial themes related to the fact that conflict and violence are central to much of children's television programming, and therefore similar themes in advertising merely present children with familiar concepts. They also pointed out that very young children use trickery (or deception) and so hypothetically would have little trouble in understanding it in advertising.

TECHNIQUES USED TO MISLEAD CHILDREN ABOUT PRODUCTS

Children are targeted just as any other market, and, like adults, are subject to particular techniques used by advertisers to enhance their brands. As discussed in chapter three, young children are trusting of commercials, and it is possible to accuse advertisers of being unfair in taking advantage of this trusting outlook. The Independent Television Commission, regulator of television advertising in the United Kingdom, specifically mentions misleadingness in an effort to control advertisers' use of techniques that make it difficult for children to judge the true size, action, performance, or construction of a toy (see chap. 9). Areas of concern include exaggeration, fantasy, particular appeals, celebrities, use of metaphors, and special effects.

Exaggeration

General concern about misleading tactics that advertisers employ is centered on the use of exaggeration or puffery. Consumer protection groups and parents believe that children are largely ill equipped to recognize such techniques and that often exaggeration is used at the expense of brand information (Bandyopadhyay, Kindra, & Sharp, 2001). Claims such as "the best," or "better than" can be subjective and misleading; even adults may be unsure as to their meaning. Barcus (1980) pointed out that these attributed qualities represent the advertiser's opinions about the qualities of the product or brand and, as a consequence, are difficult to verify. Disclaimers/disclosures may offset such exaggerations, but research has shown that children often have difficulty in understanding these. Comstock, Chaffee, Katzman, McCombs, and Roberts (1978) suggested that less than a quarter of children aged between six and eight years old understood standard disclaimers used in many toy advertisements and that disclaimers are more readily comprehended when presented in both audio and visual formats. Kunkel and Gantz (1992) found that although disclaimers were common in advertisements for breakfast cereals ("part of a balanced breakfast"), they were mainly presented in audio format only. In addition, Barcus (1980, p. 279) pointed out that children may interpret the phrase "part of a balanced breakfast" to mean that the cereal is required as a *necessary* part of a balanced breakfast.

Fantasy

The use of fantasy is one of the more common techniques in advertising that could possibly mislead a young audience. Child-oriented advertisements are more likely to include magic and fantasy than advertisements aimed at adults. In a content analysis of Canadian television, Kline (1993) observed that nearly all character toy commercials featured fantasy play. Bandyopadhyay et al. (2001) pointed out that children have strong imaginations and the use of fantasy brings their ideas to life, but children may not be adept enough to realize what they are viewing is unreal. Fantasy situations and settings are frequently used to attract children's attention, particularly in food advertising (Barcus, 1980; Lewis & Hill, 1998). Advertisements for cereals have, for many years, been found to be especially fond of fantasy techniques, with almost nine out of 10 including such content (Barcus, 1980).

On U.K. television, many advertisements for confectionery use fantasy techniques, a good example being the Bassett's and Beyond series of advertisements. Here, an animated young character, Ben and his dog Barkley, have several adventures in a fantasyland where the landscape is constructed from Bassett's products (chews, sherbet, lollipops). The way to enter this land is through a sweet shop where a choice has to be made about which Bassett's product to purchase. Entering the magical world of Bassett's and Beyond helps Ben to make up his mind as he and Barkley try lots of different sweets. Extensive pre- and posttesting was carried out before this commercial was finalized and broadcast on television, as Bassett's wanted both mothers and children not only to understand and like the advertising but also to recall the brand and the specific products. Focus groups were undertaken separately with girls, boys, and mothers to ensure the level of fantasy was seen as exciting rather than dangerous and to check that children could relate to the animated figures of the child and dog. As a campaign, the fantasy advertisements were successful, leading to an increase in both awareness and purchase (J. Ellyatt, 1999).

Generally, there is uncertainty as to whether very young children can distinguish fantasy and reality in advertising. Certainly, rational appeals in advertising aimed at children are limited as most advertisements use emotional and indirect appeals to psychological states or associations (Barcus, 1980; Rajecki et al., 1994).

Appeals

The range of appeals advertisers use can be broadly categorized into a small number of main themes according to Kunkel and Gantz (1992). They identified three "pitches" commonly used in children's advertising: fun/happiness, taste/flavor/smell, and product performance. These accounted for the most prevalent themes in almost two thirds of all advertising to children. Each theme was closely aligned with a particular product category; for example, product performance was most often associated with toy commercials, fun/happiness with fast food, and taste/flavour/smell with breakfast cereals. Interestingly, the theme of fun/happiness was also the predominant approach for the promotion of healthy food products, whereas health/nutrition appeals were rarely employed. This suggests that advertising for healthy food has adopted a similar approach to the one used by fast food, possibly because this has been such a successful approach for the latter. Connor and Armitage (2002), however, suggested that healthy products are often promoted using a more rational appeal. This contrast in findings between the two studies might be due to differences in U.K. and U.S. advertising practices and also to the tradition that government messages about nutrition are likely to be framed in an educational style, whereas other agencies might adopt more subtle promotional strategies. Lewis and Hill (1998) pointed out that food advertisements in general are more likely to use animation, stories, humor, and the promotion of fun compared with other product ranges. Barcus (1980) found that the fun appeal was used in at least 70% of advertisements for food.

Marketers are aware that advertising will be more successful if they can appeal both to children and their parents. Advertisers encourage children to view products such as toys as fun, whereas parents are approached via a more educational route to persuade them to consider toys as learning tools (Szymanski, 2002). The developmental stages of children are familiar to marketers and inform subsequent promotional activities. For example, toys may be advertised to certain age groups as helping to improve abilities such as thinking, social skills, motor skills, or character development. According to Szymanski (2002), however, the appeal that is most attractive to children is simply fun.

Celebrities

The use of celebrities is common in advertising. The intention is for the positively perceived attributes of the celebrity to be transferred to the advertised product and for the two to become automatically linked in the audience's mind. In children's advertising, the "celebrities" are often animated figures from popular cartoons such as the Flintstones or Disney characters. In the recent past, the role of celebrities in advertising to children has often been conflated with the concept of host selling. Kunkel (1988a) showed that the practice of host selling, which involves the appearance of characters from adjacent programs in an advertisement, reduced children's ability to distinguish between advertising and program material, and it was found that older children responded more positively to products in host-selling advertisements.

Regarding the appearance of celebrities who do not feature in surrounding programs, the evidence is mixed. Atkin (1980) found that children believe that characters such as Fred Flintstone and Barney Rubble (from the Flintstones cartoon) know about cereals and accept them as credible sources of nutritional information. This finding was even more marked for heavy viewers of television. In addition, children feel validated in their choice of product when a celebrity endorses that product (Bandyopadhyay et al., 2001). A study of children in Hong Kong, however, found that the presence of celebrities (pop singers, actors) in advertisements could negatively affect the children's perceptions of the advertised brand if the children did not like the celebrity in question (Chan, 2000). This concept will be discussed further in chapter four.

Metaphors

Metaphors are frequently used in advertising as a linguistic tool in which the qualities of one object are transferred to another (Pawlowski, Badzinski, & Mitchell, 1998). In a content analysis of British children's television commercials, Young (1990) found that nearly a third featured metaphors. As an example of a metaphor, Pawlowski et al. (1998) cited the advertising slogan of Skittles (chewy, multicolored sweets), which is "taste the rainbow." Metaphors are used to create strong visual images that can stimulate the imagination and therefore aid recall of the product. There is some debate as to whether children understand metaphors, but nevertheless, they are common in children's advertising. Metaphors are popular because they relate an unfamiliar product or attribute to something that is familiar and which constitutes shared knowledge between the advertiser and consumer. The concept of metaphor implies that ideas have accustomed contexts and that recognizable changes from these standard contexts occur (Young, 1990). In general, it is believed that young children can understand metaphors if the meaning of the metaphor is within the child's experiences and if additional information is given to facilitate interpretation. However, Pawlowski et al. (1998) found that children have difficulty in interpreting metaphors and that advertisements featuring metaphors have little advantage over their more literal equivalents in terms of recall and perception.

Special Effects

Special effects used in children's advertising include sound techniques, speeded-up action, animated figures interacting with real children, and "camera magic" (i.e., transforming objects, appearance and disappearance, distortion, and so on). Such techniques gain children's attention and imbue the products with excitement. However, they can also mislead children into expecting certain results from using or eating the featured products, especially when the child is too young to recognize the techniques involved. Disappointment with advertised products not living up to their exciting image is evident in children as young as eight (Oates et al., in press). As discussed in chapter four, children easily recall products that use special effects, and older children realize the purpose of such effects is to enhance the product (Preston, 2000).

STEREOTYPING

Television in general is a powerful medium in that it can affect viewers' perceptions of social reality. As part of this medium, advertising contributes to how we think about other people. The danger is that advertising may encourage viewers to form unrealistic and clichéd opinions on a range of issues, from body size to gender roles and racial stereotyping. Currently, concerns about the portrayal of body size stem from the statistics on childhood obesity (see earlier discussion) and from young children's (especially girls') preoccupation with dieting. Advertising aimed at adults contains images of thin, attractive woman and the nature of children's advertising is no different, putting the emphasis on physical attractiveness, as does children's television programming in general. The stereotypes of thinness as attractive and desirable and fatness as neither are common and well established in children before the age of nine years (Lewis & Hill, 1998).

Children as young as three years who are heavy television viewers have been found to hold more rigid attitudes about "appropriate" jobs for men and women compared with their peers who watch less television. The nature of advertising in relation to gender generally demonstrates the following features (from Fox, 1996):

- Voice-overs are spoken or sung by men
- Men are shown in more roles than are women
- Women are shown more in family roles
- Women do activities in the home, and men are the beneficiaries of such activities
- A man's world is outside the home, a woman's within it.

With specific reference to advertisements aimed at children, women and girls are seen less than men and boys. This point is supported in research by Furnham, Abramsky, and Gunter (1997), who compared children's television advertisements in the United Kingdom and the United States. They found that males were more numerous than females in both American and British advertisements but that girls outnumbered boys in American commercials. The opposite was true of British advertisements. Also, in the

United Kingdom, more characters were identified as gender neutral than in the United States. Like Fox (1996), Furnham et al. noted that males held more central and authoritative positions, and this applied to the advertisements in both countries. They also summarized earlier research that showed how advertising aimed at girls and boys used different features. For example, advertisements for boys' products contained more cuts, loud music, and boisterous activity. Those aimed at girls, by contrast, featured more fades and dissolves, soft music, and quiet play. Marketers generally tend to use boys (either real or animated) rather than girls when advertisements are aimed at both genders. Girls will accept both girl and boy characters in advertising but boys will not accept girl characters (Ellyatt, 1999a). The confectionery advertisement described earlier for Bassett's and Beyond is a good example.

It appears that gender in children's advertising has not developed in line with changes in wider society. Research in Denmark, which has only shown children's advertising since the launch of TV2 in 1988, has concluded that things are no different than they were many years ago:

> If we look at TV commercials—both those aimed at adults and those aimed at children—we see a universe of men and boys engaged in actions such as walking, running, eating or hitting nails into a board, while girls and women are washing the husband/father's shirts and the children's clothes, washing their hair, looking into a mirror or sitting on a sofa. In commercials for children, girls are playing in pink universes filled with dolls and horses, while boys are playing with war and space toys while deep male voices talk about fights and competition in the background. (Tufte, 1999, p. 20)

Tufte (1999) pointed out that there is every reason to believe that such representations in advertising contribute to reinforcing stereotyped perceptions of gender roles and should be seen as a step backwards in relation to parents' upbringing of and influences on their children. Other researchers in the field support her negative findings, notably Seiter (1995) who wrote about both gender and racial stereotyping in children's advertising. She found gender stereotyping similar to the Danish study, noting the blatant gender identification of all children in advertisements manifested in soft close-ups of girls and bold, rugged images of boys. But it was the racial nature of advertising that preoccupied Seiter. Her view of American television was that the nature of its advertising was predominantly and positively white. The stability of the image of blonde, pale-skinned, blue-eyed children dominated commercials, and Seiter cited examples to illustrate this. Black children, however, were generally absent but on the occasions when they were present, they were portrayed as passive and silent and always outnumbered by white children.

Fox (1996) found similar features in the advertisements on the U.S. school television station, Channel One, where white teenagers dominated the commercials, and viewers generalized from the commercials to form real-life judgements about people. Furnham et al. (1997) also found that white characters were more frequent than black characters in children's advertising in both the United Kingdom and the United States. In a quantitative analysis of several thousand characters in children's television commercials, Barcus (1980) found a consistent bias toward both gender and race: more than 60% of all characters were male, and more than 90% of all characters were white. Spokespeople were male in nine out of 10 commercials overall. The stereotypical nature of advertising is discussed further in chapter eight.

SUBTLE FORMS OF ADVERTISING

The preoccupation of researchers of children's advertising has always been with television, the most visible and some would say most persuasive medium. Traditionally, television has taken the largest slice of the marketing communications budget and has attracted advertisers because of the opportunity to target carefully around particular programs or times (e.g., Saturday morning). However, the threat of a ban on advertising to children in the United Kingdom (Kemp, 1999), although not implemented, has focused marketers' minds on alternative ways of communicating with a young audience while still using the medium of television. The traditional 30-second spot advertisement has been supplemented with other means of reaching children. The two most common methods are sponsorship and merchandising. These more subtle forms of advertising mean that children may often be unaware of the marketing messages.

SPONSORSHIP

The rules governing sponsorship on U.K. television were initially set out in the Broadcasting Act of 1981 and the Independent Broadcasting Authority's 1990 Guide to Television Sponsorship (IBA, 1990). Several conditions are associated with sponsorship, for example, the type of program that can be sponsored, the nature of the sponsor, the influence of the sponsor on the program, and how the sponsorship is to be declared. In 1990, the role of the IBA was taken over by the ITC, which subsequently produced its own sponsorship code (ITC, 1991b). The ITC defines a sponsored program as "a programme that has had some or all of its costs met by a sponsor with a view to promoting its own or another's name, product or service" (ITC, 2000, p. 6). The ITC urges caution about sponsorship, acknowledging that young children may have difficulty in recognizing a sponsorship relationship.

Pecora (1998) identified the 1980s as the key decade in which the relationship between sponsorship and programs became blurred. At that time, producers looked to toy manufacturers in an effort to spread program production costs, and toy manufacturers turned to the media as a way to control the uncertainties of a fickle young market. Programs were developed with the consultation and financial backing of toy manufacturers and licensing agents. This genre of program, usually animated, was linked to existing or new toys, for example, *He-Man and the Masters of the Universe*, and *Transformers*. However, Pecora also pointed out that the seeds of sponsorship were sown as far back as the 1930s, during the era of children's radio, when 50% of programs were sponsored by the major cereal manufacturers and another 40% by other product affiliations. Children's programs have always been sponsored, but it is the relationship between producers and manufacturers that has changed.

Sponsorship can be more apparent than the rather less obvious link between toy manufacturers and animations discussed earlier. It is common to see products explicitly sponsoring television programs, featuring characters such as Frosties' Tony the Tiger at the beginning of *Gladiators* (an early Saturday evening family entertainment show), for example, or mobile telephone brands sponsoring the mid-week film on ITV1. Two of the most popular soap operas aimed at adults on U.K. terrestrial television are currently sponsored, and children watch both programs. Awareness of sponsorship of television programs has been researched with adults (IBA, 1990), but there is less research on children's awareness of or understanding of sponsorship.

Aitken, Leathar, and Squair (1986a, b) suggested that it is not until the age of 10 or 11 years that children have some understanding of the meaning of sponsorship. A more recent study confirmed that young children do not understand the concept of sponsorship or recognize its purpose. Oates et al. (2003) found that although children at the age of eight can recall many examples of programs and their sponsors, it is not until the age of about 10 years that the relationship between the two is identified in terms of promotional or financial meaning.

Piepe, Charlton, Morey, Yerrel, and Ledwith (1986) considered the effects of sponsorship on children's behavior and investigated whether sponsored sport leads to children smoking. They carried out a survey of more than 800 children aged between 11 and 15 years, dividing them into smokers and nonsmokers and testing their exposure to sponsored sport and recall of branded cigarettes. Piepe et al. found a causal link between viewing sponsored sport and recall of the Benson and Hedges brand. Ledwith (1984) carried out a study of nearly 900 children aged from 11 to 16 years in the United Kingdom. Ledwith found that the children were most aware of those cigarette brands that frequently sponsored sporting events on television, and as a result, sponsorship by tobacco manufacturers acted as cigarette advertising, despite the fact such advertising is banned in the United Kingdom. The effects of advertising and other means of promotion will be discussed in chapter eight.

MERCHANDISING

Buckingham (2000) pointed out that the relationship between merchandising and children's media is not a new phenomenon. In the 1930s, Disney established Mickey Mouse Clubs for children with the aim of building brand identity and loyalty but also with the intention of selling merchandise related to its films. This it did successfully, using the foyers of cinemas as extensions of the department store to display and sell the products. Indeed, Disney continues to excel at merchandising and each new children's film is heavily promoted via a whole range of activities (merchandising, tie-ins, sponsorship, licensing agreements, as well as traditional advertising).

In the recent past, there was occasional spin-off merchandise from popular children's shows, for example Dougal pillowcases from the Magic Roundabout (Lynn, 2002). Now, shows and products are an integrated campaign, with program producers admitting that the program is effectively an advert. Lynn (2002, p. 40) quotes a program maker who acknowledges that "when we invest in a new project, we want to know that there will be substantial merchandising on the back of it." For this reason, more recent children's television programs, especially animations, have engaged the critical attention of media researchers and commentators. For example, Kline (1993) pointed out that merchandising no longer seems to be a spin-off from films or programs but is really the primary activity.

Toy manufacturers have been criticized for commissioning and/or producing children's programs with an explicit view to creating new products (see earlier discussion). Programs such as *Transformers, My Little Pony,* and *Teenage Mutant Ninja Turtles* provide opportunities for children to collect many characters and accessories associated with the shows. These multiple character lines and associated accessorizing have extended the shelf life of a toy to about 10 years, a privilege previously only enjoyed by exceptional toys such as Barbie (Pecora, 1998). For this reason, many critics have labeled the animations as program-length commercials, unrecognized as such by regulatory bodies or by children. Parents are possibly more aware of the commercial nature of the programs. Such animations might be seen as deliberately deceiving children by disguising the advertising content under a cloak of neutral program material. Kunkel (2001, p. 376) noted that these "program-length commercials" allow advertisers to promote products directly within the body of the program, thus blurring the boundary between commercial and noncommercial content.

SUMMARY

There are many issues around children's advertising, ranging from the products advertised to more subtle means of reaching children. The points discussed in this chapter indicate widespread concern over the nature of children's advertising and its possible negative effects. Food advertising in particular has been singled out as potentially damaging in its relentless promotion of fatty and sugary products, but as pointed out, such promotion is not a new phenomenon. Discussions around advertising to children have been present for several decades, and the product categories advertised have remained the same. However, it is clear that more contemporary research is required, particularly because of the changing environment. Much of the existing research relates to a time characterized by a less-fragmented media with restricted viewing choices and fewer available channels. As Bandyopadhyay et al. (2001) note, more empirical evidence is needed to supplement and update the original research from the 1970s and 1980s.

The nature of advertising to children is inseparable from children's understanding of advertisements, and this will be discussed in the following chapters. In the next chapter, the focus is on young children and their understanding. Research on this concept has often resulted in contradictory findings, with academics disagreeing about the extent to which children under the age of about six or seven years can grasp the persuasive intent of advertising. The age of understanding has policy implications for the regulation of advertising, illustrated by the approach of countries such as Sweden, which has banned television advertising to children under twelve.

3

Children's Early Understanding of Television Advertisements

Concerns about young children's lack of understanding of television advertising have frequently been voiced by parents, regulatory bodies, and politicians who, in turn, have been reassured by advertisers and marketers that children fully understand such advertising and there is no need for further research or regulation. In publications such as *Marketing* (Hanson, 2000) and *Marketing Week* (Shannon, 2000), marketing practitioners have defended advertising to children, citing research claims that children as young as three or four years of age understand that advertising has a persuasive agenda (e.g., Donohue, Henke, & Donohue, 1980; Gaines & Esserman, 1981). On the other hand, Sweden has defended its current policy of banning television advertising to under-12s by stating they have difficulty in understanding the purpose of advertising (Bjurström, 1994; Edling, 1999). The key points that dominate the existing research in this area include young children's ability to differentiate advertising from surrounding programs, their early understanding of advertising, how this understanding is measured and factors that may mitigate this understanding. Research with very young children has certain difficulties because of their language capability, and different researchers have used various methodologies, which has led to contradictory results. Consequently, there is much disagreement both among academics and between academics and practitioners regarding the ages at which children can differentiate between program and advertising material and when they can understand the persuasive intent of advertising.

In this chapter, young children's awareness and early understanding of advertising will be explored. The main theoretical perspectives will be introduced and then the empirical evidence on children's ability to recognize advertising, their levels of attention and memory for advertisements, and their recognition of persuasiveness intent, will be examined. The concept of advertising literacy will also be introduced in this chapter. The discussion of children's early understanding will be developed in chapter four with regard to older children and their more advanced understanding of television advertising.

THEORETICAL PERSPECTIVES

Many researchers have used the theories of cognitive development proposed by Piaget to suggest that the child's ability to comprehend advertising is determined by their current cognitive stage. Piaget identified four stages of child development—sensorimotor (birth to two years), preoperational (two to seven years), concrete operational (seven to 11 years), and formal operational (11 to adulthood), and each stage is characterized by certain cognitive abilities or limitations. We discuss Piaget's theory and the way it has been used in advertising research in more detail in chapter five.

Although Piaget did not apply his theories to the understanding of commercial messages, many researchers have adopted his stages to help explain the development of children's comprehension of advertising (see chap. 5). For example, John (1999a) suggested that children in the preoperational stage can distinguish advertisements from programs based on perceptual cues, and they regard advertising as truthful and funny. Children in this stage also show a positive attitude toward advertising. In other words, young children might distinguish commercials on the basis of perceptual cues rather than any understanding of persuasive intent. In contrast, children in the concrete operational stage have a better understanding of advertising and are less likely to take advertisements at face value.

In a development of the stages suggested by Piaget, work by Roedder (1981) focused on children's ability to process information. (Roedder's theory is discussed in full in chap. 5.) Roedder suggested that as children grow older, they become more adept at information processing, that is, the acquisition, encoding, organization, and retrieval of information from memory. Children aged less than eight years are "limited processors" who are more dependent on short-term memory. "Cued processors" are aged eight to 12 years and can retrieve information if prompted. "Strategic processors" are those aged 12 and over who have the ability to store and retrieve information efficiently. The implication for identifying children in this way is that "limited processors," that is, children under eight, cannot bring a critical perspective to their consumption of advertising, simply accepting it at face value as entertaining, informative, and truthful.

Lawlor and Prothero (2002) pointed out the similarity in both Piaget's and Roedder's research in terms of the age at which children could begin to understand persuasive intent—in the concrete operational stage (from seven years) for Piaget and in the cued processor stage (from eight years) for Roedder. Therefore, in terms of cognitive development, several researchers have argued that seven to eight years of age is when children begin to understand that advertisements are designed to influence their audience. As pointed out in chapter five, most research into children's understanding of advertisements has been conducted with reference to either Piaget's or Roedder's theories. That chapter also argues that these theories are limited and that more contemporary theories of child development offer better approaches to the study of children and advertising. In this chapter, however, the focus is on the empirical results from the research into young children's understanding.

CONCEPT OF TELEVISION ADVERTISING

Very young children initially have a limited concept of television advertising. At first, it is indistinguishable from the surrounding programs, as the two merge in a montage of sounds and images. Some researchers have shown that the visual attention of very young children (around five years of age) remains stable when viewing advertisements and programs, indicating a lack of differentiation between the two (Ward & Wackman, 1973). But other researchers have suggested that children at this age do have the ability to differentiate (Wartella & Ettema, 1974). As children get older, changes in levels of attention can be observed, although this difference does not necessarily indicate an understanding of advertising and programming—it may be a response to the perceptual variations that are evident such as changes in music, sound effects, color, action, and so on.

PRE-SCHOOL YEARS— IDENTIFICATION OF TELEVISION ADVERTISING

The ability to distinguish television advertising from surrounding programs is seen as one of the key stages in understanding advertising (Gunter & Furnham, 1998; Kunkel, 2001). Before a child can comprehend the nature and intent of advertising, they should be able to identify advertisements as distinct from programs, but there is much disagreement in the literature about when this ability is evident in children. Estimates range from as young as three years (Jaglom & Gardner, 1981; Levin, Petros, & Petrella, 1982) to more than six years (Bjurström, 1994) and depend very much on the methodology used. Researchers who have suggested that very young children have this ability tend to rely on nonverbal methods, whereas verbal testing has resulted in higher estimates (Gunter & Furnham, 1998).

MEASURES USED TO ASSESS CHILDREN'S ABILITY TO DIFFERENTIATE ADVERTISING FROM PROGRAMS

Most research used to assess children's ability to differentiate between program and commercial material on television uses verbal, nonverbal, or observational means. Verbal methods involve questioning children and asking them to explain the differences between the two. This method therefore demands a certain level of verbal skill from children. Consequently, researchers relying on verbal methods have tended to find that only older children can articulate such differences (Gunter & Furnham, 1998).

Nonverbal methods rely on gestures such as raising a hand (Dorr, 1986), or placing a hand on a colored square when an advertisement appears (Bijmolt, Claassen, & Brus, 1998; Stutts, Vance, & Hudleson, 1981). Other methods involve only minimal verbal skills such as calling out (Butter, Popovich, Stackhouse, & Garner, 1981) or responding yes/no to a researcher's question (Levin et al., 1982). Researchers using nonverbal methods have generally concluded that awareness of advertisements and programs is evident at a younger age than researchers who have used verbal means.

Observational methods rely on researchers monitoring changes in children's visual and auditory attention levels between programs and commercials (Gunter & Furnham, 1998). Such studies tend to find that children exhibit a drop in attention when an advertisement appears compared with their previous levels of attention during a program, indicating recognition of some difference between the two (Zuckerman, Ziegler, & Stevenson, 1978). In addition to the three methods outlined above, researchers have also used memory to test children's abilities to differentiate between advertisements and programs. Children might be asked to decide whether specific characters were previously seen in a program or in a commercial (Zuckerman & Gianino, 1981). Alternatively, children can be shown a program including advertisements and then asked yes/no questions about events in both to compare the accuracy of their recall for the program with their recall of the advertisements (Oates et al., 2002). Evidence relating to all these methods will now be discussed in more detail.

Nonverbal Methods

The research by Levin et al. (1982) is often cited as a key study that demonstrates young children's ability to differentiate program and commercial material on television. Children aged three, four, and five years were asked to identify videotaped television segments as either programs or commercials using minimal verbal skills. The segments were 10 seconds long. The proportion of correct identifications was four fifths for the five-year-olds, two thirds for the four-year-olds, and two thirds for the three-year-olds. These percentages were better than chance, although the authors noted much variability in children's individual performance. They also suggested that had longer segments of both programs and commercials been used, the children's performance might have improved as they would have had more information on which to make a judgement. Nonetheless, Levin et al. (1982) demonstrated that children from about three years of age could distinguish advertisements and programs, and other researchers have found similar results. For example, Butter et al. (1981) found that children aged four and five years were able to identify commercial content. They placed four 30-second advertisements in a children's program, and asked children just to say when a commercial came on. Butter et al. found that all four advertisements were correctly identified by three quarters of the four-year-olds and by nearly all the five-year-olds.

Bijmolt et al. (1998) tested whether children aged from five to eight years could distinguish advertisements from programs and their understanding of advertisements. Children were asked to place their hands on a red square during a commercial. Bijmolt et al. found that almost 90% of the children recognized both transitions, that is, from program to commercial and from commercial to program. However, when asked to verbalize the difference between commercials and programs, only 8% of the five- and six-year-olds gave correct and relevant answers. Bijmolt et al.'s study used a similar methodology to that of Stutts, Vance, and Hudleson (1981) who also asked children to place their hands on a red square when they saw a commercial. When the program came back on, they had to return their hands to their laps. In this study, three-year-olds did not recognize commercials as distinct from the program, but five and seven-year-olds did.

A slight variation on the methods discussed above was used by Gaines and Esserman (1981) who showed children a video featuring a short cartoon that included two animated 30-second advertisements. They used a freeze frame technique—that is, the video was stopped during the second airing of the commercial and children were asked whether it was part of the program. The majority of the four to eight-year-olds could identify the advertisements as distinct from the surrounding program. However, a similar study by Palmer and McDowell (1979) found that five- to seven-year-olds had difficulty identifying commercials and programs. The children managed to identify only half the commercials and three quarters of the programs.

Attention

Another way to measure awareness of advertising includes observation of young children's levels of attention when watching television. Wartella and Ettema (1974) tested three- to eight-year-olds who viewed a program into which 12 commercials had been inserted. The researchers observed the children's attention as they watched the program and found that all the children were aware of shifts between the program and commercials. "Their attention behavior indicates that they have learned the visual and auditory cues signifying the interruption of the program by a series of commercials" (p. 81). This effect was most noticeable for the three- and four-year-old children. Levin and Anderson (1976) also found that the visual attention of young children shifted when a commercial break interrupted a program.

Attention can be observed directly, as in the studies discussed, or children and/or parents can be asked to report viewing behavior. Parents often estimate higher levels of children's attention to television advertising than more independent observers. This may be because of less rigorous measures being used and a reliance on memory. When Bechtel, Achelpol, and Akers (1972) used video cameras in children's homes to record viewing patterns, they found that children under 10 years watched advertisements nearly half the time that they were broadcast.

In a study with children that used self-completed questionnaires and diaries, Greenberg, Fazal, and Wober (1986) reported that two thirds of four- to 13-year-olds watched all or most advertisements on television, indicating awareness of both program and commercial content. They did not find any age differences, but there was a difference between girls and boys because girls showed greater attention to advertising.

Memory

Memory for television advertising can be tested in several different ways. Randrup and Lac (2000) questioned Danish children in an effort to understand how they process television commercials. They suggested that children watch commercials to be entertained and they chiefly react to peripheral cues, exhibiting memory for jingles, tunes, and slogans. When asked about the central message, the children often failed to respond, even though they had been attentive for the full length of the commercial. Randrup and Lac (2000) concluded that young children need to be exposed to the same advertisement a number of times before they recognize the central message, although peripheral cues are quickly remembered and are the main focus of children's attention. Levin et al. (1982) also found that children aged between three and four years remembered more peripheral than central information from commercials aimed at both adults and children. Five-year-olds also remembered peripheral information from adult commercials, but remembered central information from children's commercials.

Research by Oates et al. (2002) illustrated that young children have a poor memory for novel advertisements. In an experiment with six- to 10-year-olds, children were exposed to a video featuring a cartoon with advertisements inserted at the beginning, in the middle and at the end of the program. Three novel advertisements from South Africa and the United States were used, presented in a counterbalanced order so that a third of the children each saw one product advertised once, one advertised twice, and one advertised three times. One day later, recall memory was tested by asking the children to name the brands they had seen in the advertisements and to answer six yes/no questions about the advertisements. Children were also shown seven stills, two of which came from the advertisement and were asked to select the stills from the advertisements to test recognition memory. This was repeated three times. For six-year-olds, brand name recall was very poor, even when an advertisement had been seen three times. Recall of advertising content measured by the yes/no questions was also poor, as children seeing an advertisement once performed no better than chance, although repeat viewing led to increased accuracy. However, recognition of stills yielded more impressive results, with 72% of the six-year-olds correctly selecting the appropriate still for an advertisement they had seen only once. This figure rose to 83% when choosing a still from an advertisement they had watched three times. Oates et al. concluded that six-year-olds have poor recall of novel advertisements but good recognition skills.

The research discussed above points to preschoolers' ability to differentiate between program and advertising material on television. However, some authors put the age when children have this ability much later. From a review of the evidence, Kunkel and Roberts (1991) suggested that children under five years of age were unable to identify commercial as opposed to program material. However, they also acknowledged that studies using nonverbal techniques have raised questions about this finding, and to account for such discrepancies, they suggested that there may be different levels of functional discrimination that warrant further investigation.

The debate about distinguishing commercial from program content is important. Although some of the studies discussed earlier demonstrated children's ability to make this distinction, the studies do not show that the children can explain the difference between the two types of television content. When asked to do so, young children are often unable to offer any explanation to account for the difference between programs and commercials. In terms of attention, it might be that children are reacting to differences in physical features between programs and commercials without making a conceptual distinction (Gunter & McAleer, 1997). Superficial perceptual responses may account for changes in the child's viewing patterns. In some nonverbal tests, children may choose a program or commercial based on perceptual cues rather than understanding. Perceptual cues might include the short length of an advertisement, its colors, the speed of action, adult voice-overs, and the presence of a jingle. In other words, factors that catch and maintain the attention of the audience may help children to first identify advertisements.

ADVERTISING FACTORS AFFECTING DIFFERENTIATION

Certain factors can reduce the ability of children to differentiate between programs and commercials. The concept of host selling, that is, using popular television characters in commercials that also feature in the adjacent program can blur the boundaries between an advertisement and the surrounding program (Kunkel, 1988a). This is especially pertinent when animated advertisements are shown within and between cartoon programs. Also, some perceptual similarities between children's programs and advertisements may confuse children in their attempts to recognize the differences between them (Kunkel & Roberts, 1991). Another factor to consider is the development of product-related shows, which feature characters available for purchase. These programs, often cartoons, have been criticized as no more than program-length commercials, designed as vehicles to market brands to young children (Kunkel, 2001).

The use of alternative marketing communications such as sponsorship may also lead to confusion, although this is an underresearched area. However, such forms of marketing are an increasingly popular way to break through the clutter in traditional advertising media (see chap. 2).

Other factors may make it easier for children to differentiate between programs and advertisements. For example, the presence of bumpers or separators is required by broadcast regulators to act as a marker to separate advertisements from surrounding program material. Kunkel and Roberts (1991) suggested that bumpers typically employed by broadcasters do little to aid young children in differentiating between the two because of the lack of sufficient contrast. Indeed, it might be argued that the beginning of the advertisement itself provides more contrast than separators and so children have a greater chance of recognising an advertisement without such intervention (Verhaeren, 1991). Other studies, however, have found that separators can lead to increasing children's awareness of advertisements and programs. Successful separators need to be constructed with the young audience in mind; for example, Dorr (1986) found that the design of a red stop sign with the phrase "OK kids, get ready, here comes a commercial" increased recognition of advertisements in four-, six- and eight-year-olds.

In addition to bumpers or separators, children can also be helped to discriminate between advertising and other television content by clustering advertisements in blocks before and after programs but not during programs. Nevertheless, Gunter and Furnham (1998) pointed out that this technique of scheduling advertising is open to criticism on the grounds that it leads to a cluttering effect and also poor memory for the advertisements. A study by Duffy and Rossiter (1975), using changes in visual attention as a measure, found that clustering did not enhance the ability of five-year-olds to discriminate between advertising and program material.

EARLY UNDERSTANDING
OF THE PURPOSE OF ADVERTISING

Children's understanding of television advertising moves through several stages. At first, they are unaware of advertising and cannot distinguish it from the surrounding program content. Once a distinction can be made, usually by the age of five, and based on perceptual cues, children view advertising as entertaining and fun.

It is not until after this stage that children begin to recognize the informative (assistive) function of advertising, followed by a realization of selling or persuasive intent. Being able to understand the purpose of advertising is important to judgements about its truth or falsity (Young, 1990). This type of understanding progressively develops through a number of stages. Robertson and Rossiter (1974) illustrated these stages in a study of boys aged between six- and 11-years-old. By asking the children questions about the existence of commercials and their purpose, Robertson and Rossiter identified several antecedents of attributions of advertising intent. These included discrimination between programs and commercials, recognition of commercial source, and personal experience of a discrepancy between products as advertised and products in reality. They found awareness of assistive intent across all age groups but only half of the six- and seven-year-olds were able to attribute persuasive intent to advertisements. One of the factors in children demonstrating the latter understanding was prior personal experience of disappointment with a product not living up to its advertised claims.

Robertson and Rossiter's (1974) findings have been replicated by other researchers who also place the age of understanding for most children at about seven to eight years (e.g., Brucks, Armstrong, & Goldberg, 1988; Chan, 2000; Kunkel & Roberts, 1991). However other researchers suggest this understanding occurs much earlier (e.g., Donohue et al., 1980) or considerably later (e.g., Bjurström, 1994). The researchers who have emphasized early understanding have often used nonverbal tasks, and these tasks are discussed in the next section. The age at which understanding is achieved has been debated extensively and has influenced policy decisions on banning television advertising to children (Kemp, 1999). Gunter, McAleer, and Clifford (1992a) reported qualitative research with children and teenagers that revealed some understanding of the selling intent of television advertisements. While advertising was amusing and entertaining, its primary purpose was to raise product awareness. This purpose was seen as being especially significant for new products—even for children as young as seven years.

NONVERBAL TASKS USED TO ASSESS UNDERSTANDING OF PERSUASIVE INTENT

The age at which a child can demonstrate awareness of persuasive intent of advertising has varied with the method used (Young, 1990). One of the studies that has been frequently cited as evidence for early understanding of persuasive intent was carried out by Donohue et al. (1980) and used a nonverbal method. They showed children a cereal advertisement that included a character called "Toucan Sam." After seeing the advertisement, children were asked to choose between two pictures to indicate what "Toucan Sam" wanted them to do. The choice was between a picture of a woman and child selecting the cereal in a shop and a picture of a child watching television that did not feature the cereal. If children chose the shopping sketch, it was assumed that they understood that the purpose of the advertisement was to persuade people to buy the product. Donohoe et al found that 75% of two- to three-year-olds, 70% of four-year-olds, 76% of five-year-olds, and 96% of six-year-olds chose the picture of the shopping trip, and they concluded that even young children understand the commercial intent of an advertisement.

However, Macklin (1987) pointed out that Donohue et al. (1980) might have overestimated children's abilities because they showed children one picture (the shopping trip) that included the cereal product that the children had seen in the advertisement and one that did not (the child watching a television). The children in Donohue's experiment may have chosen the shopping trip picture because it was the only one that included the product they had just seen in the television advertisement. If so, this might indicate some recognition of the product but did not necessarily mean that the children understood the nature of the advertisement. Macklin therefore repeated Donohue et al.'s experiment but used 10 pictures rather than two. One of the 10 pictures showed a shopping trip. The children in her experiment saw a television advertisement for cereal and were then asked to point to a picture that showed what advertisements "want you to do after you watch them" (1987, p. 235).

Macklin (1987) found that none of the three-year-olds in her study pointed to the shopping trip, and only 8% of four-year-olds and 20% of five-year-olds chose this picture. These results stand in marked contrast to Donohue et al.'s (1980) original study and lend support to Macklin's suggestion that the young children in Donohue et al. were only picking a picture because it included the product and not with any greater understanding. Certainly Macklin found little understanding of advertisements in three- and four-year-olds who performed at chance levels in her study.

However, Macklin (1987) suggested that as 20% of the five-year-olds in her study selected the shopping trip picture, they had some understanding of advertising intent because this percentage was better than chance. Macklin's results are often cited as evidence that five-year-olds have some understanding of the persuasive intent of advertisements. However the five-year-olds in Macklin's study only performed better than chance if all 10 pictures were equally likely to be chosen (in which case chance was 10%). But Macklin's study is open to the same criticism that was leveled at Donohue et al. (1980). Only three of the 10 pictures she used included the product, and if the five-year-olds simply chose a picture because it included the product they had just seen in the television advertisement, they had a 33% chance of picking the shopping picture by chance. In other words, Macklin's study did not provide strong evidence for understanding persuasive intent.

Harvey and Blades (2002) replicated Macklin's (1987) study using exactly the same procedure that she used. Four-, five-, and six-year-olds watched an unfamiliar television commercial for cereal and were then shown six pictures of family activity, including one picture showing a shopping trip. The key point was that all the pictures included the cereal product, and therefore children could not be biased to selecting some rather than other pictures simply by choosing the ones that included the product. Harvey and Blades found that four- and five-year-olds only chose the shopping picture at chance levels. In other words, when all the pictures included the product, even five-year-olds were no more likely to choose a picture of a family going shopping than any other picture. This suggests that five-year-olds do not understand the intent of television advertisements. In Harvey and Blades's study, the six-year-olds did perform better than chance but only a third of this age group chose the correct picture of the shopping trip—a much smaller proportion than the six-year-olds in Donohue et al.'s (1980) original study.

Bijmolt et al. (1998) carried out a similar nonverbal study to test understanding of advertising. Five- to eight-year-old children saw an advertisement for a chocolate drink and were then asked to choose one of three pictures to indicate what the advertisement wanted them to do. The three pictures were a mother and child buying the chocolate drink, the chocolate drink shown on a shelf in a shop, and children watching the chocolate drink advertisement on television. If children picked either of the first two pictures they were scored as correct. Sixty-nine percent of the children did choose one of those two pictures, and Bijmolt et al. concluded that this percentage of children was slightly above chance and went on to say that the children had some understanding of advertising. However, this is not a valid conclusion because children were scored as correct if they chose either of two out of the three pictures, and if they had guessed randomly, the children would have scored 66% correct. The figure of 69% found by Bijmolt et al. was therefore not significantly better than chance and no conclusions can be drawn from their results. The lack of a significant result in Bijmolt et al.'s study is surprising given the age of the children in their study. They included five- to eight-year-olds, and given the other evidence for older children's understanding of advertisements (see chap. 4), it might have been expected that a group that included seven- and eight-year-olds would have done well on a nonverbal task.

We have emphasized the details of the nonverbal studies in which children had to choose pictures to indicate understanding because many authors have claimed that such nonverbal tasks have demonstrated that young children have an appreciation of the persuasive intent of advertisements. But as we have stressed above one reason for children's apparent success on nonverbal tasks has been the failure of experimenters to consider chance effects. In nonverbal tasks that involve choices between a small number of pictures children may appear to perform well because even if they are guessing they are likely to pick the correct picture by chance. Studies such as Donohue et al. (1980) and Macklin (1987) are frequently cited in the advertising literature, but their validity is questionable.

In another study, Macklin (1987) designed a novel nonverbal task to assess three-, four-, and five-year-olds' understanding of advertising intent. The children watched a television advertisement for cereal and were then taken to a room that included three play areas. One play area had a kitchen layout, one had a hot dog stand and outdoor eating area, and one had a shop. The cereal product was present in all three play areas. The children were shown all the play areas, and then they were asked to show what the advertisement wanted them to do. Macklin scored the children for acting out a shopping event or indicating that the cereal should be bought. None of the three- and four-year-olds gave any indication of purchasing behavior, but six (out of 15) five-year-olds did so.

On the basis of this result, Macklin suggested that the five-year-olds had some understanding of the purpose of advertising. This may be the case, but unfortunately Macklin did not include a control group of children who were

asked to carry out the same task *without* watching the television advertisement first. Such a control group would have established whether the five-
year-olds who carried out the shopping behavior did so because of the advertisement or for some other reason. For example, the five-year-olds may simply have found the play shop a more attractive layout and preferred to spend
their time there rather than in one of the other play areas. Macklin's procedure offers an intriguing way to assess young children's understanding of advertisements, but without the necessary control group, Macklin's results
have to be treated with caution.

UNDERSTANDING PROMOTIONAL INTENT

The concept of understanding, as discussed earlier, has often been used by
academics in a specific way, that is, to mean children's comprehension of
persuasive intent by advertisers. To broaden this debate, Young (2000)
looked at a different aspect of understanding—that of the promotional nature of advertising and marketing generally. Marketing is promotional in the
sense that positive claims are made about a product and advertisers rarely
intentionally present negative information about their own brands. If they
do so, it is to be expected that the advertisement is deliberately ironic or rule
breaking in an attempt to gain attention.

Young (2000) tested children's ability to choose the "correct" (i.e., promotional) ending to a number of television commercials. Children aged
from four years to nine years were shown seven advertisements that had
been edited to cut out the final shot. The children were then asked to choose
between three possible endings presented as stills (promotional, neutral,
and entertaining) and to justify their choice. The majority of four- to
five-year-olds selected the entertaining option, but by the age of six, a third
of the children chose the promotional ending. Young suggested these results
demonstrated young children's emerging ability to understand that advertising is different and follows alternative rules to other kinds of communication such as programs. In a review of the literature, Young (1998) concluded
that children under the age of six see advertising as entertainment before
developing an appreciation of assistive intent. It is not until about eight
years of age that most children recognize that this information is presented
in an advocatory way to show only the benefits of brands.

ADVERTISING-RELATED FACTORS

Additional indicators that very young children are aware of advertising or
that it has impacted on them in some way are presented in studies on logo
and brand recognition. Dammler and Middelmann-Motz (2002) showed

brand logos and packaging to preschool children. Three- and four-year-olds could describe a product after having seen just the logo. For example, two thirds of this age group could name and describe Milka products and two fifths could do the same for Kinder chocolates. These brands are both aimed at children, but even for a more adult brand such as Nivea, nearly a third of the children could name and describe the products. These findings are not unusual—in a 1995 study, Hite and Hite (1995) discovered that children as young as two years of age recognized and chose branded products rather than unbranded alternatives. However, in a study of young children's letters to Father Christmas, Pine and Nash (in press) found that 90% of toys advertised in the build-up to Christmas did not feature in the children's letters. This suggests that brand name recall is poor for children under seven years of age. Nonetheless, children who watched more commercial television requested a greater number of items in their Christmas letters and included more requests for branded products.

DIFFERENCES IN DEFINING ADVERTISING INTENT

In general, there is a problem with studies on advertising intent because of the lack of clarity about what is meant by "understanding" advertising. The concept of "advertising literacy" (Young, 1986, 1990) is useful, as it offers an indication of what is meant by understanding. Young suggested that for a child to understand advertising, they must realize there is a source deliberately creating television advertisements and be aware that this source intends to persuade an audience to purchase (and for this, children must be able to comprehend that others have different intentions). This is a basic level of understanding, and it becomes more sophisticated as the child begins to comprehend who pays for advertisements, who makes them, who benefits from them, why they are present on certain channels and not others, and so on. Macklin (1987) further distinguished between the informational function of advertising (showing products that are available in-store) and the persuasive function, which involves understanding four attributes: that the source has other interests than the receiver, that the source intends to persuade, that persuasive messages are biased, and that biased messages demand different interpretation strategies than do informational messages. Differences in the age at which children achieve this understanding might be attributed to how complex a definition of persuasive intent is used by the researcher.

Methodological differences may also account for variation in results. Martin (1997) carried out a metaanalysis of the literature addressing children's understanding of advertising and suggested that several methodological factors moderated the relationship between age and understanding of advertising intent. Three main factors were identified: first, the use of nonverbal or verbal assessments. Nonverbal measures of assessment may detect levels of understanding that verbal measures cannot, although, as we have noted above there are difficulties in interpreting some of the nonverbal studies. Second, the distinction between types of intent (e.g., is the study measuring assistive or persuasive intent). The literature has not treated different kinds of understanding in a consistent way, as some researchers regard assistive and persuasive functions as distinct, but others view them as a con-. tinuum of understanding. Third, the type of exposure before understanding is measured (advertisement only, no advertisement, or advertisement and programs together). This is important because children who see an advertisement in isolation may be more confused than those who watch advertisements in a more usual context, that is, within and between programs. Martin concluded that these moderating variables should be manipulated in future research.

MEDIA AND ADVERTISING LITERACY

The debate about children's understanding of advertising needs to be placed in the wider context of media literacy, practices which enable children to access, analyze, and produce media texts (Marsh & Millard, 2000). This is because younger children do not possess the critical abilities that allow them to be skeptical toward advertising but they can be taught to acquire such skills via literacy programs. And although older children can recognize the persuasive function of advertising, they do not necessarily critique commercials spontaneously while viewing them (Strasburger & Wilson, 2002). There is a clear role for educating children about advertising to facilitate their critical abilities and a need to research how those abilities can be triggered during viewing. Media literacy can be defined as:

> analytical, reflective understanding of print and electronic mass media … critical viewing skills is one major component of media literacy, referring to understanding of and competence with television, including its aesthetic, social, cultural, psychological, educational, economic, and regulatory aspects. (Brown, 2001, p. 681)

Advertising literacy is only a small part of media literacy and has been considered under the broader remit of television research, with particular attention paid to broadcast advertisements. Most commonly, in the 1970s and 1980s, a few questions on advertising were incorporated into studies on television literacy (Dorr, Graves, & Phelps, 1980; Singer & Singer, 1981). The results were encouraging and demonstrated that after only a short course children could be helped to understand and evaluate television content.

With specific reference to advertising, an early study was carried out by Christenson (1982) in which children aged between nine and 13 were divided into two groups—one group viewed an instructional film called the *Six Billion Dollar Sell* and the other group watched a film unrelated to advertising. After viewing, results showed that the first group was more skeptical toward advertising than their peers in the control group—this was particularly evident with the nine-year-olds. A second, similar study with younger children (aged seven, eight, and 10 years) also showed increases in scepticism, again particularly in the youngest age group.

Children can be taught about advertising but this does not mean they employ a critical perspective when viewing advertisements. Research by Brucks, Armstrong, and Goldberg (1988) found that older children, who were aware of the persuasive nature of advertising, did not necessarily use any cognitive defenses when viewing advertising. Implicit in much of the research on children's understanding is an assumption that children who possess cognitive defenses (an understanding of the selling intent and an associated distrust of advertisements) will actually use them against advertising. However, Brucks et al. pointed out that although children of about seven years of age may have a general awareness of advertising intent when watching advertisements, they may still later behave in such a way as to suggest that this awareness was not used as an effective defense. The implication is that it is insufficient just to test children's awareness of advertising intent—we need to know if they use this awareness and indeed what activates their defenses. Brucks et al. suggested three possible kinds of defense that could be employed by children:

- counterarguments (but children need prior knowledge of the product to argue against current advertising),
- support arguments (in favor of current advertisements),
- source derogation (critical of specific advertisements and/or advertising in general).

Children may not necessarily have the knowledge to produce counterarguments and so source derogation may be an easier cognitive defense for them to use. Brucks et al. (1988) found that when nine- and 10-year-old children watch advertisements, they do not spontaneously retrieve prior knowledge about advertising but can do so when cued. Neither do knowledgeable children generate skeptical thoughts during exposure to advertisements unless prompted. The authors concluded that nine- and 10-year-olds need more than just a skeptical attitude toward advertising—they also require knowledge about the nature of advertising that then has to be cued to generate advertising counterarguments. The authors suggested several possible ways in which children might be helped to use their cognitive defences effectively, for example, via literacy programs in school, prompts from parents as commercials begin, and cues from broadcasters reminding children to watch advertisements carefully.

Advertising literacy has emerged as a key issue in the United Kingdom because of the introduction in November 2002, of Media Smart, an advertising industry-led initiative aimed at educating young children about advertising (Rogers, 2002). Media Smart has the backing of several major advertisers (e.g., Cadbury, Hasbro, Kellogg's, Masterfoods, Mattel, Trebor Bassett) and is intended to deflect criticism from parents and pressure groups unhappy about the industry's targeting of children. The program is designed to be taught in schools to six- to 11-year-olds as part of the National Curriculum and provides teachers with a short video and teaching notes, activities, pupil certificates, an educational Web site, and a leaflet for parents. Topics covered include constructing an advertisement, finding advertisements in different media, differentiating between needs and wants, advertising regulation, the use of slogans, and planning a campaign. The program has yet to be evaluated, but its creators hope it will encourage children to take a critical approach to advertising, whether on television, radio, or in the press.

SUMMARY

Children's awareness of advertising can occur at a very young age, as researchers have found that some children at the age of three can distinguish programs and commercials (Levin et al., 1982). Conclusions about young children's awareness, however, depend on the methodology that researchers use (Macklin, 1983). Conceptual and methodological issues also affect conclusions about children's understanding of the persuasive intent of advertising, and various ages have been suggested for the achievement of this understanding—with estimates ranging from three years (Donohue et al., 1980) up to 12 years (Bjurström, 1994). But many researchers agree that most children recognize the persuasive intent of advertising about eight years of age (Kunkel & Roberts, 1991)—see chapter four.

Goldstein (1999) argued that debates about the recognition and understanding of advertising are flawed for several reasons. First, research results are highly variable and inconsistent because of differences in researchers' definitions of "understanding." Second, research can be poorly conducted and open to different interpretations. And third, age is immaterial as there is no magic age at which a child understands advertising because learning is a continuous process which depends upon other factors such as family and peers. Goldstein claimed that no research exists that demonstrates that children who cannot understand advertising are more affected by it than those who can understand it. However, the debate around children and advertising is not necessarily restricted to effects. As Kunkel and Roberts (1991) argued, if children are unaware of advertising's intent, then by implication all advertising to them is unfair. Therefore, it is important to continue investigations of children's ability. Although Goldstein was correct to point to the discrepancies in results, previous researchers have helped to define the field and have provided material for the information of policy makers and advertisers, and studies such as Martin's (1997) metaanalysis have identified the factors that may account for variance in results.

Lawlor and Prothero (2002) proposed an alternative way of looking at young children's understanding of advertising. Unlike the previous studies discussed earlier, they hypothesized that the advertiser's purpose of information and persuasion is just one perspective and that it does not take into account the impact of advertising on the consumer over and above a purely marketing focus. Rather than asking what advertising does to people, they argued the focus should also encompass what children actively do with advertising. Thus, in addition to exploring traditional persuasive intent, researchers should also be asking themselves about the existence of advertising through the eyes of the child. The intention of the advertiser is to elicit a particular response from their audience, but the audience may not react in expected ways. For example, O'Donohoe (1994) found that young adults use advertising as a social resource as well as entertainment. Lawlor and Prothero suggested that children might take a similar view, using advertising for social purposes, for convenience, to convey popularity, and to affect interaction with parents and peers. In other words, additional uses to the expected commercial outcomes may exist. This in itself, however, does not deflect from the argument about when understanding of the advertiser's intent occurs—just because children may have other uses for advertising does not mean the advertiser's purpose can be ignored. But by incorporating Lawlor and Prothero's perspective, a more holistic view of the child's understanding of advertising may be achieved.

John (1999a) summed up the research on young children and advertising by concluding that there is little reason to believe that the majority of children below the age of seven or eight years have a command of advertising's persuasive intent. The next chapter continues with an examination of children's advanced understanding of advertising and the stages they pass through to achieve a full understanding.

4

Advanced Understanding of Advertising

Understanding advertising clearly develops with age and cognitive abilities. In the previous chapter, early understanding (up to the age of about six to seven years) was discussed, and it was concluded that after this age, some children begin to demonstrate a more sophisticated level of comprehension. Many studies have also investigated older children's understanding, mostly relying on verbal or written methods given older children's ability to articulate their knowledge. Studies with older children have focused on whether they can comprehend advertising, the truthfulness of advertising, and the influence of famous characters in advertisements. Most researchers would agree that with increased understanding comes more cynicism toward advertising, doubt about its veracity, and a growing dislike of advertisements. Why children develop these negative attitudes toward advertising will be addressed in this chapter.

INTERPRETATION OF INTENT

By the time children reach the age of about 10 years, it is generally assumed that their understanding of advertising has developed enough to appreciate the persuasive intent of advertisers. Some studies place this understanding as occurring much earlier, others somewhat later, depending on the researcher's definition of understanding. Martensen and Hansen (2001) carried out a survey of 1,600 Danish children aged between eight and 18 years.

Their choice of age group was based on the premise that children under eight are only able to see advertisements from a limited perspective. Not until children are a little older are they able to see advertisements both from their own point of view as consumers, that is, adverts as information, and from the perspective of the advertiser, that is, adverts as persuasion. Martensen and Hansen found that two thirds of the eight- and nine-year-olds reported understanding the intention of advertising, and this proportion increased to three quarters of 10- to 12-year-olds. It might be argued that both figures are lower than expected when compared with studies by other authors (discussed in the previous chapter) that suggested understanding was evident in some children as young as five years of age and in the majority by eight years. However, Martensen and Hansen's findings are supported by those of Oates et al. (2002) who concluded that even by the age of 10, not all children demonstrate understanding of advertising's persuasive intent. Bergler (1999) also found similar data with German children, pointing out that even by the age of 11 years, some children did not understand that advertisements aim to sell more.

Chan (2000) asked Chinese children in grades kindergarten to grade six (aged between five and 12 years) about their general knowledge of television advertising, and she divided their responses into four categories—low, medium, high, and do not know. A low response included the naming of specific products and the fact that advertisements interrupt programs, medium responses included assistive intent, and a high awareness involved knowledge of persuasive intent. Chan commented that the age of eight was a watershed in development of knowledge and understanding, as her results showed a marked increase on both these measures after this age, and children below eight had difficulty in verbalizing what constituted a commercial. By the age of 12, two thirds of children demonstrated medium knowledge of television advertising, and when asked specifically about the purpose of advertising, nearly two thirds of this group showed understanding of promotion and persuasion.

Further studies on children in China have found similar results. Using three in-depth focus groups with 22 children, Chan and McNeal (2002) reported that children aged nine to 12 years demonstrated some understanding of the functions and selling intention of television advertising. Children of this age also showed awareness and understanding of public service announcements and could explain the difference between these and other advertisements. Nevertheless, they remained confused about the financial aspect of advertising, suggesting, for example, that advertising slots cost millions of dollars.

What are studies measuring when they look at understanding of intention? This is an important point because the definition of understanding can vary widely and might range from a simple concept that advertisements want the audience to buy products to a more complex understanding of the economy. It might be expected that young children express a straightforward concept of advertising, whereas older children demonstrate more elaborate knowledge. Gunter and McAleer (1997, p. 137) suggested that children must be able to make a number of discriminations in order to understand advertising, including:

- distinguish advertisements as separate from programs;
- recognize a sponsor as the source of the commercial message;
- perceive the idea of an intended audience for the message;
- understand the symbolic nature of products, character, and contextual representation in commercials;
- discriminate by example between products as advertised and products as experienced.

Points such as these are not always explicitly identified in studies of children's understanding and even adults have difficulty at times with some of them.

The ability to discern persuasive intent is important because it affects the child's overall perspective of advertising. Robertson and Rossiter (1974) proposed three hypotheses to investigate potential factors that might be related to intent. The first hypothesis linked children's ability to perceive assistive and/or persuasive intent in commercials with age, older siblings, parents' education level, parental interaction with the child, and peer integration. The second hypothesis proposed cognitive factors that would precede attribution of intent, including discrimination between programs and commercials, recognition of an external source or sponsor, perception of an intended audience, awareness of the symbolic nature of commercials, and experiences of discrepancies between advertised and actual products. The third hypothesis dealt with the consequences of perceived intent and proposed that persuasive intent would be negatively related to trust in, and liking of, commercials and desire for the advertised products.

Robertson and Rossiter (1974) found that children's attribution of persuasive intent to commercials was very much related to age and a high level of parental education but that other factors (siblings, etc.) were not relevant. However, the children who recognized persuasive intent met all five of the cognitive criteria these researchers proposed. For the last hypothesis, the results indicated that children understanding persuasive intent placed less trust in commercials, disliked them, and demonstrated a diminished desire for advertised products. Children who saw assistive intent in advertisements trusted them more and tended to like them. Robertson and Rossiter found that virtually all in a group of 10- to 11-year-old boys attributed persuasive intent to advertisements and consequently were less trusting, liked advertisements less, and made fewer purchase requests.

Understanding can also be expressed in terms of how children actually process commercials, that is, to which parts of the advertisement do they respond and what do they remember? Randrup and Lac (2000) carried out a small-scale qualitative study with 20 Danish children to investigate how advertisements are processed. They found marked differences in how children aged seven to nine years understand and process advertisements compared with older children. Seven- to nine-year-olds processed advertisements via the peripheral route, demonstrating memory for features such as jingles and slogans but exhibiting little understanding of the central message. In this age group, advertisements were mainly watched for their entertainment value. Children aged between 10 and 12 years paid more attention to the central message of an advertisement and demonstrated greater product knowledge.

The aforementioned studies show the degree of interest in children's understanding of advertising, especially in terms of persuasive intent. A related issue is children's understanding of the promotional function of advertising, that is, the making of positive claims about a product. Pine and Veasey (2003) investigated this concept in a way that was understandable even to young children. They tested children's comprehension of self-promotion, reasoning that the role of self-promotion is to induce in others a particular belief about oneself, making it analogous to promotional messages in advertising. Pine and Veasey found that the ability to self-promote was evident in most children from the age of six or seven. Children younger than this had difficulty in producing a self-promoting statement. But they found some understanding of the bias in promotional messages by children as young as four or five years old. In a similar experiment, Young (2000) demonstrated that when children were asked to choose an ending for an advertisement, more than 90% of seven to eight-year-olds selected a promotional ending rather than an entertaining or neutral end. By this age, it appears that children are aware that in advertising there are certain communicative rules that are not to be broken.

In addition to understanding the advertiser's perspective, that is, their desire to persuade consumers to purchase, Lawlor and Prothero (2003) argued that other aspects of advertising also need to be considered. When they probed eight- to nine-year-olds on their understanding of television advertising, the children showed awareness of some of the wider issues around advertising. They discussed the role of television channels in selling space to advertisers, the financing of programmes by advertising, advertising as aspirational, advertising as entertainment, and the convenience of advertising breaks. The latter is sometimes dismissed as a rather unsophisticated response and as something that much younger children would say (but often this is the *only* answer young children will offer as to the purpose of advertising). But Lawlor and Prothero argued it is a valid point from the child's perspective because advertising breaks permit children to plan other activities during the break, such as consuming food and drink.

COMPARISON WITH PRODUCT EXPERIENCE

One of the cognitive criteria of Robertson and Rossiter's (1974) study was the recognition of discrepancy between a product as advertised and the same product in reality. Gunter and McAleer (1997) also highlighted this as a factor in affecting children's understanding of advertising. Young children do not make this distinction, but as children get older, it becomes a frequently cited reason for not believing advertisements. Bever, Smith, Bengen, and Johnson (1975) reported that the responses of nine- and 10-year-olds to television advertising depended largely on their personal experience with misleading advertising. Bever et al. offered some typical comments from the children, including "No More Tangles actually gave me knots" and "The box didn't contain the gift it was supposed to," both from 10-year-old girls. Most of the children interviewed had been misled by advertising claims, but despite this, they continued to have high expectations of advertising. Bever et al. suggested the children's ambivalence toward advertising was because some commercials do actually live up to their claims, as the children remarked of hypothetical products "there is a chance that they might do the job" and "we want to try them" (p. 161). John (1999b) supported this concept, arguing that knowledge about advertising cannot be expected to dampen a child's enthusiasm for an enticing toy or new chocolate bar.

More recent studies have found similar results to those of Bever et al. (1975) but have suggested a slightly younger age for when children experience product discrepancy. Oates et al. (2003) interviewed children in small focus groups and found that the eight- and nine-year-olds discussed their personal experiences of a product not living up to its advertised expectations. For example, a girl of nine suggested that the L'Oreal shampoo for children was advertised as kind to your eyes, but in reality it hurts. When prompted to explain this discrepancy, she replied, "it is so you will buy it." A girl of eight and a half years of age remembered a television advertisement for toothpaste that "makes your teeth totally white, but it doesn't really happen." Again this was explained as an encouragement to purchase. But at this age, children's complaints were restricted just to a particular product and not to a disenchantment with advertising as a whole. The 10-year-olds, however, stated that products generally look better on advertisements than in reality with the specific purpose of encouraging a purchase. They were very dismissive of advertising claims and disillusioned with many products, both on their own behalf and on behalf of siblings, friends, and parents. A girl of 10, clearly relating a product experience of an older person, reported that when you buy cream to take wrinkles away, sometimes it doesn't take them away at all.

Comparison with product experience was also mentioned in Preston's (2000) study of older children in Scotland and always in a negative way. Taking five of the advertising codes imposed upon television advertisers in the United Kingdom (ITC, 1991a, 1993, 1995, 1997) aimed at children (see chap. 9), he carried out focus groups in which children aged 10 and 11 years discussed each code in turn and were encouraged to think of advertisements that contravened these regulations. Preston chose the five codes because he expected their concepts would be easily understood by children, and he reworded them slightly to be more comprehensible to children. The codes used by Preston included:

adverts must not make anything seem better than it is in real life by using special effects;

adverts should not show toys that look easy to put together in the advert, but back home aren't easy at all;

advertising should not make children pester their parents into buying something;

children must not believe from adverts that having or using a product will make them popular;

children in advertisements should be reasonably well mannered and well behaved.

The children, who had previously been unaware of advertising codes, recalled advertisements where the products were smaller in reality (Cinderella Barbie), less flexible (Barbie), less colorful (Gameboy Colour), and simply inferior (tape recorder, Kinder Eggs, Barbie caravan). The ease of construction and assembly of toys was also explored, with children annoyed at the difficulty of putting together apparently straightforward toys such as K'Nex, Lego, and Meccano. Again, Barbie products came in for some criticism, with children unaware from the advertisements that any construction was involved at all. Preston concluded that children perceive advertisements in many instances to be in violation of the ITC codes, and he suggested that children should be integrated into the process of advertising regulation.

Discrepancy between a product as advertised and the same product in reality is an important factor in children's assessment of advertising's truthfulness. Older children, as the aforementioned studies demonstrated, are more likely to use their product experience to judge advertisements, often in a negative way. A further aspect of product experience is the ability to recognize when an advertisement demonstrates a feature or property of a product that is unlikely to be true, thus warning the child that the product will probably not meet its advertised expectations.

Smith (1983) suggested that as children display a growing awareness of the persuasive intent of advertising, they also begin to appreciate the techniques used by advertisers to enhance their products, for example, the use of sound effects. Martensen and Hansen (2001) supported this, suggesting that 11- and 12-year-olds mention factors such as tone of voice, choice of words, exaggeration, and visual tricks as indicators of credibility. This ability leads children to develop increased cynicism toward the product claims in advertising. Preston's (2000) focus group study explored this issue in depth. The children had no problems in recalling advertisements that used special effects and noted that such effects were often used to make a product look better. A Kellogg's Frosties advertisement was cited as an example of endowing a product with particular properties (Tony the animated Tiger is able to score in spectacular fashion in a basketball game after eating Frosties) that the children perceived as suggesting they too could have that ability after consuming Frosties. The children's reaction to Frosties indicated that the advertisement, at least in the children's eyes, was misleading as it implied better sporting performance after eating the cereal.

Toy advertising in particular is open to criticism that the reality of the product might not live up to its advertised image. In a study by Hanley (1996), both parents and children took part in research about the information presented in such advertising and how it was understood. The children were able to judge the size, scale, and movement of advertised toys by comparing them with similar products they already owned. The potential to mislead children arose when the advertised toy defied classification or if the scale references were unclear. Special effects were understood to be theatrical elements designed to enhance the toy and were not expected in real life. Similarly, children recognized that the role of fantasy in advertising was to fuel their imaginations with ideas for playing with the toy. However, the more practical features of toys, such as assembly, accessories, and batteries, could cause frustration because children were unable to play with them immediately but did not understand from the advertisements that this would be the case.

An alternative view of creative license was offered by Moore and Lutz (2000), who studied children in second grade (seven- to eight-year-olds) and in fifth grade (10- to 11-year-olds). They suggested that the older children were interested in the creative elements of advertisements, readily acknowledging that advertisers do employ creative license in presenting the positive aspects of their products. Although the children recognized product discrepancy from their own experiences with certain advertised products, they failed to relate this to a broader view of marketers' responsibilities to portray product performance fairly in advertising. Moore and Lutz (2000, p. 43) commented that the older children's "celebration of creativity in advertising was at times offered without concern for limits" and identified gaps in children's knowledge about acceptable standards of commercial persuasion.

ATTITUDES TOWARD ADVERTISING

Young children generally demonstrate a positive attitude toward advertising, displaying none of the cynicism so evident in older children. When asked if they believe what people say in advertisements, the majority of six-year-olds respond positively or at least believe some of the time. But over half of children aged between 10 and 13 believe advertisements some of the time or not at all (Bergler, 1999). At the age of 10, most children are skeptical of advertising claims and few 12-year-olds still believe advertisements tell the truth (Gunter & Furnham, 1998). These figures demonstrate a clear change in perception of advertising as children grow older.

Martensen and Hansen (2001) pointed out that children become more critical of advertising with age and also more skeptical. From the age of 13, children no longer perceive advertisements as entertaining, and advertising frequently fails to catch their attention. Martensen and Hansen investigated children's perceptions of the credibility of advertising using six criteria: how the advertisement is presented, whether an advertisement tells the truth, whether there is any exaggeration of the product, how well the product meets its promised expectations, comparison between product in advertisements and in reality, and the general honesty of advertisements. Children aged from eight to 18 years were questioned and the findings pointed to widespread cynicism about advertising. Eighty percent of eight- and nine-year-olds thought that advertisements were not honest or believable, and this figure rose to 90% for the 13- to 18-year-olds.

Earlier research (Ward, Wackman, & Wartella, 1977) found that children had difficulty in explaining how it is exactly that advertisements "cheat," but Martensen and Hansen (2001) showed that for the eight- and nine-year-olds, three criteria were important in their judgement of advertising's credibility. These criteria were that the product does not live up to its promise in the advertisement, that things look better in advertisements than in real life, and that you cannot trust what they say in advertisements. The more subtle cues in advertisements, such as the way things are said or the tone of voice, were only discerned by children over the age of 13. This research was supported by Hansen (1999) who also suggested that children below the age of 10 cannot understand the subtleties and ambiguities used by advertisers, but older children can "see through" such devices. For Bever et al. (1975), 11- to 12-year-olds were also found to be discriminating, citing suspicion of advertisements which overstated product benefits, used visual tricks, and presented too much detail about the product. The children in Smith's (1983) study, however, appreciated details unless they were irrelevant to their own requirements for basic information about the product (price, accessories, etc).

The exaggeration of products presented in advertising is irritating for older children and makes them critical of advertisements that they perceive to be promoting false or unrealistic claims. Children of about nine and 10 years of age may take a literal interpretation of advertising and question the language used. For example, Chan and McNeal (2002) cited a boy of nine criticizing a commercial that claimed a product could make the consumer "doubly beautiful." How, the child asked, could a person become doubly beautiful? He decided this was meaningless and dismissed both the advertisement and the product. Randrup and Lac (2000) found that older children criticized commercials containing exaggerated or unrealistic features, distancing themselves from such advertising, although this negative attitude did not necessarily extend to the product or brand being advertised. Generally, children disapprove of overemphasis or exaggeration in advertising (Randrup & Lac, 2000; Smith, 1983).

The use of celebrities in children's advertising has mainly been investigated with reference to cartoon characters and the danger of blurring the boundaries between advertisements and programs (Kunkel, 1988b). Lawlor and Prothero (2003) found that children identified celebrity endorsers as powerful components in the persuasiveness of an advertisement. Football players and pop groups were specifically mentioned as attracting an audience and as having the effect of making a product "cool" by association. The presence of a celebrity, however, does not guarantee trial of the endorsed product—children in Lawlor and Prothero's study pointed out that although they were attracted to and enjoyed advertisements featuring celebrities, this alone would not persuade them to buy the product.

Another aspect of celebrity endorsers is related to trust and liking. As mentioned previously, celebrity attributes are intended to infuse the advertised product with certain qualities that are valued by the intended target audience. According to Chan (2000), older children like commercials because of the celebrities involved, especially television, film, and pop stars. Conversely, children criticized advertisements featuring celebrities they did not like, generating polarized reactions from fans and nonfans of particular pop singers who promote competitive brands of mobile telephones. A later study (Chan & McNeal, 2002) found that some children used the presence of celebrities as an indicator of trust and to gauge the truthfulness of com-mercials. Other, older children (11 years) were more cynical, suggesting that commercials featuring celebrities were doubtful because the celebrity prob-ably had not even tried the product. This seems to be the more common re-sponse, with Smith (1983) also finding older children dismissive of celebrity endorsers, particularly where essential product information is lost though the dominance of the character. He found children of all ages preferred car-toon endorsers, especially those with strong brand identities. Evidence on the influence of celebrity endorsers is mixed, with some studies suggesting the influence is greater among younger children who lack the necessary cognitive defenses and others finding the influence was equally strong between older and younger children (Gunter & Furnham, 1998).

Cynicism is evident in adolescents' attitudes toward advertising. Adoles-cents are a difficult audience for advertisers both in terms of reach and ap-peal, yet they are also an attractive audience because of adolescents' spending power. Adolescents may also be a significant influence on family purchasing, although some authors would suggest that this influence is ex-aggerated (Bergler, 1999). What are the reasons behind adolescents' skepti-cism toward advertising? Several factors may be involved—peer influence, parental attitudes, exposure to television, and marketplace knowledge are four possible areas Mangleburg and Bristol (1999) investigated to identify the source of adolescent skepticism. In a questionnaire survey of 300 high school students, with an average age of 16, Mangleburg and Bristol analyzed these factors and found that skepticism toward advertising was an attitude learned through interaction with parents, peers, and television. Market-place knowledge gave adolescents a base from which to evaluate advertising, and with this knowledge, they were able to recognize persuasive techniques that advertisers use.

To retain control over their interaction with advertising, older children may claim to avoid advertisements, although they are still able to recount many advertisements in great detail (Bartholomew & O'Donohoe, 2003). A distanced and critical stance regarding advertising means that children do not see themselves as persuaded by advertising; nevertheless, they concede that advertisements can be amusing and entertaining. Bartholomew and O'Donohoe found that 10- to 12-year-olds were able critically to analyze ad-vertising targeted at different ages and genders, identifying their particular characteristics. The children in their study felt superior to adults, especially parents, who were seen to be easily persuaded by advertising.

Children's and adolescents' attitudes toward advertising concern adver-tisers as well as researchers. If children have a negative assessment of adver-tising in general, does this lead to a dismissal of all advertising and advertised brands, or do attitudes differ according to product category? Riecken and

Yavas (1990) specifically addressed this question, pointing out that although the relationship between attitude to advertisements generally and attitude to particular products or brands has previously been studied with adults, there is little such research with children.

Consequently, Riecken and Yavas (1990) investigated the question of attitudes to advertising with 150 children aged between eight and 12 years. A questionnaire with seven questions relating to television advertisements in general was self-administered (but the younger children received help from teachers), with responses to each item recorded on a four-point scale. The children were then shown three films featuring a cartoon and advertisements for cereal, toys, and pills. Evaluation of each brand was measured by a single question recorded on a five-point scale.

Riecken and Yavas (1990) found that children's general attitude toward advertising was very negative, with two thirds believing that advertisements do not tell the truth and that they are annoying, and most reporting that advertisements only tell the good things about products. However, with specific product categories this negative attitude varied, with toy commercials more favorably evaluated than the other two categories. And within the product categories, there was further variation, as the children viewed particular brands in a positive, negative, or uncertain manner. Riecken and Yavas concluded their findings by suggesting that "the transfer of affect from attitudes towards advertising in general to attitudes toward product advertising and finally to attitudes toward brands does not necessarily hold true in the case of children" (p. 144). This result is important for advertisers if they want to understand why children express negative attitudes toward certain commercials even when the brands advertised might be favorably received. Some support for Riecken and Yavas's findings comes from a study by Randrup and Lac (2000) who concluded that children hold negative beliefs and attitudes toward a brand if the television commercial contains complex or incomprehensible messages. Inability to decode such messages leads to frustration and influences the children's attitudes toward the brand.

Advertisers might also be concerned by children's perception of advertised brands as somehow inferior to nonadvertised brands. Older children in a study by Chan and McNeal (2002) in China reported doubt about the quality of brands and their need to advertise. A 12-year-old suggested that "quality brands have good sales and they don't need to advertise. Only brands of poor quality or those overproduced need to advertise." A nine-year-old girl claimed that "advertised brands are those that can't sell well." In other words, Chan and McNeal found that the children did not agree that television advertising would enhance their confidence in the products. But Chan and McNeal stressed that more research needs to be carried in China because the regulatory and historical contexts for advertising there are very different from those in the West. Chan and McNeal also pointed out that their findings differed from their own similar research with, for example, children in Hong Kong.

Do older children's negative attitudes toward advertising affect their purchase requests? It might be expected that a cynical response to advertising leads to a decline in requests because of previous disappointments, lack of trust in advertisers, ability to see through advertising techniques, and so on. Robertson and Rossiter (1974) found that only 7% of fifth-grade boys (about 10 years of age) trusted commercials and only 6% wanted all the products they saw advertised.

SUSCEPTIBILITY TO TELEVISION ADVERTISING

Given children's cynical attitudes toward advertising as discussed previously, it might be appropriate to conclude that older children are no longer susceptible to advertisers' persuasive messages. However, this is not necessarily the case. Like adults, children continue to be susceptible to subtle influences, despite their critical response to advertising. Martensen and Hansen (2001) found that children who were able to discern that advertising is not always credible continued to want advertised products although the desire for products declined with age. In an investigation of the direct effect of advertising on purchase behavior, they suggested that one in five teenagers agreed that they often buy products that they have seen advertised despite the fact they perceive advertisements to be untrustworthy. As a caution, Martensen and Hansen added that this result may partly be because of peer pressure rather than as a function of advertising effect. They concluded that "even though many children from age eight are able to discern the intention of ads, as well as the fact that ads are not always truthful, they still let themselves be influenced by ads to want the advertised products. The more often they watch ads, the more pronounced the wants created by advertising are … just as ads influence adults, they also influence children and youngsters" (pp. 29–30).

Riecken and Yavas (1990) found a more cautious attitude among older children. When evaluating advertised brands, the children tended to choose the "not sure" response rather than assuming a product to be good. This response varied according to product category, suggesting that on the whole, children do not automatically accept commercial messages that emphasize good things about a product. The researchers concluded that children from eight to 12 years are far from credulous when it comes to television advertising.

The stance taken by older children in relation to advertising can vary according to their perception of the appropriate response required. No longer

seen as a passive audience, older children (i.e., 10- to 12-year-olds) are recognized as engaging with advertisements and using them for particular purposes, for example, to negotiate status and relationships with others
(O'Donohoe, 1994).

A study by Bartholomew and O'Donohoe (2003) illustrated children's
competence with advertising. Using small focus groups, individual interviews, and photo diaries, the authors explored the children's understanding
and use of advertisements and asked them to create an advertisement for an
imaginary drink. The children emerged as "ad masters," using advertising to
demonstrate their cultural competence. The role of ad master indicated
there were three subsidiary roles to be adopted: meaning masters, style masters, and performance masters. As meaning masters, children enjoyed de-
coding advertising messages and demonstrating their interpretative powers.
Failure to "get" a message was only admitted reluctantly. Children in the role
of style master illustrated their awareness of different advertising approaches, such as humor, the use of music, and means of attracting attention, and applied such knowledge to creating their own advertisements. The
role of performance master indicated children's delight and competence at
acting out advertisements, imitating voice-overs, singing jingles, and so on,
all skills valued by their peers. Bartholomew and O'Donohoe concluded
that children have the ability to slip in and out of roles as the occasion demands, each role offering a degree of power in their experiences with advertising. They suggested this finding supports the view of those advertising
practitioners who have argued that children are sophisticated consumers of
advertising.

STEREOTYPES IN ADVERTISING

Television programming has been shown to portray several types of stereotyping including gender, family role, and race, and many studies have been
carried out to investigate the effects of such stereotyping on children and
how these can be challenged (Gunter & McAleer, 1997). There is less research into advertising stereotypes, and the research that exists tends to focus on advertising content or on the effects of stereotypes on older children
and young adults (see chap. 8). The studies of content analyses are mainly
about gender stereotypes and tend to show a bias in favor of women as
homemakers although the actual influence of such role portrayals on advertising effectiveness is rather unclear, with different studies finding contradictory results (Gunter, 1995).

Children are affected by stereotypes in television advertising as Martin et
al. (1999) noted in relation to gender stereotyping. Much of the research is
undertaken with girls, although studies have shown that boys may also be

susceptible to gender-role stereotyping in advertising (Lury, 1996). Adolescent girls in particular are adversely affected by images of beauty in advertisements, especially if they already have a poor body image. Advertisements featuring physically attractive models are more likely to create a desire for the product in girls with poorer body images. For example, Fox (1996) reported the results of a study in which teenage girls were shown fifteen commercials emphasizing physical beauty, and another group was not exposed to the commercials. The former group was more likely to agree with statements such as "beauty is desirable for me" and "beauty is important to be popular" than the latter group. The cumulative effects of advertising may, therefore, condition children to accept conventional gender roles, and the situation regarding gender-specific advertisements has not changed over time. As mentioned earlier, contemporary children are adept at spotting features that identify advertisements aimed at males and females (Bartholomew & O'Donohoe, 2003). The influence of stereotypes in advertising are discussed at greater length in chapter eight.

Contemporary advertising is often characterized by self-parody, particularly advertisements for traditional household products, and because these are executed and presented in a knowing, self-referential style, advertisers deny they perpetuate stereotypical representations. Given this type of advertising, it would be useful to analyze contemporary advertising to assess whether stereotyping is still evident and to investigate whether children's ability to discern stereotyped advertising has any bearing on the actual effects of that stereotyping.

The conclusion from this chapter is that older children are both more cynical about television advertising than their younger counterparts but still susceptible to its persuasive messages. Adolescents are a hard-to-reach, cynical audience who see through advertisers' techniques yet (possibly because of peer pressure) continue to desire advertised products. In this, they are like adults who, even after years of experience with advertising, are prepared to try new brands on the strength of their advertisements.

5

Theoretical Approaches to Studying Children's Understanding of Advertisements

In chapters three and four, the research into children's understanding of advertisements was discussed. In chapter three, young children's attention and memory for advertisements, whether they could distinguish between advertisements and programs, and the early recognition of brand names was considered. Chapter four looked at more advanced forms of understanding, in particular children's recognition of the persuasive nature of television advertising as well as their attitudes toward advertising. In both chapters, many of the results from the research into children's understanding were summarized, and it was pointed out that there has not been much agreement about when children achieve different levels of awareness. As was pointed out, most of the research into children's understanding of advertising has been conducted without any theoretical framework.

This chapter suggests that the lack of a well-developed theoretical framework has weakened the research into children's understanding of advertisements. Two theoretical approaches that are referred to most frequently—Piaget's theory of cognitive development and the information processing approach to cognitive development (see Smith, Cowie, & Blades, 2003)—are the main focus though other theoretical approaches are discussed. Although the latter frameworks are helpful, they are limited in generating testable hypotheses about children and advertising. A final topic concerns the idea that the best way forward is to investigate children's understanding of advertising in the context of their developing understanding of others' minds (Smith et al., 2003). This contemporary paradigm of developmental psychology offers insights into children's abilities that can be applied to their understanding of advertisements.

PIAGET'S THEORY AND ADVERTISING RESEARCH

The theory that has been most frequently cited in the literature about children's understanding of advertisements is Piaget's description of the development of children's logical thinking (for a description of Piaget's theory, see Smith et al., 2003). Piaget developed his theory over several decades and in many books, and, therefore, any summary of his work loses the richness of what he proposed. Nonetheless, we will outline one or two aspects of his theory and explain how those aspects have influenced the research into children and advertisements.

Sensorimotor Stage

Piaget described children's development in terms of four "stages" of logical thought. The first of these is known as the "sensorimotor" stage (0–2 years of age) and includes that period of children's development from birth to the development of early independent thought and simple problem solving about the age of two years. Simple problem solving means children being able to plan limited series of actions (e.g., to work out how to reach a toy that isn't immediately available). During this period, children have some language and by two years of age may be producing two and three word sentences. Nonetheless, children's limited language and cognitive development in this period precludes any possibility of understanding advertisements.

Preoperational Stage

Piaget's second stage of cognitive development is called the "preoperational" stage. Piaget described children's reasoning in terms of performing logical operations to solve problems. Because Piaget thought that young children had limited reasoning in this period, he referred to the period as the preoperational (or prelogical) one. This period occurs between two and seven years of age (though Piaget himself did not specify precise ages for any of the stages). According to Piaget, children's cognitive abilities develop rapidly during this period, but they are also limited in a number of ways. He identified these limitations from several key experiments. For example, he noted that children had difficulty in tasks that involved the transformation of materials. To give one example, if children are shown two identical glasses with the same quantity of liquid in each a child will, of course, agree that there is the same quantity in each glass. But if the liquid from one glass is then poured into a taller, but narrower, glass, many preoperational children will think there is now more liquid in the taller glass. In other words, the appearance of the liquid in the new glass overcomes children's ability to reason that the liquid cannot really have increased in quantity. Therefore, one of the limitations of the preoperational period is children's inability to overcome the perceptual qualities of a stimulus.

Without the ability to overcome superficial changes (the height of the liquid) that are not relevant to the problem (of deciding whether the quantity of liquid has changed), children in the preoperational period find it hard to reason logically in problem-solving tasks. To reason logically, children need to consider both the height and width of the new glass. In other words, children need to consider two dimensions at the same time and realize that the greater height of the liquid is compensated for by the narrower width of the glass. But Piaget claimed that children often focus only on one dimension of the task, and this limits their reasoning. Some researchers have suggested that children's inability to consider more than a single aspect of a task is one of the reasons why children in the preoperational period do not have a well-developed understanding of advertising. Kunkel (1988a) suggested children who cannot consider different aspects of television will view television as a "monolithic entity" and will therefore have difficulty distinguishing advertisements from programs. Young (1990) pointed out that if young children only concentrate on a single aspect of what they are watching they might have more difficulty switching attention between programs and advertisements because they will be less sensitive to the differences between the two.

Piaget suggested that another limitation of children in the preoperational period is their "egocentrism." Piaget placed a toy landscape, with several different features, on a table and asked a child to sit at one side of the table (Piaget & Inhelder, 1956). Then he placed a doll at the opposite side of the table and asked the child to describe what the doll saw. Children in the preoperational stage found this a difficult task. They were unable to describe the view seen by the doll and often just described their own view of the landscape. This is another example of children's inability to reason logically, and because they often reported their own view, Piaget called them egocentric. Piaget pointed out that children were egocentric in other contexts as well. For example, in conversation, preoperational children may have difficulty appreciating the viewpoint of another person if that viewpoint is different from the child's own. Piaget used the term *egocentric* to emphasize that children could not work out logically how another person viewed the world when that view was different from their own.

Children's egocentrism may be an important aspect of understanding advertisements (Kunkel, 2001). If children in the preoperational period cannot appreciate viewpoints other than their own, it is likely that they will have difficulty understanding the persuasive nature of advertising. To understand persuasive content, children need to be aware of the aims of an advertiser whose purpose is to sell products. The advertiser's view of a television commercial is quite different from a child's view of an advertisement. A young child may see an advertisement from one point of view (e.g., as a source of information—see previous chapters), but this is not the same as the advertiser's point of view. If egocentric children can only consider one point of view, they will not be able to understand that the advertisement they see as informational can also be interpreted in a different way as a persuasive message. We will discuss this issue further in the section on understanding minds below.

Concrete Operational Stage

Children after the preoperational period can reason logically in problem-solving tasks, and they can consider two aspects of the task at the same time. For this reason, they have no difficulty considering the relationship between the height and width of the glass in the liquid task. Piaget argued that children's ability to consider more than one dimension of a task reflected their developing logical thought. When children have achieved such logical thought, they are in the stage of concrete operational thought (seven–11 years of age). This period is called "concrete" because children can usually solve tasks like the liquid task because they are tasks that the children can see or experience directly. In other words, the tasks are concrete ones because their components (e.g., glasses and liquid) physically exist in the world (i.e., they are real or "concrete" components). According to Piaget, children develop their reasoning abilities by experience and by interacting with materials in the world. For example, young children develop their reasoning about the liquid task through playing with liquids and containers. They learn that it does not matter how many times you pour the same quantity of liquid into differently shaped containers, the quantity of liquid will not change. In this way children learn about the properties of the world.

Applying Piaget's theory to children's understanding of advertisements in the concrete stage is not self-evident. On one hand, children's reasoning is developing, and therefore we would expect an increasing ability to understand advertisements. On the other hand, Piaget argued that children's reasoning is better in concrete contexts—ones in which they can experience or manipulate materials directly. But children's experience of television is usually as a passive receiver of the medium without the opportunity to question the images they view. Without direct experience, we might expect children's reasoning about television to be less well developed than their reasoning in other domains that involve more opportunities for interacting with stimuli.

Formal Operational Stage

Although children can achieve a degree of logical thought in the concrete operational stage, they still have difficulty in tasks that require abstract reasoning. For example, children in that stage have difficulty solving a problem such as "all cats with pink eyes have six legs. Fred is a cat with pink eyes. How many legs does Fred have?" Children have difficulty giving the logical answer because the components of the task are abstract, imaginary ones that do not have any counterparts in real life. According to Piaget, children only begin abstract reasoning after about 11 years of age as they move into the formal operational stage of development. It is called the "formal" operational stage because it encompasses all aspects of abstract, hypothetical reasoning that can be applied to any task that can be solved by logical thought. Although the formal stage extends from about 11 years throughout adulthood, teenagers' logical reasoning is not as sophisticated as adults' reasoning. Nonetheless, the start of the formal period reflects the potential of children to think about problems in a similar way to adults and to develop their reasoning from experience and learning (see Smith et al., 2003). We can assume therefore that children's understanding of advertising after the age of about 11 or 12 years should be similar to adults' understanding. Any differences between children's and adults' understanding in the formal operational period are more likely to be the result of different experience rather than the consequence of different cognitive abilities.

In summary, Piaget described children's development as series of ever more sophisticated periods of logical thought, culminating in the adult achievement of abstract reasoning after about 11 or 12 years of age. Piaget demonstrated the levels of logical thinking in each stage by describing what children could or could not do in problem-solving tasks. The liquid task and the syllogism given earlier are examples of such logical problem-solving tasks (for others, see Smith et al., 2003). To describe what children have to achieve to solve a particular problem requires an analysis of that problem, and Piaget offered analyses of many different problems. On the basis of these analyses, he drew conclusions about children's abilities or lack of abilities in each stage.

Influence of Piaget's Theory on Advertising Research

Piaget's theory is probably the most frequently cited theory in papers about children's understanding of advertisements (Young, 1990). However, it is difficult to assess the theory's influence on the research. This section suggests the influence of Piaget's theory has been quite limited despite the number of citations it receives.

The majority of advertising researchers who cite Piaget's work do so only as a token reference without discussing his work at all. A few researchers do include descriptions of Piaget's stage theory but without explaining why this framework is useful or appropriate. In other words, many authors seem to feel obliged to mention Piaget's theory, perhaps as a reflection of his importance in the history of developmental psychology, but do not use the theory to advance particular hypotheses or expectations about children's understanding of advertising.

Linking Piaget's theory to understanding advertisements is difficult. Piaget did not carry out any research into children's understanding of television advertising and therefore assumptions based on his theory have to be extrapolations from his research in other domains. As pointed out previously, the focus of Piaget's work was the analysis of children's reasoning on problem-solving tasks. One way to apply Piaget's work to children's understanding of advertising is to consider that understanding as problem solving. For example, children's ability to distinguish advertising from programs or their ability to understand advertisements as persuasive messages would have to be analyzed in terms of problem solving. But children's ability to distinguish advertisements is not of the same nature as the problem-solving tasks that Piaget set children. To succeed in problem-solving tasks such as Piaget's liquid task or like the syllogism given earlier requires logical reasoning to achieve a correct conclusion. In contrast, distinguishing advertisements or realizing they are persuasive messages does not necessarily involve the same type of logical reasoning. For instance, there are no obvious premises by which a child can work out that one television scene is a program and one scene is an advertisement. Nor are there "correct" answers because the borderline between advertisements and programs (that include sponsorship, product placement, and so on) are not always clear and well defined.

Therefore, the application of Piaget's theory to advertising research is not straightforward, and this may be why the precise relationship between Piaget's work and children's knowledge of advertising is often left unspecified. Most commonly, his theory is invoked in a general manner as a way of indicating that young children have limited cognitive abilities (e.g., in the preoperational period) with the implication that if children have limitations, they will also have a limited understanding of advertising (e.g., Bijmolt et al., 1998; Chan, 2000). Only a few authors have tried to draw specific reasons from Piaget's theories to explain why children's understanding of advertising might be limited. To repeat the examples used earlier, some researchers have suggested that children's egocentrism and their inability to consider more than one dimension of a problem are both reasons why we would expect young children to have difficulty understanding advertisements (Kunkel, 1988a; Young, 1990).

Piaget's theory has been much criticized in the years since it was first proposed (see Smith et al., 2003). Piaget argued that preoperational children's lack of success on his problem-solving tasks was a reflection of their lack of logical reasoning. But other researchers have suggested that children may fail Piagetian tasks because they are confused about the instructions they are given or about the nature of the language used during the tasks. There is now much evidence that altering the instructions and questions in Piaget's tasks can result in an increase in children's success (Donaldson 1978; Siegal 1997). This means that the difficulties that Piaget found and interpreted as a lack of reasoning may not reflect a lack of reasoning at all. The difficulties may reflect children's confusion about what they were expected to do in the tasks that Piaget set them. Once children understand the nature of the tasks, they are often able to perform them successfully and demonstrate the reasoning that Piaget thought was lacking. This is not to say that young children have the same reasoning abilities as older children or adults, but they may be more capable of logical thinking than Piaget assumed.

The nature of many of Piaget's tasks might have led to an underestimation of children's cognitive abilities. For example, children's ability to consider more than one dimension of a problem is an earlier achievement that Piaget suggested. If children are more capable of reasoning than Piaget assumed this has implications for research into advertising. His theory can no longer be cited as evidence that children's lack of understanding is "automatically" a result of their lack of reasoning. More important, the fact that children can perform some tasks earlier than Piaget found, weakens the framework of the stage theory he proposed, and contemporary psychologists put much less emphasis on descriptions of children's development that place children in particular stages at particular ages. Nonetheless, as we noted earlier, many researchers still refer to children's understanding of advertisements in terms of Piaget's stages.

Children's difficulty with the language in many of Piaget's tasks reflects a wider concern about the use of language in any task with young children. Much of the research into children's understanding of advertisements has been based on questioning, interviews, and focus groups (see chaps. 3 and 4). This methodology is necessary to find out about children's understanding. Issues like the persuasive nature of advertising and broader issues about the influence of advertisements on children's behavior can usually only be addressed by talking to children about their own ideas. But several researchers have argued that any method, like Piaget's, that is particularly dependent on language understanding may have underestimated children's abilities. Children may have knowledge that they are unable to express in verbal responses. As noted in chapter three, some researchers have attempted to use nonverbal tasks with young children to elicit their understanding without the complication of asking them to express their understanding in words (Bijmolt et al., 1998; Donohoe et al., 1980; Macklin, 1983, 1987). The nonverbal tasks included children pointing to pictures to indicate the purpose of advertising or acting out shopping behavior. As pointed out in chapter three, these nonverbal tasks have methodological problems, and there was little evidence that the tasks demonstrated an early understanding of advertisements. Nonetheless, future researchers may be able to find valid nonverbal measures to overcome the general concern that verbal measures on their own result in children being underestimated.

The use of nonverbal tasks were a specific response to the criticisms of Piaget's methodology (see Macklin, 1983). Other researchers have responded to criticisms of Piaget's theory by adopting alternative frameworks for studying children's understanding of advertisements. The most influential of these has been the information-processing framework, initially proposed by Roedder (1981) and this approach is discussed in the following section.

How useful has Piaget's theory been for research into children's understanding of advertising? We suggest that Piaget's framework has contributed little to the research. The majority of citations of the framework are only token acknowledgments to the theory. Those authors who have made links between the theory and the results from studies of advertising have usually done so only in a post hoc way so that findings are explained by reference to Piaget's theory after the empirical work has been completed. Nearly all studies of children's understanding could have been planned and carried out without any reference to Piaget's theory at all.

Put another way, Piaget's framework has not been used to *predict* children's understanding at different ages or in different contexts in advance of carrying out a study. Such predictions require an analysis of advertising tasks in Piagetian terms, and depending on that analysis, predicting from the theory which tasks would be completed in which stages of development. This would mean a consideration of the "logical operations," or reasoning, needed to carry out a task related to advertising. But as noted above, it is not obvious how Piaget's analysis of reasoning can be applied to children's understanding of advertising. Advertising depends on factors such as image, presentation, emotion, persuasion, entertainment, and so on (Moore & Lutz, 2000). Understanding advertisements depends on understanding such factors. But these are not the same factors that Piaget considered in most of the tasks that he set children—his tasks were usually structured, logical, and "scientific" tasks that could be solved with a single (correct) answer.

Even if appropriate task analyses could be used to relate advertising tasks to Piaget's framework, any use of his theory means taking into account the criticisms that have been leveled at the theory. The criticisms have been wide-ranging ones that have much weakened his stage theory. Few developmental psychologists would now support the notion that all aspects of children's reasoning at any given age can be explained by reference to what "stage" they are in. The decline in the support for Piaget's theory during the last two decades of developmental research makes it all the more surprising that his theory is still frequently, and positively, cited in the advertising literature.

THE INFORMATION APPROACH
TO ADVERTISING RESEARCH

Information processing refers to the way that children attend to and take in information about the world around them. How they interpret that information, remember it, relate it to their existing knowledge, how they recall it at a later time, and how they apply that information in new contexts. Not unlike Piaget's approach any investigation of information processing depends on task analyses. But whereas Piaget discussed children's abilities in terms of the reasoning (or lack of reasoning), the focus of the information-processing approach is on children's abilities in terms of their attention, memory, and recall.

People have only limited memory capacity and attention, and researchers have pointed out that young children have more limited attention and memory than older children and adults. If young children have limitations, they will be less able to process information, and this may account for age related differences in ability and reasoning. For example, if young children have a more limited memory capacity, they will be able to hold less information in memory at one time, and therefore they will be less able to deal with complex problems (Schneider & Pressley, 1997). Information processing also refers to the cognitive strategies that children use. These may be strategies that can be applied across a range of tasks. For instance, when trying to remember new information children may apply mnemonics to help them remember the information, and the same mnemonic can be used to learn different types of information. Older children are likely to have more effective mnemonics than younger children (Schneider & Pressley, 1997).

As well as strategies, like mnemonics, that are applicable in different contexts, there will be strategies that are specific to particular tasks. Some researchers have analyzed the strategies needed to solve tasks (like the problem solving tasks used by Piaget) and described how, as children develop, they use progressively more sophisticated strategies to solve a particular problem. For example, children might be shown a balance scale with various weights placed on both sides of the fulcrum. If they are asked to say whether the balance scale will tip one way or the other, the children need to consider factors such as the number of weights, their distance from the fulcrum, and perform various mental calculations (Siegler, 1998). Children's performance on such a task will depend on whether they have the appropriate strategies (e.g., mathematical ones) to carry out those calculations and will also depend on whether they have the memory capacity to complete those calculations. Put another way, even if children know the mathematical procedures for working out balance scale problems, those procedures may involve so much mental arithmetic that children will not be able to hold all the information needed for the calculations in their memory at the same time.

In summary, according to the information processing approach, children's development depends on finding effective ways to deal with the world. These ways will depend on children learning about specific aspects of the world, and, in turn, this learning depends on the development of cognitive factors such as the capacity of children's memory and their ability to apply memory and other strategies in different contexts. The information-processing approach does not preclude stage theories of child development (Case, 1985), but contemporary researchers in the information-processing tradition place most emphasis on gradual rather than stage like development. For example, Siegler (1998) suggested that as children develop a better understanding of a task, they may think about that task in more than one and perhaps several different ways at the same time. With age and experience, children come to learn which is the best or most reliable way to think about the task. For this reason children may, for a period of time, be willing to come to different conclusions about a task each time they think about it. But gradually they will achieve a consistency and consider the same task in the same way each time. The emphasis on children gradually exploring different (and usually progressively better) ways to deal with a task over a period of time stands in contrast to the earlier approaches, like Piaget's, which described children's development as a series of distinct stages.

Influence of Information Processing Approaches on Advertising Research

In a frequently cited paper in the advertising literature, Roedder (1981) described information processing research up to that date and discussed its implications for investigating children's understanding of advertisements.

Roedder (1981) suggested that children could be divided into three types of processors, those who were "strategic" those who were "cued" and those who were "limited." According to Roedder, the strategic processors are children who are able to select and encode information appropriately (presumably, as well as adults). Cued processors are children who have the necessary encoding and learning strategies but do not apply those strategies unless they are prompted to do so. Limited processors are children who do not have the necessary strategies, and therefore do not benefit from being prompted.

Roedder (1981) then applied the three categories (strategic, cued, and limited processors) to two aspects of children's development. First, to children's "central-incidental" learning. By central-incidental learning, Roedder meant children's ability to distinguish what is central to a particular task from what is peripheral to that task. The implication being that children who can ignore peripheral information can focus on just the central information that is important for understanding a task. Children who focus on the central aspects of advertisements will be able to process the information about the product and ignore the less relevant peripheral content of the advertisement. According to Roedder, only strategic processors (aged 13 or more) are able to ignore peripheral information. In contrast, cued processors (eight- to 12-year-olds) will need help to ignore the peripheral content of an advertisement, and limited processors (children below the age of eight years) will be unable to ignore peripheral messages with or without help. This has implications for advertising regulation, and Roedder argued that cued processors need help to focus on the central message of an advertisement—either by having that message highlighted in some way or by specific media education to teach children about the purpose of advertising. Although such approaches might help cued processors they will be ineffective for limited processors. Roedder did not suggest ways to help limited processors except to suggest very simplified advertising messages in which the central, product information is presented with little or no distracting peripheral information.

Second, Roedder (1981) applied her three categories to children's memory development and argued that strategic processors are better at learning new information and remembering that information. Cued processors can only learn information when they are given help and support to do so, and limited processors will have difficulty in many tasks. Roedder suggested that for memory development, children achieved strategic processing after about 10 years of age, cued processing after six years, and were limited processors before the age of six years. These ages are, of course, different from the ones that Roedder proposed for different aspects of central-peripheral processing (given previously). Although Roedder suggested how there might be a relationship between learning processes and the ability to make central-peripheral distinctions, she did not make the relationship explicit.

We have described Roedder's (1981) information processing approach to advertising in some detail because her theory is still very frequently cited (e.g., Bandyopadhyay et al., 2001; Bijmolt et al., 1998; Chan, 2000; Clark, 1999; Marshall & Ffelan, 1999; Moore & Lutz, 2000; John, 1999a). However, because Roedder described children's understanding in terms of limited, cued, and strategic processors and attached specific age bands to these terms, her theory is in effect a stage theory. The theory is most often cited as a way of saying that children are in the "limited stage," the "cued stage" or the "strategic stage" of development. But describing children's development in these terms is not much of an advance on previous stage theories (like Piaget's) and is open to the same criticisms. As Schneider and Pressley (1997) pointed out, the way that children approach a task will depend on the nature of the task and children's familiarity with the task as well as their information processing abilities. For example, children who are expert chess players can remember chess positions better than adults who are not chess players (Chi, 1978). Examples such as this demonstrate the limitation of any stage theory that implies that younger children will always perform less well than older children who, in turn, will always perform less well than adults.

A stage theory, such as Roedder's that is based on assumptions about children's information processing at a particular age but which does not take into account the factors that are specific to particular tasks and contexts and children's past experience of a task, is, therefore, likely to be limited. Because children of a particular age have been shown to be, for example, "cued processors" in a particular task of memory performance, this does not necessarily mean that children of the same age will also be cued processors on a different task. The best way to establish whether children's level of processing is the same across different tasks is to test the *same* children on several tasks. This would mean testing children on various information processing tasks and testing the same children on various advertising tasks. If children showed the same processing limitations across a range of different task, this would provide some support for a stage theory of understanding. However, advertising researchers have tended to measure children's performance only on advertising tasks. This is a limitation in understanding the development of children's awareness because we do not know whether children's performance on an advertising task will be related to their performance on another task. What is needed is research showing that children's understanding of advertising parallels their understanding of similar tasks that do not involve advertising. But as yet researchers have not made comparisons between different types of tasks.

Most researchers have focused on the stages described by Roedder (1981) and have ignored the information processing basis of her theory, and for this reason, the influence of the theory has been limited. Most researchers have not adopted an information processing approach, and tasks involving advertisements have not been analyzed with reference to concepts such as attention, encoding, and retrieval of information. Without such analyses, it is difficult to know how these components of the task affect children's understanding. The information processing approach might provide insights into children's understanding of advertising, and this approach may be particularly useful for considering some aspects of children's developing awareness. For example, a systematic analysis of how children distinguish between advertisements and programs may help to identify the strategies that children use to first identify advertisements (John, 1999a). But as yet, task analysis in advertising research is lacking.

Although Roedder (1981) referred to central and incidental learning, these terms are not often used in contemporary developmental psychology. The main problem with the terms *central* and *incidental* is the difficulty of defining them. The terms imply different aspects of processing, but there has been little agreement about the meaning of terms such as *incidental learning* (Parkin, 1993). Alternatively, the terms might imply different elements of a stimulus, such as an advertisement. But if they are used in this way, researchers need to specify which aspects of a particular advertising task are the central ones and which are incidental ones—a difficult task. The briefest television advertisement involves many images, references, music, words, and sounds, and all these are presented to enhance the attractiveness of the product. If a child does not encode the full details of an advertisement, but recalls an image, a logo, a jingle, or a slogan, the advertising has been successful. For this reason, it is not easy to determine what is central and what is incidental in an advertisement. Roedder implied that the term *central* refers to understanding the "main product message" (1981, p. 146), but this requires a conceptual understanding of the purpose of advertising, and Roedder did not explain how such conceptual awareness develops from children having better information processing abilities.

The following section explores an alternative way to examine children's understanding of advertising in the context of contemporary theories of child development that offer novel ways to examine children's ability to interpret advertisements.

UNDERSTANDING OTHER MINDS

An important aspect of interpreting advertisements is the ability to consider the aims and purpose of the advertisement. This means adopting the perspective of the advertiser. But many researchers have pointed out that children have difficulty appreciating another person's perspective. Piaget and Inhelder's (1956) perspective-taking task was described earlier. On the basis of such tasks, Piaget argued that children in the preoperational period of development (up to about seven years of age) were egocentric because they could not appreciate that other people can have different views of the world from their own. Other researchers, following Piaget, have also stressed the egocentrism of young children (e.g., Selman, 1980). Young children's failure to appreciate other perspectives implies that they would have difficulty understanding that advertisements are designed from a particular point of view—the advertiser's desire to market a product (John, 1999a).

Despite some acknowledgment of the early research into children's perspective taking, most researchers investigating the understanding of advertisements have ignored the more recent research into children's perspective taking. Since the 1980s, one of the dominant paradigms in developmental research has been the "theory of mind" paradigm (see Smith et al., 2003). Researchers within this paradigm investigate how a child develops an awareness of other people as individuals who have minds that include knowledge, desires, and beliefs that may be different from the child's own. Put another way, how does a child come to realize that other people have minds? This question has prompted a large amount of research, and this research is the most relevant in any discussion of children's understanding of advertisements.

Research into theory of mind is best explained by describing one of the most commonly used tasks that have been employed to test young children's ability to adopt other perspectives. This task is called the "Sally-Anne" task (Baron-Cohen, Leslie, & Frith, 1985). In this task, a child is shown two dolls, Sally and Anne. Sally has a basket and Anne has a box. Sally puts a marble in her basket and then leaves the scene. While she is away, Anne takes the marble out of the basket and puts it in her box. Sally returns and the child is asked "Where will Sally look for her marble?" Most children from the age of four years will say, correctly, that Sally will look for the marble in the basket. But most three-year-olds say that Sally will look in the box. In other words, children before the age of four years do not appreciate that their own knowledge of the world (that the marble is in the box) is different from Sally's belief (that the marble is in the basket).

The Sally-Anne task is described as a "false belief" task because for children to answer correctly, they need to appreciate that Sally has a false belief about the location of the marble. False belief here means a belief that is incorrect because it does not reflect reality. When children are able to appreciate that others have incorrect beliefs, they are starting to realize that other people have minds that interpret (not always correctly) the world around them. Another way of saying this is that children realize that different people can interpret the world in different ways—that is, different people can have different perspectives.

Three-year-olds typically fail false belief tasks and show little awareness that their perspective and another's perspective might be different. Four-year-olds are generally successful in such tasks and are, therefore, said to have an understanding of other perspectives, at least in tasks like the Sally-Anne task. As children have such an understanding from about four years of age, the earlier suggestions (Piaget & Inhelder, 1956; Selman, 1980) that children before six or seven years of age are unable to appreciate other people's perspectives may have underestimated young children's abilities.

Understanding that different people can have different beliefs is a crucial step toward understanding other aspects of people's minds. Once children are capable of appreciating that a person can hold a false belief in their minds, then, potentially, children can implant an incorrect belief in another person's mind. In other words, they can manipulate how the other person interprets the world. For example, if a person is looking for a marble that is hidden in a red box, a child could tell the person that the marble is in a blue box. If the other person has no other source of information and is willing to believe the child, then the child has successfully given the other person a false belief. Implanting a false belief depends on giving another person deceptive information (saying the marble is in the blue box) when that person does not have any other source of information (i.e., does not know in which box the marble has been placed). The ability to deceive by implanting a belief can sometimes be achieved by four-year-olds and by five years of age children are consistently good at such deception (Peskin, 1992). Therefore, by the age of about five years children can manipulate the perspective of another person. Understanding different perspectives (and manipulating them) are early achievements and occur well before the age when previous researchers (e.g., Piaget & Inhelder, 1956) thought that children could adopt other people's perspectives.

Despite young children's early achievements in understanding other minds, they may not have a full appreciation of all aspects of mind. It takes children several years to achieve adult-like levels of understanding of mind. For example, some aspects of persuasion depend on changing another person's beliefs. This requires more than just implanting a belief in someone else's mind (as in the case of deception) because changing someone else's mind means considering what they already believe and then offering a counterargument to that belief to suggest a new belief.

Little research has explored how children attempt to change beliefs in the context of manipulating another person's existing beliefs. One of the few studies is by Bartsch and London (2000) who asked children to invent arguments to change someone else's mind. For example, the researchers told children a story in which a boy wanted his parents to buy him a bird, but his father thinks the bird will be messy, and his mother thinks the bird will be noisy. The children were asked what the boy in the story should say to persuade his parents to buy the bird. To be correct, children needed to consider the existing beliefs of the boy's parents and suggest counterarguments to those beliefs. For instance, they could suggest that the boy should say that the bird is in fact clean and quiet. If children could do this successfully, then they appreciated the need to manipulate someone else's existing beliefs. Bartsch and London found that four-, five-, and six-year-old children had difficulty in this task and could not consistently formulate appropriate ways to persuade the parents to buy the bird. Even though they used several story scenarios and used different ways to test the children, young children were generally unable to offer consistent ways to change the parents' minds.

Taken together, the results of the studies summarized in this section show that children's understanding of minds and beliefs develops gradually during the preschool and early school years. Children from about four years of age can understand that other people may have incorrect beliefs in their minds (Baron-Cohen et al., 1985). Children from about five years of age can do more than this and realize that if another person does not have an existing belief, then you can instill a belief in their minds (Peskin, 1992). But it is not until after six years of age that children begin to realize the need to present appropriate arguments to change someone's preexisting beliefs (Bartsch & London, 2000). The following section suggests that children's gradually developing understanding of other minds has implications for their understanding of advertisements.

If young children do not appreciate the importance of changing some one else's beliefs as a form of persuasion, what type of persuasive techniques do young children use? Weiss and Sachs (1991) asked three- to six-year-olds how they would persuade a friend to share a toy with them or how they would ask their mother to buy them a toy in a supermarket. They analyzed the persuasive strategies that the children used. The most frequent ones were what Weiss and Sachs called "positive sanctions" which included strategies like bargaining (the child offered to reciprocate in some way) or by promising things that were not in the child's control. The next most frequent strategies were "negative sanctions" such as nagging, begging, or crying. There were only a few examples of children trying to change someone else's mind. Using a similar methodology, Clark and Delia (1976) asked children and adolescents (aged seven to 14 years) to describe how they would ask their parents for something that they wanted. Clark and Delia combined several parameters in their coding system, and therefore children's individual responses were not reported, but there was little indication that many of the children before the age of eight years used counter arguments to overcome their parents' beliefs.

Trawick-Smith (1992) carried out a naturalistic study by recording the persuasive strategies used by four- and five-year-olds as they interacted during play sessions. Trawick-Smith categorized the children's strategies as various types of requests, demands, and threats. Nearly all the examples of these strategies were ones in which children made direct appeals to their peers, and they did not involve attempts to change minds. It is not until children are older that they demonstrate the spontaneous use of strategies that involve considering another's belief or point-of-view and providing counterarguments (Erftmier & Dyson, 1986).

In summary, the research into children's understanding of other people's minds has shown that young children do have some appreciation that other people have thoughts and beliefs and that these might be different from their own. Children achieve this awareness at a younger age than suggested by earlier theorists like Piaget. Nonetheless, an awareness of other minds involves more than just realizing that other people might have different beliefs. A full understanding of mind means realizing that other people can have beliefs that are inaccurate or that another person's beliefs can be changed depending on the type of information they receive. Such a rich understanding of mind takes several years to develop. In particular, both the research related to understanding of minds (Bartsh & London, 2000) and the earlier empirical research that focused on children's persuasive strategies (Trawick-Smith, 1992; Weiss & Sachs, 1991) have shown that young children do not employ persuasive strategies that involve changing other's minds. To change someone else's mind means considering their current beliefs and then presenting them with counter beliefs to overcome their present beliefs. Such persuasion requires a sophisticated understanding of the relationship between minds and beliefs. But young children do not have the necessary awareness of others' minds to have an effective understanding of persuasion based on altering others' beliefs.

Implications of Understanding Other Minds for Advertising Research

Most of the research into children and advertising has been conducted in the context of traditional theories of children's development (e.g., Piaget's), but more recent theories have superceded such frameworks. In particular, the information processing approach to children's development has been one of the most influential paradigms. This framework has influenced some of the research into children and advertising (Roedder, 1981), but its use has been limited. More recent frameworks of child development have largely been ignored, and yet some of these are particularly relevant to children's understanding of advertisements. Some of the research described previously related to children's understanding of minds because this framework could provide insights into the way that children think about and interpret advertisements.

Advertisements aim to persuade. Although there are many types of persuasion, we suggest that the principle way that television advertisements influence children is by offering beliefs and images about products. There may be a few instances when advertising provides new information to a child (e.g., for a novel product the child will not have experienced previously), and this can provide new information or beliefs for the child when none were present before. But the majority of advertising aims to promote existing product images. This may include persuading children to change brands (i.e., change their beliefs about what is an appropriate product choice) or persuading them to use a product more (i.e., change their beliefs about what is an appropriate level of use). These aims are therefore about changing the beliefs of the viewer.

Children can only be said to understand the nature of advertising when they have a full appreciation of these aspects of belief manipulation. As described in the previous section, children's understanding of beliefs and belief change develops only gradually during the early school years. It is not surprising that young children have a limited understanding about the purpose of advertising (see chap. 3). This is not because children have specific problems understanding advertisements per se, it is because young children have cognitive limitations in understanding all aspects of belief manipulation (see discussion of persuasive strategies earlier). We predict that as children develop progressively more sophisticated understanding of minds and beliefs in general, they will also develop a better understanding of advertising. This is why placing advertising research in the context of contemporary theories of child development would be a step forward in understanding the way that children interpret advertisements.

An important empirical question is whether children's understanding of advertisements parallels their understanding of beliefs and persuasion in other domains. Advertisements are the products of minds, and understanding advertisements means understanding the mind and the beliefs that created them. This may be more difficult than understanding another person's mind because an extra step is involved (the awareness that an advertisement is a creation of a mind). It may be the case that even after children have developed an understanding of other people's minds, they may need longer to realize that an advertisement is also an aspect of mind.

Children's understanding of beliefs and persuasion develops, in part, from the experience of interacting with others, and several researchers have shown that the more people that children have contact with, the more developed will be their understanding of beliefs (Dunn, 1999; Lewis et al., 1996). For example, interaction is important for finding out that people usually act on their beliefs. If Jack thinks that Jill likes a particular toy, he will expect Jill to buy that toy when she goes to the shop. In other words, Jack can learn the relationship between beliefs and actions from observing the correlation between his belief about other people's beliefs and their subsequent actions. To give another example, learning about persuasion is only possible through interacting with others. If Jack wants to persuade Jill to buy a different toy he will need to develop an appropriate persuasive strategy to get Jill to change her beliefs about her preferred toy. Children do not interact with advertisements in the same way that they interact with other people and this may be another reason to expect children's full understanding of advertisements to lag behind their understanding of minds and beliefs in other domains. Such issues are empirical questions that can be addressed by new approaches to the research into children and advertising—ones that take into account the contemporary theories of child development.

As this chapter has emphasized, the dominant paradigm in research with young children focuses on their interpretation of minds and beliefs. This paradigm considers topics that are close to the issues which have been raised in the advertising literature. Issues such as the interpretation and understanding of advertisements, the persuasive effects of advertising, the manipulation of beliefs and images through advertising, and the relationship between beliefs and behavior. All these are topics that can be considered in new frameworks that are more relevant and potentially more useful than the traditional frameworks that have been used in much of the advertising literature.

6

Advertising Impact: Knowledge, Attitudes, and Values

This chapter considers the impact of advertising on children. The main concern of advertisers is that their commercial messages are effective. Advertisements can influence children in a number of ways. They can increase young consumers' awareness of brands and product attributes, influence attitudes toward brands and products, and influence intentions to purchase or actual purchase behavior. Advertising on television represents a particularly important product information source (Barry & Sheikh, 1977; Howard, Hulbert, & Lehmann, 1973; John, 1999a). Research evidence indicates that exposure to advertisements can increase children's desire for products and may encourage them to ask their parents to make purchases on their behalf (Atkin, 1982).

Although advertisers are ultimately concerned about the effectiveness of advertisements in enhancing purchase levels and the overall market share attained by their products or services, the effects of advertising can be measured at other psychological and social levels. Some effects are intended and others occur incidentally. These different kinds of advertising influences will be examined in this and the next two chapters.

The importance of examining the influence of advertising at a number of different levels is underpinned by the hierarchy of effects model that has been endorsed over many years—at least conceptually—by a number of researchers in the field (Lavidge & Steiner, 1961; Rothschild, 1987). According to two early writers, awareness leads to knowledge that influences liking, which, in turn, affects preferences that produces conviction and eventual purchase (Lavidge & Steiner, 1961). How detailed and elaborate this stage-by-stage decision-making process about brands turns out to be is mediated by the degree of involvement or psychological (and financial) investment in the product. Low-cost and therefore often low-psychological involvement products, such as soap powders, may be selected swiftly with minimal thought. The cost of making a mistake in this sort of case is not great and is easily recoverable. With a high-cost and high psychological involvement item such as obtaining a mortgage or buying a car, more careful thought is needed because a mistake at this level of expenditure is more serious.

This chapter focuses on the effects of advertising on young viewers' perceptions and knowledge of brands and products and on their wider consumer-related values. Chapter seven examines evidence for the influence of advertising on children's product choices and actual consumption, and chapter eight considers incidental effects of televised advertising. These effects are unintended, spin-off perceptions or behavioral responses related to the messages that advertising contains. These messages may be of a social as well as of a consumer nature.

Before turning to the ways in which advertising can exert direct effects upon young consumers, it is worth beginning with a review of the most significant models of advertising effects that have emerged over the years. These models do not apply nor were they developed exclusively to explain the effects of advertising on children and teenagers. Instead, they were developed to enhance our understanding of the key processes that underpin the way that advertising can influence consumers in general. Nonetheless, it is useful to describe how conceptual thinking about advertising has evolved because this description provides a background to the review of advertising influence that follows later in the chapter.

THEORIES OF ADVERTISING EFFECTS

This review of theories of advertising effects is not exhaustive, but it does cover the models that have dominated thinking about advertising impact. The models that follow were grounded primarily in psychology. They consider the way consumers process information from commercial messages, the ways that advertisements can invoke emotions and motivations in consumers, and the behavioral reinforcement mechanisms advertisers apply to invoke, shape and condition consumer behavior.

Hierarchical Models

Hierarchical models conceive of advertising influences as operating through a series of stages that involve a number of distinct psychological processes. One early version of a hierarchical model identified such stages as attention to the advertisement, awareness and knowledge of the product, liking for the product, preferring the advertised product over others, desire to possess the product, and finally the action of purchasing the product (Lavidge & Steiner, 1961). Another stage model was put forward by McGuire (1969) who identified several decision-making processes between initial exposure to a commercial message and eventual product purchase. These stages included: exposure, attention, comprehension, yielding, retention, and decision to buy. Each stage must be successfully negotiated before progressing to the next one.

Hence, in a classic hierarchical model, the consumer must first become aware of the product through exposure and attention to advertising. Second, the consumer evaluates the product and the brand and forms a set of beliefs and attitudes about it. Third, if convinced that the brand is superior to others in the competing product range and if the purchaser is also in the market to consume this type of product, then an intention to buy will become established, followed by eventual purchase (Preston, 1982).

Multiattribute Model

The multiattribute model is based on the premise that a consumer's attitude toward a brand is the aggregate of the opinions the consumer holds toward specific product attributes multiplied by a subjective estimate of the probability that the brand in question actually possesses each of those attributes. The more favorable the attitude toward the brand, the greater the likelihood that the consumer will purchase it (Fishbein & Ajzen, 1975). Advertising influences brand-related attitude either by causing the consumer to believe that a brand really does possess a specific attribute or by changing the consumer's evaluation of the attractiveness and importance of specific attributes that the brand is believed to possess.

Involvement Models

Involvement models focus on the idea that behavior is influenced by outside factors to the extent that there are situations in which specific kinds of behavior are required, expected, or encouraged and have significance to individuals. The more important a situation is deemed to be by individuals, the more involved they become in performing the most appropriate or advantageous

behaviors in that situation (Sherif & Hovland, 1961). In the context of advertising, involvement has been defined with reference to the types of verbal responses consumers make about products during exposure to advertisements
(Krugman, 1965), as a motivational state (Mitchell, 1981), and in terms of
commitment to a brand or product type (Lastovicka & Gardner, 1979).

One writer observed that television viewing was usually a relatively low-
involvement activity. Viewers seldom made powerful links between what
they watched on screen and their own experiences (Krugman, 1965). Such
low involvement meant that advertising on television could not be expected
to affect consumers' core values and may, therefore, have fairly superficial
influences on consumer behavior. Later involvement models emerged that
challenged the low-involvement view of television advertising and recognized that advertising could involve varying degrees of consumer involvement. The level of involvement was significant, however, in relation to the
way consumers processed information from an advertisement and
responded to it in emotional terms.

Ray (1973) proposed a Hierarchies of Effects Model that at first glance
appears to be a hierarchical model but which also distinguishes between levels of consumer involvement. Ray distinguished between cognitive, attitudinal, and behavioral responses to advertising. Consumers who are highly
involved are motivated to learn more about a product, develop attitudes toward it, and may eventually purchase it. Under conditions of low involvement, however, changed cognitive responses toward the brand precede
behavioral action, with attitude changes following on.

The best known involvement model of advertising impact is the Elaboration Likelihood Model (ELM) that Petty and Cacioppo (1979) developed.
Although this model has evolved over time, the basic idea is that attitudes
towards products may be formed either via a central route or a peripheral
route of persuasion. The central route is adopted by highly involved consumers and focuses on quality of arguments that support the product. These
arguments affect the consumer's thinking about and evaluation of the product, and when highly involved, the consumer will expend considerable effort elaborating on the arguments for and against a particular brand.

Under some conditions, though, involvement is low. When this occurs,
the consumer adopts a more peripheral processing route in taking decisions
about whether to purchase a brand. Low involvement consumers engage in
a relatively superficial level of analysis of product attributes. Little attention
is paid to arguments for or against a product. Instead, consumers may be
more influenced by the attractiveness of models or celebrities associated
with a brand or with incidental benefits that may derive from brand purchase than by whether the product is functionally superior. Although initially conceiving of information processing from advertising as being either

central or peripheral, a later conceptualization acknowledged that degree of consumer involvement was continuous rather than dichotomous in nature (Petty, Cacioppo, & Kasmer, 1987).

Attitude Toward the Ad (Aad) Models

Aad models allow for the fact that consumers' attitudes toward advertisements can influence attitudes toward brands and intentions to purchase (Mitchell & Olson, 1981; Shimp, 1981). Aad models have similarities to multiattribute models. They do not simply consider a holistic or global attitude of like versus dislike that consumers develop about advertisements but examine specific features in advertisements (e.g., various aspects of visual production treatment, music and sound effects, types of endorsers) and the different feelings they generate in consumers. Any positive feelings generated by the advertisement may become associated with the brand and through repeated exposure rub off on the brand itself. Some writers have suggested that attitude toward the advertisement may affect brand attitude directly or indirectly via specific thoughts held about the brand. MacKenzie, Lutz, and Belch (1986) further argued that attitude to the advertisement may exert a direct influence on brand purchase without being mediated by brand cognitions or attitudes.

Behavioral Models

A number of researchers have noted that advertising can influence consumer preferences and purchase intentions via behavioral conditioning processes. In classical conditioning, associative learning can take place between a particular stimuli and a behavioral response, such that the presence of a particular stimulus automatically gives rise to the conditioned response. For example, some stimuli and responses are biologically connected whereas others are not. When hungry and presented with a plate of our favorite food, we begin to salivate in preparation for food ingestion. If a passage of music (which biologically does not give rise to the salivation response) is played every time we are presented with food when we are hungry, then through a process of associative learning the music alone may result in the salivation response.

This form of behavioral conditioning can be used in advertising to influence brand-related thoughts, attitudes, and eventual purchase. The depiction of an attractive, scantily clad model may give rise to various positive arousal responses among consumers. The repeated association of that model with a hair shampoo may lead to those responses become conditioned to the advertised brand. Such positive feelings may enhance the image of the brand

and its appeal to consumers (Mitchell, 1983). For example, Gorn (1982) showed that consumers were more likely to select the color of a ball point pen they had seen advertised with pleasant rather than with unpleasant music. In line with traditional classical conditioning research, the strength of this type of influence becomes greater with increased exposure to such stimulus-response pairings in advertising (Stuart, Shimp, & Engle, 1987).

Information Processing Models

Information processing models are also sometimes referred to as attentional models. They offer a variety of explanations for the importance of effective information processing from advertisements. The formation of brand-related beliefs and attitudes and intentions to purchase depend on how much detail from advertisements consumers are able to process during exposure. Involvement models indicate that consumer involvement with advertisements is a significant factor linked to style of information processing. Other factors, however, are linked to the way that information is presented within advertisements, that also affect attention, information encoding and comprehension, and emotional responding.

The greater the amount of information an advertisement presents within a specified period of time, the more likely it becomes that certain details will be lost to the consumer. Limited capacity attention theory has been used to explain why and how processing of information from a stimulus deteriorates if the individual's attention is divided between the stimulus in question and another task that also requires a certain amount of mental concentration. In addition, the more complex the stimulus, the greater attention it demands to enable effective processing and encoding to take place. This phenomenon has been repeatedly observed in connection with processing information from advertisements. The greater the narrative and visual production complexity of a commercial, the more information processing capacity it demands (Thorson, Reeves, & Schleuder, 1985, 1987), and presenting advertisements at faster speeds, which involves more rapid processing of information, also requires more attention (Schleuder, Thorson, & Reeves, 1988).

The processing of information from advertisements is also affected by the nature of the adjacent programming. Program content can affect viewers' mood states (Axelrod, 1963; Goldberg & Gorn, 1987; Kamins, Marks, & Skinner, 1991) or excite them in a way that interferes with effective processing of the informational content of advertisements (Singh, Churchill, & Hitchon, 1987). A program can also involve viewers so powerfully that they are unable to redirect their attention to adjacent advertising sufficiently to facilitate the encoding of the commercial messages (Bryant & Comisky, 1978; Park & McLung, 1986; Schumann & Thorson, 1990).

Program environment has been found to exert both positive and negative effects on viewers' memory for televised advertising. Some results have indicated that program context can facilitate advertising recall (Johnson, 1992; Lloyd & Clancy, 1991), but others have found a negative effect (Bryant & Comisky, 1978; Gunter, Furnham, & Beeson, 1997; Gunter, Furnham, & Frost; 1994; Norris & Colman, 1992).

Inconsistencies in the ways key variables such as attention, memory, and exposure to stimulus materials have been operationalized have been invoked to account for some of these differences in results (Norris & Colman, 1993, 1994). In addition, involvement may interact with the nature of surrounding program content to affect advertising recall in different ways. Thus, whether a surrounding program environment has facilitative or inhibitory effects upon cognitive processing of embedded advertising material can also depend on the nature of differences or similarities between programs and advertisement, with "psychological involvement" in the program magnifying these effects (Furnham, Gunter, & Walsh, 1998).

Bushman (1998) reported that viewers' memory for advertisements was impaired by adjacent violent movie content as compared with a nonviolent program environment. This effect has also been observed by other researchers (Prasad & Smith, 1994; Shen & Prinsen, 1999). Bushman explained this interference in the cognitive processing of the advertising message being the result of the hostility-related ideas invoked by the surrounding violent film content. Bushman suggested that cognitive effort becomes deflected from processing the advertising to calming the anger brought on by the adjacent program violence. This effect was attributed to cognitive responses generated specifically by violent content, given that the violent and nonviolent film sequences used in this research had been pretested to produce nonsignificant differences in self-reported excitement and physiological arousal. Further research confirmed these results in respect of effects of violent programming on nonviolent advertisements but also indicated that memory for advertisements that contained violence could be enhanced by adjacent program violence (Gunter, Tohala, & Furnham, 2001).

The notion of construct accessibility has been invoked to explain how programs and advertisements that contain semantically congruent material can enhance information processing from the advertisement (Sanbonmatsu & Fazio, 1991). A construct has been defined as "a representation in memory consisting of coherent information about some entity" (Higgins & King, 1981, p. 74). Thus, a construct is a mental representation involving a category that divides a domain into positive and negative instances. Researchers have suggested that the initial use of a construct increases the accessibility of that construct and the possibility of its use in later judgements and impression formation (Herr, 1986). This accessibility can also be increased indirectly through the activation of constructs that are associated with the representation. For example, the construct of dog can be primed by presenting the construct of poodle (Srull & Wyer, 1979).

The construct accessibility model has developed from a belief that semantic memory can be represented as an abundance of networks consisting of nodes that represent constructs, which are connected by associative pathways (Anderson, 1976). Each network represents elements of thoughts and feelings, and internetwork connections are determined by factors such as similarity, congruity, and semantic relatedness (Bryant & Zillmann, 1994). Upon activation of a node, other semantically related nodes are activated as the activation travels along the paths of the network. This view states that the presentation of a specific stimulus will prime other, related thoughts by activating the connections between the memory networks.

Research with teenagers has yielded little evidence of construct accessibility effects in the context of recall of television advertisements. In one study, advertisements for cars or foods were placed either within a program about cars or a program about food. Advertisement recall was better when commercial messages were placed in a program of dissimilar than of similar content. There were gender-related differences because males had better brand recognition than did females for car advertisements, but females were superior in recognizing food brands (Furnham, Gunter, & Richardson, 2001). In another experiment, teenagers and young adults were tested for recall of advertisements for alcoholic beverages (beers) placed in a popular TV soap opera against scenes that either contained or did not contain drinking behavior. Semantically congruent program content enhanced recall of the beer advertisement when it occurred subsequent to the advertising break but impaired recall of the beer advertisement when it was shown before the advertising break. This effect, however, was confined to conditions when the beer advertisement was shown in first position in the advertising break and the interfering program content occurred immediately before the advertisement (Furnham, Bergland, & Gunter, 2002).

Similar effects have been found for advertisements aimed at children. For example, cartoon advertisements may be generally more memorable than noncartoon advertisements, but this effect depends on whether the advertisements are placed in a cartoon or noncartoon program. The placement of cartoon advertisements in a cartoon program can impede children's memory for the commercial messages, while placement in a noncartoon program makes them stand out more (Gunter, Baluch, Duffy, & Furnham, 2002).

LEVELS OF ADVERTISING INFLUENCE

Before considering behavioral level and incidental effects of advertising, the more direct reactions children display when exposed to commercial messages will be discussed. Before any consumer responds, if they do at all, in terms of product purchase, the advertising imparts to them certain information about the brand being promoted. Advertising is, therefore, a source of consumer learning. This type of impact occurs at cognitive and emotional levels rather than at a behavioral level. Such effects can be conveniently considered to occur at three distinct, though sometimes interacting or interdependent levels:

1. brand level learning,
2. product level learning, and
3. wider consumer socialization.

Brand level responses refer to ones connected to specific models or brands of a product or service. That is, is one bank, car, breakfast cereal, cosmetic, or soap powder preferred over another? To make such choices, consumers must consider the attributes of different brands as presented in advertisements. One assumption in relation to this level of effect is that the consumer who is making a preference judgement is in the market potentially to purchase a product or service. Understandably, where younger consumers are concerned, the range of products or services they might be interested in buying is much narrower than the range available to adult consumers. Major child or teenage consumer items include toys, confectionery, breakfast cereals, eating at fast-food outlets, cartoons, music, and computer or video games (McNeal, 1992). Advertisements try to render their brand more appealing than competing brands by associating with it certain desirable attributes known to be valued by young consumers.

Product-level responses refer to the information that young consumers learn about product categories rather than a specific brand. Nonetheless, brand-level learning may feed in to product-level learning. Hence, children may learn about products and services and their characteristics as a genre through watching advertisements. For example, children may learn about the range of brands of video games available in the marketplace and may be able to evaluate specific brands by comparison with other individual brands. But they may also be able to evaluate a particular brand by comparison with a broader genre-wide standard that children extrapolate from their experiences with many brands within the product category. Children may also learn about products not yet aimed at them, such as cars, which they may one day purchase for themselves.

Wider consumer socialization refers to a more general form of learning through which children recognize and come to understand the role of consumerism in society (Gunter & Furnham, 1998). In market-driven, democratic societies, this represents an important area of learning because consumerism permeates the lives of virtually everyone. At this societal level, young consumers may become aware of the role that consumerism plays in the home and in relation to business. Consumerism enables people to maintain certain lifestyles for themselves. It also forms the basis of business activity that in turn creates employment. The ability to consume rests significantly on the disposable income an individual possesses. Income is generated primarily by work. Hence, the idea of obtaining paid employment in the service of consumerism can begin to surface in teenage years—a time during which youngsters often embark on their first paid work.

As discussed in previous chapters, children pass through various stages during which their understanding of the nature and purpose of advertising on television evolves (Ward, Reale, & Levinson, 1972; Wartella, 1982). Initial understanding is manifest in recognizing distinctions between programs and advertisements (see chap. 3), but understanding the purpose and intent of advertising emerges only gradually after about seven or eight years of age (see chap. 4). During the teenage years, however, young consumers develop the ability to make more sophisticated judgements about specific appeals and subtle tactics advertisers use to grab the attention of consumers and enhance the image of advertised products (Boush, Friestad, & Rose, 1994; Paget, Kritt, & Bergemann, 1984).

During adolescence, a significant degree of scepticism can emerge about advertising. This may take the form of critically appraising the aesthetic qualities of an advertisement, questioning the veracity of its central appeal or sales message, or perhaps rejecting the brand on the basis of personal experience (John, 1999a). Peer groups may also influence the reactions of adolescent consumers to advertisements. As fashion sense becomes more important for young consumers struggling with their self-identity, advertisements become a source of conversation among teens who are monitoring their environment to keep up with the latest trends (Ritson & Elliott, 1998, 1999).

As well as the three domains (brand-related, product-related, wider consumer awareness) in which consumer learning takes place, there are other nonbehavioral advertising "learning" effects. First, there is factual learning about brands and products. Second, there is the acquisition of attitudes about brands and products. Third, there is the conditioning of wider values about consumerism as a concept. The first two kinds of learning may be precursors of eventual product purchase. Consumers learn that certain attributes are associated with brands (facts) and decide whether these are attributes that they like or dislike (attitudes). If the attitudes formed are positive in nature, this sets up the conditions under which purchase may take place. It does not automatically follow that product purchase will occur once a positive attitudinal disposition has become established because relationships between attitudes and behavior are complex and far from consistent (Ajzen & Fishbein, 1980).

Any discussion of the research into the impact of television advertising on knowledge, attitudes, and values must consider the methodologies of that research. Many studies have been based on survey interviews with children who report not only on their brand awareness and attitudes but also on their perceived exposure to relevant advertising. Such studies use correlational analyses to examine links between advertising exposure and brand or product-related perceptions. There are limitations to using reports from children or from their parents about children's exposure to advertising because these reports may not always be accurate and subjective measures of advertising exposure also vary in how specific and detailed they are. Nonetheless, bearing these reservations in mind, some weak relationships have been found between reported exposure to advertising and consumer-related attitudes (Atkin, 1980; Goldberg, 1990).

Correlations between advertising exposure and attitudes toward products cannot prove cause-effect relationships. To establish such relationships other methodological approaches are required. For example, researchers have manipulated children's exposure to specific advertising under controlled conditions, both in laboratory settings and under more natural viewing circumstances. However, as discussed later, findings concerning the effects of advertising on children's brand- or product-related attitudes have been mixed.

BRAND-RELATED EFFECTS

At the level of the brand, interest in children's reactions centers on the degree to which children learn to associate particular attributes with the specific product being advertised and how this learning, in turn, might influence their attitudes toward the brand (Haedrich, Adam, Kreilkamp, & Kuss, 1984). One technique is to show an advertisement to children who are then interviewed immediately afterward for their retention of information from the message and their judgements about the brand that was promoted.

The first step in advertising influence is for a commercial message to raise consumer awareness of the advertised brand. Research has shown that brand name identification can be enhanced through advertising. As described in chapter two, even very young children recognize logos and brands (Dammler & Middelmann-Motz, 2002; Hite & Hite, 1995), but such recognition tends to be more pronounced among older children who begin to ask parents not just for products but for specific brands (Ward, Wackman, & Wartella, 1977).

Atkin and Gibson (1978) interviewed children for their views about a breakfast cereal called Honeycombs after they had watched a television advertisement for it. The brand was endorsed on screen by a character called Big Boris. The strength displayed by this character was associated with the brand and established a belief among young viewers that they too would grow to be big and strong if they ate this cereal. The same study showed the children another cereal called Cocoa Pebbles that was endorsed by the cartoon characters Fred Flintstone and Barney Rubble. This cereal also proved to be popular but not because of any attractive attributes that were associated with it. Instead, the children liked it because the two characters—who were well liked by this group—apparently enjoyed it.

Another feature that has been investigated in relation to the attractiveness of brands to children is whether brands are promoted on screen by other children. This feature, however, has been found to enhance liking for the advertisement, though not invariably for the brand being advertised (Loughlin & Desmond, 1981).

PRODUCT-RELATED EFFECTS

At the product level, children learn to make judgements assessing the claims made about the advantages and benefits of specific products. Much advertising aimed at children is for food products (see chap. 2). Exposure to these advertisements has been found to have specific and general effects on young consumers. Advertising can influence what children think and feel about food products and enhance their desire to consume advertised products. The most frequently advertised foods, for example, may emerge as the best liked among children. The more children are exposed to such advertising, the more they come to like the advertised brand, and several early studies found that increased exposure to advertising resulted in greater desire for the product (Goldberg & Gorn, 1978; Resnik & Stern, 1977).

Researchers have shown that children and teenagers may sometimes condemn advertisements for making unrealistic claims about products. In one qualitative study, in-depth interviews with groups of children aged between seven and 14 years found, for example, that the cleanliness and softness claims made by various advertisers about their cleaning products (e.g., shampoo and soap powder) were found difficult to believe (Gunter, McAleer, & Clifford, 1992a).

Gunter et al. (1992a) also considered how children considered the truthfulness of specific advertisements that they were shown. Children appeared to adopt specific strategies to enable them to make an assessment. The strategy tended to depend initially on whether the advertisement was for a product or a service. Advertisements that promoted a service were frequently perceived as being unlikely to make exaggerated claims or to fabricate information. Reactions to product-based advertisements depended on whether specific claims were made. For example, a hamburger restaurant advertisement offered no information about its food items, so the children felt unable to comment on its truthfulness. Real-life experience was a salient factor for children assessing the truthfulness of toy advertising. In the case of a toy truck that was promoted as being "indestructible," many seven- to 10-year-olds maintained that this was a realistic claim and offered examples from their own experience with the product.

Gunter et al. (1992b) found that nearly all the children who were interviewed could remember being motivated enough by a television advertisement to ask their parents to purchase products they had seen. Most purchase requests were for toy products. However, the children rarely relied solely on television for their information about new products. They also consulted friends and other sources of information (e.g., some mentioned looking through mail-order catalogs).

A number of product-related studies have investigated the impact of television advertisements for medicine products on children's wider beliefs and attitudes about medicines (see Winick, Williamson, Chuzmir, & Winick, 1973). This research has found little support for the suggestion that advertisements for over-the-counter (OTC) or nonprescription drugs can encourage excessive reliance on pills (Milavsky, Pekowsky, & Stipp, 1975). In research with eight- and nine-year-olds, Butter et al. (1991) investigated the influence of advertisements for OTC medications on children's preferred brands. In one experiment, 100 children were shown televised advertisements for six different OTC medicines along with advertisements for other products. Afterward, they were asked to recommend either a medicine or nonmedicine remedy for a child and an adult with various illnesses or health problems. The OTC medicine advertisements appeared to influence their recommendations only with respect to the use of sleeping pills but not for the other five products. In another experiment, 200 children were exposed either to fever and cold medicine advertisements intended for a child audience or to nondrug advertisements. Only the fever medicine advertisements appeared to influence the children. In both experiments, the effects of advertisements were specific to particular products.

Rossano and Butter (1987) conducted two experiments with television drug advertisements to find out whether such messages could affect children's attitudes concerning medication. This research was carried out with children aged between eight and 12 years. Children's attitudes toward drug use were measured using questionnaires and no influence of advertisements was found. In this case, however, the children were tested only once immediately after exposure to advertising. The absence of any pronounced effect of advertising on children here does not mean that effects would necessarily be absent in the longer term following repeat exposure to relevant televised advertising (Young, 1990).

In experimental research, the most effective design is to compare participant knowledge or attitudes before and after exposure to a media stimulus. This approach has been taken in research investigating the impact of advertising on young children's toy preferences. Observing children's choices as they play freely with toys allows the researcher to establish naturally occurring preferences. Fischer (1985) did this in a study of children aged five to six years and eight to nine years. The children were shown a television program in which was embedded an advertisement for one of a set of toys that they had previously played with. After seeing the advertisement, the children were asked to rank their preferences for the original set of toys, including the one that had been advertised. The younger children's toy preferences were unaffected by exposure to the advertisement, but the older children liked a toy more if they had seen an advertisement for it.

In a quasi-experimental study conducted in the field, Goldberg (1990) examined French-speaking and English-speaking children living in Montreal. At the time of this investigation, Quebec law had eliminated all advertising aimed at children on local television stations which meant that exposure to advertisements for toys and children's breakfast cereals could only occur through watching U.S. television stations. English-speaking children watched the American stations more than did French-speaking children, and Goldberg compared the two for their awareness of advertised products. Results indicated that the English-speaking children exhibited greater recognition of toys available in the marketplace and had more children's cereals in their homes compared with the French-speaking children.

The difference in product awareness in Goldberg's (1990) study could not be confidently attributed to the effects of televised advertising alone. There were other differences between English- and French-speaking children in Quebec concerning their cultural environment, their typical eating habits, and other product purchasing habits that may have contributed to the differences between them in their product recognition, quite independently of their patterns of exposure to relevant television advertising. Notwithstanding these other factors, the children who had the greatest exposure to American television (and the advertising aimed at children that it carried) did exhibit the greatest relevant product recognition, and this was especially true for the English-speaking children.

WIDER CONSUMER SOCIALIZATION EFFECTS

The learning that takes place following exposure to advertising can go far beyond the acquisition of factual information or attitudes about specific brands and the awareness of the range of brands available within a particular product category. Advertising represents part of a wider consumer-related experience for children that conditions a value system that underpins the nature of their consumer orientation. Through an ongoing process of consumer socialization, children acquire consumer-related skills, knowledge, beliefs, attitudes, and behavioral dispositions (Ward, 1974).

One concern about the domination of a consumer-orientation in society is that, carried to an extreme, consumerism generates a value system driven by self-centeredness; individual ambition and achievement; and, ultimately, greed. In other words, it generates a society in which people are motivated primarily by the acquisition of wealth and possessions.

During their teenage years, young people develop an understanding of concepts of working for money and business for profit (Berti & Bombi, 1979, 1981). In a retail context, it is teenagers rather than preteens who understand why customers pay shopkeepers for goods and why the shopkeeper sells goods for a profit (Furth, 1980). Although children as young as eight years can be taught to appreciate the idea of shops selling goods for profit, they cannot transfer this knowledge when considering the role of manufacturers of goods in shops (Berti, Bombi, & de Bens, 1986). By the midteens, however, understanding of relationships between shop and factory profit becomes better developed (Furnham & Cleare, 1988).

In relation to advertising itself, youngsters can exhibit increased skepticism, with age, about the motives of advertisers. This skepticism generally accompanies a growing awareness of the tactics used in advertising to influence consumers' opinions. With this enhanced awareness, as well as direct experience of products, and through conversations with parents and peers, young consumers may become less willing to believe advertisers' claims (Boush et al., 1994).

The process of becoming a consumer begins at an early age—even before children are able to purchase products for themselves or indeed before they begin to ask others (i.e., parents) to purchase things for them (Reynolds & Wells, 1977). Initial involvement in consumption itself has been observed as early as five years of age (McNeal, 1969). By this age, their mothers may have already begun to instruct children about brand preferences (Bahn, 1986). Children also observe their mothers while on shopping trips with them and acquire basic in-store behaviors through observation and imitation (Grossbart, Carlson, & Walsh, 1988). During their school years, children's television viewing behavior increases as does, in turn, its influence as a source of consumer information (Adler et al., 1980). During preteen years, use of newspapers, magazines, and books also increases, offering further information about products, services, and consumerism (Wartella, Wackman, Ward, Shamir, & Alexander, 1979). Once into their teen years, these mediated information sources are accompanied by the growing influence of peer groups (McNeal, 1969). Direct parental influence, in the meantime, changes during this period of development (Ward, Popper, & Wackman, 1977).

The role of advertising and other mass media content on children's consumer socialization is linked to parental communication style and the socioeconomic class of the child's family household. Evidence has emerged, for instance, that young children from more affluent households exhibit more advanced understanding of consumer issues than do children from poorer backgrounds (Moore & Moschis, 1978; Moschis & Churchill, 1978; Ward, 1974). Children from wealthier households may also show stronger brand preferences and seek more information about brands before deciding which one to purchase (Moore & Moschis, 1978).

How parents interact and converse with their children is linked to the child's media consumption habits and other consumer-related attitudes and behaviors. More open, democratic forms of interaction among family members in relation to decision making yields a more consumer literate young consumer. This type of communication climate can foster a form of consumer socialization that encourages youngsters to focus on the pros and cons of different brands, particularly in relation to price and value for money (Moschis & Moore, 1979c).

One family communication pattern distinction has been made between socio-oriented and concept-oriented climates. In a socio-oriented family setting, parents encourage their children to maintain a harmonious climate of personal relationships, to avoid arguments, anger, and any form of controversial expression or behavior. In a concept-oriented family, children are invited to express their ideas and feelings, even if they are controversial, and to challenge the beliefs of others (Chaffee, McLeod, & Wackman, 1973). In early research, these patterns of communication were associated with socioeconomic class. The socio-oriented climate was more characteristic of working-class families, while concept orientation was more typical of middle- class families (Wade, 1973). But the effects of family communications patterns are not wholly explicable in terms of socioeconomic class alone (Chaffee et al., 1973), and the orientations themselves have relationships with cognitive processes that are more than simply an outcome of socioeconomic class (McLeod & Brown, 1976).

Moore and Moschis (1981) examined whether motivation for television viewing could be the result of family communication patterns at home. They speculated that a socio-oriented communication orientation might implicitly encourage the child to pay attention to the mass media as a means of learning how to behave in various social settings. This expectation was supported, and Moore and Moschis suggested that some families encourage their children to turn to the media to learn social or consumer tendencies appropriate to certain roles. This might then lead to the learning of materialistic orientations because people can learn the expressive aspects of consumption from mass media (Moschis & Moore, 1982). Earlier research had also found that materialistic attitudes were related to the social motivations for watching television advertisements and programs. Put another way, advertisements are watched to learn what products to buy to make a good impression on others, with such motivations being influenced by family communication patterns (Moore & Moschis, 1981; Moschis & Moore, 1979b; Ward & Wackman, 1972).

Chaffee et al. (1973) showed that concept-oriented family communication structure was positively associated with exposure to the use of mass media for news and current affairs information that could, in turn, have a positive influence on consumer knowledge and other consumer competencies (Moschis & Moore, 1979b, 1979c). Thus, a concept-oriented family communication environment may encourage greater curiosity among children who turn to the media selectively to obtain information about social and public affairs and about consumer-related matters.

MEDIATING VARIABLES
AND ADVERTISING EFFECTS

In assessing the nature of the impact of television advertising on children's knowledge, attitudes, and values, evidence has emerged that these effects do not occur uniformly. Their influence can vary in the presence of different mediating factors (Van Evra, 1995). The latter include how often exposure to an advertisement occurs, the age of the child, the child's social class, and the role of parents. Another important observation is that factors other than advertising can affect children's knowledge, attitudes, and values about brands and products. In consequence, researchers must often disentangle the role played by these different influential variables to derive the unique and specific effects of advertising.

Advertising Exposure

In most real life contexts, children see television advertisements more than once, and usually many times. During the course of a controlled laboratory study, however, the influence of advertising may be assessed after just a single exposure. Does repeated exposure to an advertisement make any difference to brand or product-related knowledge or attitudes?

Research evidence on this point is equivocal. Different writers on the subject have disagreed, some suggesting that repetition has no effect (Gorn & Goldberg, 1980) and others claiming that the effects of repeated exposure can be negative rather than positive—in terms of attitude toward a product (Kinsey, 1987). Yet other researchers have reported that repeated exposure to an advertisement can leave very young children more positively disposed toward the advertisement and brand (Joossens, 1984). The reason is that the child's memory for the advertisement improves with repetition and leaves them feeling more pleased with themselves for being able to recognize a brand more effectively. Gorn and Goldberg (1978) produced supportive evidence for repetition effects and found that repeat exposure to advertisements for the same brand not only enhances brand recognition but also affects brand-related attitudes and purchase disposition in positive ways. In their study, children remembered information about a brand of ice cream after just one exposure to an advertisement for the brand. Three exposures in quick succession enhanced brand preference, and five exposures lead children to choose it over others to a greater extent.

It is also worth noting, however, that repeat exposure to a brand during the course of an advertising campaign may not be the only factor at play in enhancing memory for the brand and improving consumer attitudes (Young, 1990). The increased presence of the product in shops, and the greater likelihood that other consumers are talking about the product, may be other factors that become compounded with advertising exposure to enhance memory and shape attitudes. Advertising exposure may also interact with the social class of the child to shape knowledge and attitudes, with middle-class youngsters being more receptive to advertising messages than are working class children (Goldberg, 1990; Kapferer, 1985).

Age of Child

It is generally recognized within the research literature that older children and younger children respond differently to advertising. We have already seen differences in levels of understanding of televised advertising associated with different age groups. Older children also display more cynical attitudes toward advertising than younger children that again reflects a different level of understanding of advertising and its purpose on their part (see chap. 4). Increased distrust of and cynicism about advertising among older children might, therefore, be expected to reduce the influence of advertising messages on knowledge, attitudes, and values.

Role of Parents

Parents can have a significant role in moderating or modifying the influence of advertisements on children's knowledge, attitudes, and values. The degree to which this mediating phenomenon occurs, in turn, varies with the educational level and social class of the parents. Parental influence can operate directly and indirectly. Parents can control the level of television advertising exposure, especially if they actively limit how much television their children watch or the times they watch. Parents can also create an environment that imparts a certain type of consumer socialization to their children that creates a cognitive framework within which advertisements are interpreted. The higher the social class or education of the parent, the more likely it is that television exposure (including exposure to advertising) will be limited (Goldberg, 1990).

Parents may comment on advertisements themselves. Such commentary may include remarks about attributes or qualities of the advertising or the product. Such parental intervention in relation to programs has been found to be effective in managing television's influences upon children (Donohue & Meyer, 1984). It can serve to enhance the overall television literacy of the child, encouraging children to think more deeply about whatever they are viewing. The effect of this response may be to influence the messages that children take away from the medium (Dorr, 1986). Parents can also offer moral judgements and other comments on advertising messages and this may have moderating effects on influences of advertising on children's longer-term values (Robertson, 1979). This influence can occur whether parents make direct or indirect comments about advertisements (Messaris & Sarett, 1982). It does not always follow that frequent parent–child dialogue about advertising will necessarily reduce purchase requests, but the more a parent adopts a proactive role in engaging a child's thinking about advertising, the more the child will understand the nature and purpose of advertising (Wiman, 1983).

Parental interaction with children about television advertising and its effects can take place either when children are or are not watching advertisements. Some researchers have observed that the best results may occur when parents engage in conversations with their children about advertising while the are watching television together (Dorr, Kovaric, & Doubleday, 1989). In this instance, parents know for certain what their children are watching and can relate their advisory comments directly to specific aspects of the advertisement being viewed.

Despite the potential significance of this mediating role of parents, research evidence indicates that it is not a role many parents actively adopt. Parent–child coviewing has been found to be more likely to occur between parents and older children (whose viewing tastes come to resemble those of their parents) than between parents and younger children (Carlens, 1990). There are also clear social class differences as working-class parents are less likely than middle-class parents to mediate their children's viewing (Desmond, Singer, & Singer, 1990).

Cognitive Defenses

If children do not realize that advertising intends to persuade, then they likely accept advertising messages as truthful rather than question whether they have a hidden agenda. There is a debate about the age when children first start to appreciate the persuasive intent of television advertisements, or when they achieve a full understanding of advertising (see chaps. 3 through 5). But when children do understand the selling intent, they are said to have established "cognitive defences" against advertising (Rossiter & Robertson, 1974).

Knowledge of selling intent may not be not enough to impart resistance to persuasive appeals. Children must also be able to discount the advertiser's message in some way. Some researchers have studied children's judgements and preferences for advertised products as a function of their cognitive defences. Cognitive defences have been found to be associated with lower general trust and liking of advertising, a diminished desire for advertised products, and fewer product purchase requests among children (Robertson & Rossiter, 1974; Rossiter & Robertson, 1974).

But if cognitive defenses increase skepticism and moderate the influence of commercial messages, then older children should be less willing than young children to accept advertising messages. Laboratory studies have failed to support this position (Ross et al., 1984; Ross, Campbell, Houston-Stein, & Wright, 1981). In respect to advertisements for breakfast cereals, beverages, and toys, and even when a celebrity endorser was present, older children were as likely as younger children to respond the way advertisers intended. Though children gain experience and understanding all the time, they may not automatically and spontaneously call upon that prior knowledge about advertising when watching television. They can and will do so, however, when prompted. In the absence of prompting, even children who have a sophisticated understanding of what advertising is about, may fail to generate critical thoughts about advertising while watching television (Brucks, et al., 1988).

CONCLUDING REMARKS

The main function of advertising is to convey a message about a brand effectively to influence consumers' perceptions of the brand, to render the brand more desirable, and to create an intention to buy leading to eventual purchase. A number of theories have been put forward by advertising researchers to explain how advertising influences consumers. These theories were not developed exclusively to explain the effects of advertising on young consumers, but they do provide a useful background when considering how children may be affected by commercial messages. Advertising influence depends on the effectiveness with which the information about brands reaches consumers during exposure to advertising. Consumers must pay attention to advertising, understand the commercial message, and accept its arguments. Consumers' involvement with the advertising and the type of product being promoted mediates their processing of information and can determine which aspects of an advertising message are most closely attend to.

Advertising effects can occur at a number of distinct psychological levels among consumers. Advertisements can affect knowledge about products, brand-related beliefs and attitudes, the desirability of the product, and motives to consume. Finally, actual purchase behavior is influenced. Consumers are influenced in terms of knowledge, attitudes, and values, and these can be in relation to brands, products, or wider consumer socialization. Researchers have found that advertisements can enhance brand awareness and shape brand-related attitudes. Advertisements can also affect product-level knowledge and shape a broader orientation toward items in the case of some product categories. Advertising plays a part in the wider socialization of children in relation to consumerism—it raises their awareness of the availability of products and encourages thought about the significance of consumerism in the world today.

Advertising does not operate in a social vacuum, and its influences can vary with the age and cognitive development of the individual. Other important social factors mediate the effects of advertising, such as parents and peer groups (see chap. 7). Furthermore, as children grow older, their personal experience with products can lead them to reappraise commercial messages and what those message say. As children's intellectual abilities and consumer experiences develop, they may become more skeptical about brands and advertisements, establishing cognitive defenses against commercial messages. Although advertising is undoubtedly effective in raising brand awareness and drawing attention to the presence of consumerism in society, it does not possess omnipotent influence over actual consumption.

This chapter has focused on the ability of television advertising to raise awareness, create desire, and motivate intention to buy. The next chapter focuses on the behavioral effects of advertising.

7

Advertising Influence: Choice and Consumption

This chapter considers the extent to which advertisements on television can affect product choice and consumption. This subject is most central to advertisers' concerns—namely to produce enhanced awareness, preference, and purchase of the commodities they have promoted. Television advertising is designed to influence consumer behavior by entering the market for the type of product being advertised, or to switch to the advertised brand from a rival, or to remain loyal to the advertised brand. With children, these aims are the same. However, unlike adults, children may lack the independent economic ability to make their own purchases and must rely, instead, on the goodwill of others, most usually their parents. In consequence, the influence of advertising on children can be assessed in terms of how it encourages children to persuade adults to buy products for them.

Television advertising acts on consumers via a chain of psychological processes (see chap. 6). The ultimate process is to influence the decision to purchase a brand. Chapter six examined the role of advertising in enhancing children's knowledge and perceptions of products and broader consumer-related attitudes, beliefs, and values. This chapter considers the effects of advertising on the act of consumption itself. Will an advertisement cause children to choose an advertised brand over another competing brand in the same product range? Will advertisements encourage children—who do not yet have their own purchasing power—to pester others to buy on their behalf, in particular their parents?

Advertisers are concerned that their promotional messages will enhance the choice of their brand over others. But parents' groups, educationalists, and others who lobby on behalf of children's best interests have expressed concerns that advertisements can cause children to purchase things they do not really need. Another worry, as will be noted later, is that some advertising is believed to encourage consumption of products that could represent health risks to youngsters (see chap. 8).

Establishing the link between exposure to advertising and product purchase behavior, however, is not straightforward. Although it can be shown that advertisements can promote product and brand awareness and positive attitudes toward brands, neither of these achievements is a guarantee that eventual purchase or consumption will take place. A favorable attitude toward a brand does not mean that the consumer will purchase it or, in the case of young children, ask a parent to do so. Determining what we know about direct advertising influences children's product purchase behaviors is largely restricted to the available academic literature. This is not the full extent of research on this subject because many companies conduct their own research into the effectiveness of advertising, but, given its commercial nature, such research is rarely published. As Gunter and Furnham (1998) observed: "many detailed advertising studies about the effectiveness of certain advertising campaigns directed at children are never made public, which keeps away some very interesting data from most scholars" (p. 147).

Research into the effects of advertising on purchase behavior has involved a number of methodological approaches including experiments, large-scale surveys, and interviews. Experiments usually involve direct manipulation of brand choice following controlled exposure of children to specific advertisements. With surveys, data are typically collected via questionnaires and comprise self-reports of past consumer-related behavior and media exposure behavior. Interviews with children or their parents individually or in focus groups have been used to elicit information from respondents about their experiences with advertising. We will discuss these methods in turn.

EXPERIMENTAL RESEARCH

Many academic studies on the effects of advertising on children have opted for experimental designs. These permit the investigation of cause-effect relations between variables and allow researchers to control precisely the nature and extent of children's exposure to advertising in a way that would not be possible in their everyday living environment (Goldberg, 1990). Most experiments entail showing children selected television advertisements, usually embedded in a children's television program recorded on videotape.

The advertisements are generally ones recorded off-air for children's products such as snack foods, confectionery, sugared breakfast cereals, or toys. After one or more exposures to preedited video material, the children are provided with an opportunity to choose a brand from a range of product items. The aim of such experiments is to establish whether prior exposure, albeit under controlled and rather unnatural viewing conditions, encourages youngsters to choose the advertised brand over others. As the following review of evidence indicates, such studies have found evidence for the effectiveness of advertising.

One important series of experiments was conducted by Gorn and Goldberg (1980) during the late 1970s and 1980s and focused on behavioral effects of advertising. A typical study entailed showing children a television program with embedded advertisements. Afterward, the children were given an opportunity to choose from a range of brands (including the advertised one) the brand they would most like to consume.

Gorn and Goldberg (1980) examined the effects of repeating the same advertisement to children. They prerecorded several videotapes that varied in how often they repeated an advertised brand (of ice cream) within a half-hour cartoon program. The research was carried out with children aged eight to 10 years. After exposure, the children were invited to choose from a range of ice creams, including the advertised brand, and then allowed to eat the brand they chose. The amount, in weight, they ate was also measured. The results showed that the advertised brand was more likely to be chosen than others, but advertising had no effect on the amount that was eaten. Nor was there any strong indication that repeating the same advertisements more than once made any difference to brand choice.

Goldberg, Gorn, and Gibson (1987) used a similar design with very young children, five- and six-year-olds, who were given a choice of snack and breakfast foods. Once again, brand choices reflected the brands the children had seen advertised. This finding applied to sugared food products that were preferred when they had been advertised, and it also applied to public service announcements promoting healthy eating, after which children were more likely to choose nutritious snack and breakfast foods. As with any experiment of this type, there are issues about the ecological validity of the conditions under which children saw the advertisements and the way that the brand choices were manipulated. Nevertheless, these studies demonstrated the impact that advertisements can have in experimental contexts. The key question is whether these effects are likely to occur under more naturalistic viewing and product consumption conditions.

Another study from the same series was conducted outside artificial laboratory conditions with children aged five to eight years in an American summer camp (Gorn & Goldberg, 1982a). Exposure to television advertisements (for brands of food and drink) was manipulated during brief permitted spells of television viewing at the camp. Gorn and Goldberg found that children were later more likely to choose the brands that they had seen advertised.

One concern about advertising aimed at children is that it may encourage them to choose products that may not be good for them. For example, many food products aimed at children are high in sugar content, leading to concerns about the impact of consumption of children's health. Chapter eight considers this issue in more detail when we consider the incidental effects of advertising. Here, a few of the experimental studies that have tested the impact of advertising on children's choices of foodstuffs will be mentioned. Some researchers have also investigated the possibility that any negative effects of advertising can be counteracted by promotional messages for more nutritional foods.

In an early study of this kind, three- to seven-year-old children were presented with videotaped cartoon programs that included food advertisements and public service announcements (PSAs) with pronutritional messages (Galst, 1980). After viewing a version of this material, each child was invited to select a drink and a food from a range of options. Galst repeated this procedure with the same children every day over a period of four weeks. Another variable within the experiment was whether adding an adult's comment to reinforce the pronutritional PSA message would have any effect. In general, the children tended to select sugared snack foods, and this effect was reinforced by television advertisements for such products. However, this effect was partially offset by the pronutritional PSAs and by the adult advice, both of which led children to choose nutritionally healthier food options.

In another attempt to encourage children to choose a healthier food option, Cantor (1981) showed three- to nine-year-olds a children's program containing advertisements for a sweet dessert and for oranges. A humorous advertisement and serious advertisement for oranges were used in different conditions. The key measure was whether the children would choose the sugared sweet or an orange during lunch at a child-care center over a one-week period. Cantor found that presenting the advertisements for oranges immediately after the one for the sweet dessert was found to have some effect on lunchtime dessert choice. Oranges were more likely to be chosen when advertised in a serious rather than a humorous fashion.

Peer groups can strongly influence children's behavior. In the context of the influence of advertising, however, is there any evidence that peer group pressure can further enhance advertising effects? Stoneman and Brody (1982) created a condition in which children taking part in their experiment first heard other children of their age group indicate which one out of an array of foods they liked best. In this case, different foods were projected onto a screen to enable the children to indicate their preferences. The experimental participants did not know that the researchers had previously instructed the other children which foods to choose. The experimental participants subsequently viewed television advertising for selected food products and then made their own choices. Stoneman and Brody found that the advertising exerted a short-term influence on food choice and that this effect was strengthened by seeing other children making the same choices earlier on.

Researchers have sometimes been quite ingenious in the simulations they have devised to measure behavioral effects of television advertising. While many researchers have focused on whether advertisements affect immediate subsequent product selections, Dawson, Jeffrey, Peterson, Sommers, and Wilson (1985) investigated whether they could influence the degree to which children were prepared to delay making a product choice. They presented television advertisements for sugared breakfast cereals to six-year-old children to find out whether the children would be tempted to try that food immediately afterward. The children played a game in which they were required to wait before being allowed to eat the cereal. Dawson et al. found that children waited longer when they viewed an advertisement for the cereal than when they were shown no such advertisement. The explanation they gave for this effect was that the advertisement was entertaining and momentarily distracted children's attention from eating the cereal.

Experiments have their limitations. First, the behavior usually assessed is a measure of product choice but not product purchase. In all academic experiments, children are allowed to choose freely among a range of brands within a product range and may consume without purchase. In effect, children are invited to choose between free gifts rather than commercial products. Second, the effects measured in experiments are short-term effects only because children are invited to choose a product or brand very soon after seeing it advertised.

Third, experiments implicitly assume that advertisements act directly upon children who respond by choosing the advertised brand almost automatically. In real life, there is usually some delay between advertising exposure and opportunity to purchase. During this time, other factors may come into play to influence a purchase decision. Products and advertisements might be commented upon by parents or discussed with peer groups. These experiences may also shape consumer preferences and mediate advertising effects (Galst, 1980; Stoneman & Brody, 1982). There is also evidence, however, that advertisements can be more influential than the child's own mother (Prasad, Rao, & Sheikh, 1978).

Fourth, experimental studies tend not to replicate the natural viewing environment. In real life contexts, children may be engaged in a variety of other activities at the same time as they are watching the television. For all these reasons, some researchers have suggested that experiments are an inappropriate way to assess the effects of advertising on children (Young, 1990).

Experimental studies have provided evidence that television advertisements can influence children's product choices under controlled conditions and when such product choices are made immediately after advertising exposure. Their lack of ecological validity, however, means that they cannot be taken as unambiguous evidence about the way children respond to advertising when they are shopping in the real world.

Notwithstanding these remarks, some academic research has demonstrated that it is possible to gain insights into "real-world" purchase preferences from experimental evidence. Roedder, Sternthal, and Calder (1983) monitored nine-year-old children's choice of a "prize" they could take home and found that they based their choice on an evaluation of the advertised product itself rather than on a comparison of the various alternatives. Older children, aged 13 years, in contrast, were found to weigh all the alternatives before deciding which prize to choose.

Roedder et al. (1983) noticed, however, that when the range of alternatives was reduced, the younger aged group were less influenced by the advertising and relied instead on their preadvertising-exposure item preferences. Thus, it is possible that when faced with a large range of alternatives, young children may find it difficult to make choices by considering all the many varied messages about them. Put another way, when the marketplace is cluttered with many brand choices, the brand that is chosen may be the one that simply had the most memorable advertising campaign. The point is that, under information overload conditions, young children probably make efforts to simplify their product-related judgements.

SURVEY RESEARCH

Some researchers have adopted survey approaches to investigate the effects of television advertising on children (Goldberg, 1990). With surveys the evidence is based on respondents' personal reports about their behavior or, sometimes in the case of children, reports provided by their parents. Surveys make no attempt to manipulate advertising exposure or product purchase circumstances in advance. Hence, they have no control over the advertising-related experiences of individual children that may have a bearing on that child's consumer behavior. One of the strengths of surveys, however, is that they have greater ecological validity than experiments, and surveys can show how children's purchase behaviors are shaped by a range of factors, as well as by advertising.

The weakness of surveys is that they are unable, technically, to attribute causality. Their evidence is grounded in data that indicate correlational relationships between variables. Hence, a survey that investigates the potential effects of television advertising on children's purchase behavior can only establish that a correlation exists between how much relevant advertising children (or their parents) say they have seen and the extent to which they have purchased a particular product. Any relationship between advertising exposure and product purchase could be the joint effects of another variable (measured or unmeasured by the research) or could have occurred by coincidence.

Most researchers do, of course, recognize that consumers' choices can be influenced by a variety of factors. It is not just information presented in advertisements that influences consumers' choices. In any case, even if product choice was based directly on advertising information different consumers might vary in their abilities to process that information effectively. The circumstances under which consumers are exposed to advertising can vary too. In some instances, consumers may have their attention distracted at a crucial point in the advertisement.

It is, therefore, important to appreciate and to measure the range of factors that can enhance, impede, or mediate an advertisement's impact (Ross et al., 1984). Some researchers have found through surveys that children's purchase behaviors are mediated by their family or by their peer group. These social factors are sources of information about products and sources of judgement and opinion about advertisements (Moore, 1990), but these factors will be different for each individual child. For example, within the family, the way parents communicate with their children can differ from one household to another (see chap. 6), and children can also differ in the degree to which they are linked into peer and friendship networks.

Role of Parents as Mediators

The role of parents is very important in relation to a child's consumer behavior. For example, products that have been heavily promoted to the child market have failed to become established because they were unable to appeal to parents (Smith & Sweeney, 1984). The role played by parents can vary, however, from one family household to the next. As discussed in chapter six, parents can vary in styles of communicating with their children and hence also in their styles of consumer socialisation. This means that parents differ in the degree to which they intervene in their child's buying behaviors. Different patterns of parental intervention can also cultivate different attitudes toward advertising on the part of children (Carlson & Grossbart, 1988).

Parents may be negatively disposed toward television advertising directed at children (Atkin, 1978; Burr & Burr, 1976; Ward et al., 1977; Young et al., 2003) or not bothered about it (Enis, Spencer, & Webb, 1980). Given that parents have a key role in the early consumer socialisation of their children, parents' attitudinal dispositions toward advertising may be passed on to their offspring. Parental socialization instills in children certain values and beliefs that in turn can establish norms of conduct (Baumrind, 1980; Furnham, 2000). While some parents give their children a degree of latitude in how they are permitted to behave, other parents are more restrictive and controlling and possibly also more punitive of children who fail to do as they are told (Bronson, 1972; Carlson & Grossbart, 1988; Crosby & Grossbart, 1988). Parenting styles are one of the powerful forces in shaping a child's perception of the economic world. Such consumer-related perceptions may in turn affect a child's consumer behavior patterns, product decision-making processes, and attitudes to advertising (Carlson & Grossbart, 1988).

Peer-Related Factors

Apart from parents, peer groups represent the other key source of influence over a child's consumer-related values, opinions, and behavior. The influence of peers becomes more pronounced as children grow older and gradually attain a degree of social and financial independence from their parents (Coleman & Hendry, 1999). Young children, aged five to 10 years, do display peer group sensitivities, but the role of peer groups becomes more pronounced during the teenage years when adolescent preferences for products and brands are known to be influenced by peer group tastes (Lee & Brown, 1995; Ryan, 1965; Saunders, Samli, & Tozier, 1973).

The power of brands lies in what they stand for in a symbolic sense as much as in the attributes of that particular version of a product. The symbolic value of brands and the need to be seen to be actively consuming can both be triggered and shaped by peer pressure (Saunders et al., 1973). As children enter their teens and come to explore their self-identity, the range of products they wish to purchase expands to include those that are not just related to entertainment but also to projection of a particular self-image. Clothing is prominent among these. Individual tastes in styles of dress are very sensitive to current peer-related fashions. Teenagers are unlikely to choose clothes that they believe their peers would dislike (Brittain, 1963).

Peer groups may also play a part in determining young consumers' attitudes toward advertising itself, and both children and teenagers are known to talk frequently about advertising with their friends (Greenberg et al., 1986). Some advertisements may be singled out as the best or most entertaining. Peer groups may, therefore, encourage particular critical dispositions toward specific advertisements or advertising campaigns that could in turn affect the impact of those commercial messages.

Other Factors

Children can also think for themselves, and as they develop and become socialized into consumerism, they begin to make their own judgements about advertised products and the ways they have been promoted. Although children depend on their parents initially to make purchases for them, as they grow older, this changes as they increasingly go out on their own or with their friends, and shopping takes place less often in the company of parents. Research in different countries has shown that this pattern occurs in most cultures. By the time children have reached their immediate pre-teenage years, many parents report that their children make independent purchases without parental help or influence (McNeal & Yeh, 1990).

A child may have clear expectations regarding products that have been widely advertised. Under such circumstances, it is essential that the product lives up to the child's expectations, otherwise, it will quickly lose its initial appeal. Items that might be repeat purchased will be rejected and young consumer loyalty will not be established. If the product fails to live up to its anticipated quality, even endorsements by celebrity figures may not be enough to guarantee its success in the child market (Schneider, 1987).

SELF-ATTRIBUTED ADVERTISING EFFECTS

Whereas surveys explore correlations between self-report measures of media exposure and knowledge, attitudes, or behavior, qualitative approaches to the study of children and television advertising have asked respondents to indicate whether they feel they have been affected by advertising or have ever reacted to advertisements in a particular way. Such data do not represent actual evidence of advertising influence, merely a subjective impression on the part of children (or their parents) about influence. Nonetheless, these studies can reveal insights into the way children engage with advertisements.

In the United Kingdom, several qualitative enquiries of this sort have been carried out with children and their parents. In-depth interviews with children and teenagers have revealed that young consumers are aware that advertisements can invoke certain types of reactions in themselves or their friends. References are made to copying behaviors seen in television advertisements, to remembering and repeating jingles or catch-phrases, and to developing product-related likes and dislikes (Bartholomew & O'Donohoe, 2003; Gunter et al., 1992b; Hanley, 1996; Hanley, Hayward, Sims, & Jones, 2000).

Parents often express concerns about their children being misled by advertisements and also about their propensity to emulate risky behaviors depicted in advertisements. The British television advertising regulator deploys a code of practice that prohibits advertisers from depicting behaviors such as characters climbing out through windows or balancing on bridges or characters daring each other to engage in potentially dangerous actions such as walking along a precipice (see chap. 9).

Another concern is whether negative or antisocial attitudes displayed on screen can encourage children to endorse such attitudes (Hanley et al., 2000). British parents and professional or voluntary childcare workers were found to hold a widespread belief that advertising on television affects children. This manifested itself through pester power; direct copying of behavior; and a more subtle, gradual effect on attitudes. This concern was felt most strongly for children without much family support. The children themselves held less serious overall concerns about advertising but were able to identify specific advertising examples of copycat behavior. One prominent example was related to an advertisement for a fizzy soft drink—Tango Orange. In this advertisement, a young man is slapped on the face (for details, see chap. 9), and children thought that other children were likely to copy this behavior.

In another case, children reported testing the attributes of a kitchen roll. In the advertisement, a salesman was depicted demonstrating the strength of the paper towels to a customer by supporting a pot of coffee on a sheet without tearing it. The children who were interviewed about this indicated a willingness to test this feature for themselves (Hanley et al., 2000).

PARENTAL PESTERING

One particular form of consumer-related behavior among children that has been studied through survey research is children pestering their parents to buy on their behalf. As children become aware of products in the marketplace, they develop an awareness of the things they would like to possess for themselves. Initially lacking the economic independence to make their own purchases, they turn to their parents to buy things for them. Many parents may respond willingly to such demands. If parents know that other children have been bought particular games, toys, or clothes, they may not want their own child to be left out of whatever is the current fashion. Children learn that by asking you may get what you want. Furthermore, early peer group influences add to the pressures placed on parents to purchase the latest products for their children so that they will not feel disadvantaged compared with their friends. Children have become such a pervasive influence on their parents' spending, however, that marketers regularly run focus groups for consumers as young as five years (Swain, 2002).

The study of parental pestering behavior by children is important because it underlines the social context in which children's consumer behavior takes place. Research findings from several countries have shown that children pestering their parents to buy them advertised products can lead to family conflicts (Isler, Popper, & Ward, 1987). In the United States, Galst and White (1976) found that the amount of television children watched correlated with the consumption of foods advertised on television and children's attempts to influence their mothers' purchase decisions. In Australia, Morton (1990) reported that the most heavily advertised foods were most likely to be named as favorites by children and were the ones they most often pestered their parents to buy for them.

Controlled experimental studies that attempt to demonstrate an immediate triggering effect of an advertisement on children's product choices adopt a naïve notion of how children's product purchases might be influenced (Young, 1990). Children frequently reached product purchase decisions through discussion with other people. These "other people" may be friends and more usually during early childhood years, parents. Gunter et al. (1992a) carried out focus group research with children in the United Kingdom and found that preteenage children acknowledged being most strongly motivated to ask their parents to buy products they had seen advertised on television. Television advertising, however, was not the only influential source for these children. They also reported consulting friends and even mail-order catalogs.

Whether parents yield to a child's purchase requests varies from one family household to the next. Once again, parenting styles were important in this context. The age of the child was also a factor. Older children tended to make fewer requests of their parents to buy them things but were more likely to get what they wanted (Atkin, 1978). Mothers were also more likely to grant a purchase request the more involved they perceived their child to be with the product (Ward & Wackman, 1972).

What role does advertising play in encouraging parental pestering by children? One of the initial indications that advertising may influence pestering behavior derives from self-report evidence. One American survey of children aged four to 10 years asked them whether they ever asked their mothers to buy toys they had seen advertised on television (Adler et al., 1980). Many of the children interviewed did admit to pestering their parents, but differences were associated with how much television the children reported watching. Children who were classified as heavy television viewers were more likely to admit to parental pestering behavior than those classified as light viewers.

In a British survey with children aged four to 13 years, the great majority of children said that they had, at some time, asked their parents to buy them something they had seen advertised on television (Greenberg et al., 1986). But there were age-related differences, with older children making less requests (four–five-year-olds: 97% claimed to have made requests; six–seven-year-olds:

94%; eight–nine-year-olds: 86%; 10–13-year-olds: 71%). The decline in requests with age has also been found in other research (Isler et al., 1987).

The products that children request also vary with age. Young children, aged five to seven years, are most likely to ask parents to buy them advertised breakfast cereals, sweets, and toys. By their pre-teen years (ages 11–12), requests for clothing and music recordings are more prominent (Riem, 1987). Requests for TV-advertised products that are relevant to children of all ages, such as snack foods and soft drinks, also tend to decline as children grow older (Greenberg et al., 1986). Some researchers have found that the likelihood of parental pestering on the part of children can be reduced when parents discuss advertisements with their children (Dorr, 1986; Moschis & Moore, 1982).

As well as asking children, researchers have approached parents directly for their reports on how often their children pester them to purchase advertised products. In one early study, Ward and Wackman (1973) analyzed mothers' questionnaire responses and found that mothers who watched more television were more likely to yield to children's requests to buy them things. Advertisements for food products had the greatest influence in this context and represented the types of products for which children's requests to purchase would most likely be granted. Other research by Ward and his colleagues during the 1970s involved interviews with both children and their mothers. While advertising emerged as an important source of information for children and would often trigger requests to their parents, parents did not invariably accede to these requests. The granting of purchase requests was related to the type of product (Ward et al., 1977; Ward, Wackman et al., 1977).

As well as asking children or their parents how often requests are made to parents, some research has been more creative in finding out whether television advertising may act as a trigger mechanism. In one study, children completed a projective test designed to find out if they distinguished between wanting something that had been advertised on television and then requesting a parent to purchase the item for them (Sheikh & Moleski, 1977). Children were presented with a story about a child watching a television program that was interrupted by advertisements for child-related products. At the end of the story, the children were questioned about the child in the story and whether he or she would be likely to make purchase requests of a parent and with what outcome. Nearly all the children said that the child in the story would want the advertised product, but two thirds of them thought that the child would ask a parent to buy it with a successful outcome.

While most research in this area has found that children's purchase-related requests decline as they get older, one study found the opposite effect.

Observations of shoppers in a grocery store revealed that older children attempted to influence more of their mother's purchases than did younger children (Galst & White, 1976). Another study indicated that the nature of the relationship between a child's age and parental pestering may be more complicated still. Robertson (1979) found that, for toys and other child-oriented products, the relationship may be curvilinear, with the youngest and older children making fewest requests of their parents, and the greatest amount of parental pestering occurring in middle childhood.

Other research on parental pestering has derived from studies that have investigated children's requests for their parents to buy them specific food products. These are the types of requests to which parents apparently frequently acquiesce (Atkin, 1975; Galst & White, 1976; Stoneman & Brody, 1982). These studies are of interest, too, because they departed from the more usual survey methodology and conducted observational investigations within retail locations.

Atkin (1975) observed children with a parent shopping for breakfast cereals. The child was seen to initiate a purchase request in two thirds of cases, and parents were twice as likely to make the purchase as refuse to do so. In contrast to Atkin's findings, Galst and White (1976) found a lower rate of parental yielding in a supermarket—in their study, fewer than half the requests from children were granted.

Stoneman and Brody (1982) combined field observations with an experimental paradigm. Mothers and their children were observed while supermarket shopping after they had been exposed to a specially designed television program. Half the parent-child groups watched a television program that included food advertisements, but the remaining groups saw the program without advertisements. The children who had been exposed to the advertisements made more product purchase requests of their parents than did children who had not seen the advertisements. Mothers who had seen the advertisements were less likely to grant a child's request—they were more likely to refuse the request or suggest an alternative brand from the one chosen by the child.

Pestering and Conflict

As noted earlier, children's requests for advertised products can lead to conflicts, and this has been observed in several countries, including Britain, Japan, and the United States (Isler et al., 1987; Robertson, Ward, Gatignon, & Klees, 1989). Atkin (1975) found that in around one in four cases where a parent refused to grant a child's purchase request in a supermarket, some form of conflict ensued, though it tended to be brief. Parents have often reported that they are aware that pestering by their children can result in arguments, whereas advertising agency personnel behind advertisements may believe that this outcome happens only rarely (Culley & Bennett, 1976).

There are cultural differences in the overall volume of parental pestering; for example, Japanese children are less likely to make such requests than children in the United States and the United Kingdom. One reason for this might be the different levels of exposure to television advertising in Japan and other countries (Ward et al., 1984). It has been found elsewhere that greater exposure to television advertising is associated with more parental pestering by children (Greenberg et al., 1986; Riem, 1987).

Further conflict in decision making can occur on those occasions when the child is faced with discrepant information about a product from an advertisement and from a parent. This phenomenon has been studied in experimental research where some children watched a video of a television program containing a toy advertisement, and others did not see the advertisement. Afterward, some of the children's mothers presented negative information about the product in a power-assertive way, others in a warm and reasonable fashion, whereas others said nothing at all. If the product was fairly well liked and the mother's advice was presented in a warm and reasonable fashion, the child would generally comply with the mother. If the mother was more authoritative in rejecting the product, however, a conflict of opinion with the child was more likely to occur. When the product was perceived as highly desirable, though, no amount of parental argument against it, no matter how reasonably put, affected the child's purchase intention (Prasad et al., 1978).

Robertson (1979) found that children's integration with their peer group is another factor that links to parental pestering behavior. Robertson found this to be especially true of requests made to purchase toys and games. Children who watched more television (and by implication were therefore exposed to greater amounts of televised advertising) and who were poorly integrated with their peers made the greatest number of purchase requests to their parents. However, children who watched a lot of television but were better linked into peer networks made fewer such requests.

CONCLUSIONS

What has become apparent from survey research, despite its lack of control over respondents' behavior, is that advertising represents one source of information and influence over children's consumer behavior among a range of other important factors. A child's product preferences can be shaped by advertising, but equally, children can also be influenced by product attributes, personal experiences with specific brands, point-of-purchase factors such as packaging and retail promotions, the opinions of parents, and the views of peer groups. Very often, no single factor is responsible for the image that young consumers form about products and brands. The influences mentioned above can act together to determine a product's success in the marketplace. Hence, a child's consumer-related decision-making is far from dominated by television advertising.

Just how significant television advertising is alongside these other factors is a matter that has rarely been comprehensively investigated. However, a survey by De Bens and Vandenbruane (1992) considered a variety of potential influences upon children's consumer preferences and purchases. They found that televised advertising certainly played a part in children's choice of toys, but it was not as significant as other influences, including brochures, friends, and direct experience with the toy at the point of purchase. On the basis of such evidence then, it is possible to conclude that children's consumer behavior is affected by television advertising but is by no means dominated by it. It would be wrong therefore to conclude that television advertising represents a pervasive and insidious influence on children that alone shapes their consumer urges, decisions, and behavior.

This chapter has not only discussed whether advertising on television can influence children's own product purchasing but also their requests to others (i.e., parents) to purchase things on their behalf. Pestering of parents by children to buy them things is an established phenomenon. It has been observed to occur across nations and cultures. Television advertising has been implicated as an important information source that can trigger children to make such requests; however, television advertising represents just one information source among many that can influence parental pestering.

It has long been known that advertising can feed children's product ideas, but advertising itself comes in many different forms. Advertising also occurs on the radio, at the cinema, in magazines and newspapers, and on billboards and posters (McNeal, 1992). Furthermore, advertising sits alongside other factors such as peer groups, personal experience, product packaging, point-of-purchase features, and other product-related information sources. This has probably always been the case. In early studies in the United States, for example, it was found that although television advertising was children's main source of information for gift ideas, it was closely followed by friends, shops, and catalogs. The latter became increasingly important as children grew older (Caron & Ward, 1975). Other researchers have found that for some types of product (especially clothing and footwear), peer groups, store-related experiences, and catalogs were more important information sources to children than television advertising (McNeal, 1992).

More recently, one of the most important sources of product information is the Internet. Thomson and Laing (2003) interviewed children and teenagers who used the Internet and found that nearly half of them did so for "window-shopping." They would seek product information that helped them to make an informed decision before going to purchase the product in a shop. Many of the children and teenagers felt more comfortable finding information this way because they were concerned about being pressurized by sales staff in shops. As Thomson and Laing pointed out, this might have been related to the children's lack of confidence as consumers. The Internet therefore empowered them in a way that would not have been possible through other media, and we can assume that the Internet will become an ever more important source of product information, especially as access becomes easier and more universal through mobile telephones and other wireless connections. Access to the Internet also provides children with rapid access to fashion trends and peer group attitudes. However, as yet, there is a lack of studies comparing the relative importance of television advertising and the Internet as sources of product information for children.

A further source of information about products that may influence purchase requests from children comes from educational materials that retail outlets and service providers distribute to schools. These materials may be reinforced by schools visits from retail personnel, by organized field trips to stores, and by commercially sponsored educational videos that contain advertising content (Pereira, 1990). MacIndoe (1999) listed the commercial activities in U.K. schools and these included: incentive voucher schemes (e.g., to buy books); sponsorship of educational resources; sponsored stationery (e.g., lunch menus); poster and billboard advertising; and advertising on free exercise books. Such advertising not only reaches children directly, but it does so in a school context in which children are expected to pay attention and take notice of what is presented to them (Geuens et al., 2002). We can assume that such advertising is an influential source of brand and product information for children, but again, there is no research as yet investigating the relative importance of in-school and television advertising as sources of information and influence at different ages.

As we have seen in this chapter, the evidence for the effects of televised advertising upon children's and teenagers' purchase behaviors derives from two principal methodologies—experimental research and survey research. In each case, methodology limitations undermine the validity of the research and the quality of the evidence. Experiments allow researchers to manipulate the circumstances under which children are exposed to advertising and control the conditions under which product or brand selections are made. Experiments therefore allow cause-effect relations to be investigated. Their weakness is that they remove children from the natural consumer environment and create artificial conditions in which children may behave differently from the way they would in real life contexts.

Surveys can be used to collect data from consumers that reflect their personal histories in natural buying and media consumption environments. Surveys do not, however, allow any control over advertising exposure or other influences on product purchase behavior. They rely on the accuracy of respondents' self-reports, and because of the self-report nature of surveys, the quality of survey data can sometimes be questioned. Nonetheless, surveys do have the advantage that they can be used to investigate influences of a wide range of factors (of which television advertising is one) on product consumption. It is possible to collect data from respondents that relate to these other factors and to compare the relative importance of different influences on purchasing behavior.

Despite the inherent weaknesses in the methodologies that can be used to investigate the effects of television advertising on purchase behavior, it is possible, as has been described in this chapter, to derive some useful indications about the effects of television advertising on children. Advertising certainly plays a role in enhancing the young consumer's product and brand awareness, brand image, brand preference, and in turn, brand selection. Advertising does not act alone in this context, however. Its influences can vary with the demographic type of youngsters, their background, their relationship with their parents, their parents' style of parenting, their social networks, and the nature of the product itself.

8

The Incidental Influence
of Advertising

Much of the research into television advertising has concentrated on the intended effects of commercial messages. Advertising is designed to promote awareness of commodities, enhance their appeal, and ultimately to encourage their purchase and use. Commercial messages are therefore produced with persuasive appeals that are aimed at creating markets for advertised products and services and maintaining consumer loyalty. But advertising contains information that may have unintended side effects, and exposure to advertising may have social and psychological effects that are not part of the selling intent.

We have already seen that the effects of advertising can be divided into those that occur at behavioral, attitudinal, and other cognitive levels. The unintentional effects of advertising may also occur at these levels. Advertisements may influence children's perceptions of other people, their perceptions of themselves, or influence behaviors that may be potentially harmful to them. They may also contribute to a value system that emphasizes material wealth and conspicuous ownership of commodities.

Parents and child-care professionals have found that advertising has the power to make a significant impression on children. This influence does not simply take the form of mimicking the behaviors of on-screen characters or repeating jingles or taglines in advertisements, it can take on more subtle forms that may have longer-term effects. For example, parents have noted the influence of media role models connected with television advertising and other forms of brand promotion. Children may value such role models because they represent attractive values and lifestyles and provide aspirational models that children seek to emulate (Hanley et al., 2000).

Many incidental effects of advertising are related to health and social concerns, and these include the effects of advertising on nutrition, smoking, under-age drinking, social stereotyping, and self-image, and this chapter discusses these effects in turn.

ADVERTISING AND NUTRITION

Children may be exposed to many thousands of advertising messages a year for food products, and many of these products may be of dubious nutritional value (see chap. 2). In particular, advertisements embedded within programs targeted at children frequently promote food products with high sugar and fat content (Brown, 1977; Cotugna, 1988; Dibb, 1996; Dibb & Castell, 1995; Gussow, 1972; Kotz & Story, 1994). Indeed, early research indicated a period when the majority of food advertisements aimed at children on American network television were high in sugar content and calorific value (Brown, 1977). Children were encouraged to consume these products in advertisements with upbeat messages that emphasized the fun, taste, and social benefits of these products or associated the brand with other premium offers (Kotz & Story, 1994). There are additional concerns that advertising for food products aimed at children may make misleading claims about the nutritional value and health benefits of the foods being promoted (Reece, et al., 1999).

Evidence for the frequency of food advertisements is based on content analysis of advertisements and is therefore descriptive in nature and does not demonstrate the effects of advertising on children. Such content analyses, however, can identify patterns in advertising messages that might potentially exert influences over children, and these patterns can be investigated further using more appropriate audience research methodologies. There is additional evidence that heavily advertised foods can achieve high status among children, regardless of their nutritional value. Furthermore, such foods tend to be the ones that children most often pester their parents to buy for them (Morton, 1990).

The concern about the potentially harmful effects of food advertising on television must be seen in a wider perspective. In the United States, for example, surveys of children's dietary habits have indicated that many youngsters consume a nutritionally poor diet. While consumption of dairy products may be appropriate, too few children eat enough fresh fruit and green vegetables. There is, instead, a much stronger preference for foods high in sugar and fat content that can lead to obesity and dental health problems (Munoz et al., 1997). As well as having potentially significant physical health consequences in the long term, these outcomes can also damage children psychologically by affecting their self-esteem and their relationships with peers (Summerfield, 1990).

A number of contributory factors have been suggested for the growth of obesity-related problems among youngsters. A sedentary lifestyle, reinforced by cuts in physical education classes at school and linked to time spent watching television or using computers is one factor (Young, 2003). Contemporary children burn fewer calories than did earlier generations (Elmer-Dewitt, 1995; Finholn, 1997). In addition, parents may not set good examples for children. Parents may consume poor diets themselves and pay little attention to portion sizes their children consume (Elmer-Dewitt, 1995; Fabricant, 1994).

Nutrition experts and parents' groups, however, have also blamed television advertising for encouraging children to develop preferences for foods that are not healthy options (Brown, 1977; Grossbart & Crosby, 1984; Kotz & Story, 1994). Recent analyses have found that food advertisements represent a smaller proportion of advertisements in children's programs than previously, but highly sugared foods predominate among the foods that are advertised (Reece et al., 1999). As children watch many hours of television on average each day, they are likely to be exposed to large numbers of these commercial messages (Sylvester, Achterberg, & Williams, 1995). Children may, of course, also learn more positive and health-giving eating habits via public service announcements. Such health promotion campaigns may work especially well when celebrity spokespersons are used (Macklin, 1996). But as Reece et al. (1999) found such promotions are rare compared with other food advertisements.

Researchers have addressed several related questions about the effects of food advertising. Does exposure to repeated food advertising influence children's perceptions of what constitutes a healthy diet? What evidence is there that children's exposure to television advertisements can affect their food brand preferences, eating habits, and related health matters? If a child is regularly exposed to television advertising for junk foods, is consumption of these foods seen as the norm? Or are such effects weak or mediated by other factors such as the child's personality and family background, the child's social network, or the importance and credibility of television advertisements as sources of information?

One survey of American children aged five to 12 years found that two thirds believed that presweetened cereals could cause tooth decay. Heavy television viewers, however, were less likely to hold this view. In addition, heavy viewers of food advertisements on television were twice as likely as light viewers to say that sugared cereals and confectionery were highly nutritious (Atkin, Reeves, & Gibson, 1979). These findings suggest that television advertising may strengthen more positive opinions and weaken negative views about sugared food products. Adler et al. (1980), however, found that children exhibited mixed knowledge about the nutritional value of different food products and their knowledge depended upon the age of the child, family income, and their mother's educational level. Older children from higher income and better educated families were more knowledgeable about foods that were good and those that were potentially poor.

A further survey of eight- to 12-year-old American children also explored links between self-reported television viewing and nutrition-related knowledge. In this survey, the more children reported watching Saturday morning children's programs, the lower were their scores on measures of nutritional awareness. Weekday evening viewing, in contrast, was positively related to nutritional knowledge. The findings supported the idea that exposure to child-oriented advertising can have a negative effect on nutritional awareness. Saturday morning television in the United States is full of advertisements for highly sugared foods, but weekday evening programs contain relatively few advertisements of this type (Wiman & Newman, 1987).

Another investigation used nonverbal measures to assess five- to eight-year-old children's nutritional awareness. The children were asked to select foods and drinks that would be "good for you" from a range of cut-out pictures. The results showed that these children did understand some of the basics about nutrition. For example, nearly all the five- and six-year-olds thought that sweet confectionery products were bad for teeth and resulted in cavities by pointing to a picture of child with bad teeth rather than choosing one of a child with good teeth (Esserman, 1981).

Signorielli and Lears (1992) found that even when controlling for sex, reading level, ethnicity, parents' occupation, and parents' educational level, the amount of television viewing by fourth- and fifth-grade children (aged nine–10 years) was positively correlated with bad eating habits and faulty understanding of the principles of nutrition. Donkin, Neale, and Tilson (1993) found that children aged seven to 11 years made frequent requests to parents to buy them high sugar content foods, such as breakfast cereals, snack foods, and fizzy soft drinks that had been advertised recently. Such purchase requests were especially likely to occur in lower-income households in which children were heavier television viewers.

Bolton (1983) considered a variety of factors that could shape children's diets, including food advertisements, the role of parents, existing eating patterns, and other factors linked to the child and his or her environment. In a study that combined the use of diaries and questionnaires, data were collected about the characteristics and eating habits and food preferences of children aged two to 11 years. Bolton found that exposure to television advertising was linked to a greater amount of snack food consumption and that the child's viewing had an independent effect on diet and caloric intake.

A number of researchers have investigated whether television advertising can affect nutritional awareness, perceptions, and behavior under more controlled, experimental, conditions (Lambo, 1981). In this type of research, children are presented with advertisements that systematically differ in the type of message they convey. For example, Barry and Gunst (1982) created two television advertisements for a snack bar that were identical in every way except that one version promoted the product as being "chocolatey, rich, and sweet" and the other version promoted it as "healthful, vitaminey, and nutritious." These advertisements were shown to children aged five to nine years who were then interviewed about the version they had seen. The children who watched the nutritional message version rated the product high on the attributes mentioned in the advertisements and also expressed an intention to purchase it. Children in the other condition were less likely to regard the product as nutritious in this way.

Scammon and Christopher (1981) reviewed nine experimental studies of the impact of televised nutrition messages on children and concluded that different messages had different effects. But exposure to advertisements for sugared products led to greater consumption of such foods, including a greater preference for the sugared foods that had not been advertised. Exposure to advertisements for healthy foods, including foods with low or no sugar content, reduced preferences for sugared foods.

Promotional messages that combined a sugared food product advertisement with a disclaimer warning of the health hazards of excessive consumption of sugar also reduced preference for sugared foods while enhancing nutritional knowledge. But most of the experimental research on this subject has measured short-term or medium-term influences of specific food advertisements on dietary habits, and we know less about the long-term effects of particular advertisements.

Research to date has indicated that television advertising contained within children's programs is predominately for food products. These products tend to have high sugar and fat content and dubious nutritional value. There is understandable concern about this characteristic of advertising on television because advertised foods are known to have high status (Morton, 1990), and eating habits of children in western societies have been shown to exhibit low nutritional value (Dibb & Castell, 1995; Finholn, 1997). Advertising effects are not easy to isolate from other influences upon children's eating habits (Dickinson, 1997; Dickinson & Leader, 1996), but there is consistent evidence that food advertisements affect children's short-term food choices (Gorn & Goldberg, 1982b). There is also evidence that following such advertisements, children will try to influence their mothers' food purchases (Galst & White, 1976).

ADVERTISING AND ONSET OF SMOKING

Some advertisements are not aimed at children, but may nonetheless encourage them to take up behaviors that could be detrimental to their health. For instance, advertising has been blamed as an influence on young people's decision to start smoking (Brody, 1991; Pollay, 1995). The use of animated characters in tobacco advertising was pinpointed as a critical example of this trend. Such accusations were leveled against cigarette advertisers even in the early years of the twentieth century (Schudson, 1984). Early use of broadcast advertising by cigarette advertisers was seen as a deliberate attempt to reach young people (Dunlap, 1931).

It is indisputable that the tobacco industry did use young actors and models in its advertising and that it was therefore not unreasonable to conclude that there was an intention to appeal directly to the young adult market (Anderson, 1929). Some advertisers used popular music icons of the day, in the pre-World War Two era, to promote cigarette brands (Marin, 1980; Tilley, 1985). These choices were guided to some extent by market research studies that revealed the kinds of cultural attributes that were popular with young people (Pollay, 1995).

In 1950s America, as television overtook radio as the premier mass entertainment medium, the tobacco industry attempted to capitalize on this market shift by engaging in extensive sponsorship of programs. Many of these programs were targeted at young people. Sponsorship of sports-related events also extended television coverage. A number of leading tobacco manufacturers sponsored televised basketball and football (Pollay, Carter-Whitney, & Lee, 1992). Some leading tobacco industry executives were even quoted saying that their promotional strategies, including design of packaging, were in part aimed at the younger end of the market (Tide, 1955).

These developments were important in view of the well-publicized health risks associated with smoking (Pollay, 1988). Criticisms of cigarette advertising became more poignant with the emergence of statistical evidence that cigarette smoking was becoming more prevalent among teenagers (Fortune, 1963). Marketing to the young, however, was seen as strategically important to the industry in maintaining a smokers market.

By the early 1960s, the tobacco industry came under increased pressure to show restraint in its advertising where young people were concerned. Even the Tobacco Institute, sponsored by the industry, suggested that tobacco firms should no longer sponsor television programs aimed at young audiences. This was regarded as a better solution than arbitrary restrictions on advertising to certain hours of the day. Despite this apparent move toward self-regulation, some commentators noted that tobacco firms continued to sponsor programs aimed at young people (Pollay, 1994). At this time, these programs were frequently interspersed with cigarette advertising too.

Despite, the criticisms leveled against cigarette advertisers, other research has shown that smoking, historically, occurred fairly infrequently in television programs (e.g., Gerbner, Gross, Morgan, & Signorielli, 1981), and many contemporary programs and films do not include smoking at all or only do so in a negative context. Restrictions on tobacco advertising vary from country to country. In countries such as Spain, tobacco manufacturers may advertise freely across all major media, but elsewhere, televised advertising (e.g., U.K., U.S.) or advertising in any medium (Norway, Finland) is prohibited.

Other forms of promotion of tobacco products are permitted on television even in those countries that ban specific tobacco advertising on television. For example, tobacco companies may sponsor sports events that, in turn, receive television coverage. Tobacco brands may therefore receive coverage on television via such broadcasts. Although this content is not classified as "advertising" by the television industry, researchers have suggested that this type of exposure can affect tobacco brand awareness and may play a part in encouraging young people to take up smoking (Aitken, Leathar, & Squair, 1986a; Charlton, 1986; Ledwith, 1984).

The prevalence of tobacco advertising in the past gave rise to concern. This concern was backed up by some early research evidence that showed a link between reported exposure to advertising for tobacco products and children taking up smoking (Fisher & Magnus, 1981). But the link between advertising and smoking is far from conclusive.

Research on the effects of exposure to cigarette advertising on smoking behavior has consisted mainly of two types of studies—ones in which teenage smokers have been asked if their behavior was influenced by their exposure to advertising, and ones in which exposure to advertising has been linked to smoking behavior. Some studies have made comparisons between young smokers and their nonsmoking peers in respect of their cigarette brand awareness, cigarette advertising awareness, and beliefs about whether cigarette advertising should be banned. Results have not been conclusive. One early study reported no link between self-reported exposure to televised tobacco advertising and children's smoking habits (Lemin, 1966), and another early investigation failed to find any significant link between attitudes toward televised cigarette advertisements and teenage smoking behavior (Levitt & Edwards, 1970). Exposure to advertising can affect young consumers' abilities to name brands (Young, 1990). Research among teenage smokers and nonsmokers in Australia found that smokers were better at identifying brands and advertisements for different brands than were non-smokers, but no evidence emerged to demonstrate that such brand awareness influenced smoking behavior (Chapman & Fitzgerald, 1982; Goldstein, Fischer, Richards, & Creten, 1987).

Other research in the United Kingdom indicated, however, that children as young as nine were attracted to certain cigarette advertisements and enjoyed looking at them (Charlton, 1986). Charlton speculated that such initial attraction to cigarette advertising could cultivate positive impressions about smoking among children. Children who were better able to name their favorite cigarette advertisement were more likely to support positive statements about smoking (e.g., smoking helps you look tough, makes you look grown up, calms your nerves, gives you confidence, helps you to control your weight). But Charlton also found that among children who smoked, only a minority smoked the brand they named in their favorite cigarette advertisement.

Further evidence emerged from surveys among children and teenagers that smokers exhibit better brand awareness. This awareness increases with the age of the child. Awareness is also greater for brands with prominent long-running campaigns (Aitken, Leathar, O'Hagan, & Squair, 1987). Teenage smokers exhibit clear-cut brand preferences, and preferred brands are often those that are most heavily advertised at the time of the research (Aitken & Eadie, 1990; Aitken, Leathar, Scott, & Squair, 1988). Appreciation of cigarette advertising has also been linked to underage smoking, with young smokers liking cigarette advertisements more than nonsmokers did (Aitken & Eadie, 1990; O'Connell et al., 1981). But these studies also showed that other important factors in underage smoking included having parents who did not disapprove of smoking and having siblings who smoked. This research also indicated a link between liking cigarette advertisements and intention to smoke in the future, but again, this intention was also influenced by peer group pressures and the socioeconomic status of family (Aitken, Eadie, Hastings, & Haywood, 1991).

Going beyond measures of brand awareness, some studies on the influence of cigarette advertising have focused on young people's attitudes toward the advertisements themselves. Teenage smokers have been reported to hold generally more positive attitudes toward cigarette advertisements than did nonsmokers, which has been seen by some researchers as evidence of a reinforcing effect of advertising upon smoking (Aitken et al., 1986b).

Another approach to establishing whether cigarette advertising has any influence on smoking among children and teenagers has been to examine the impact of controls over tobacco advertising in different countries. Researchers have investigated changes in smoking prevalence before and after cigarette advertising bans and have also investigated variations in smoking prevalence in countries with and without restrictions. Both these approaches have failed to find an impact of restrictive legislation. Two major international studies failed to produce evidence that bans on cigarette advertising on television (and other media) had any noticeable effects upon cigarette consumption levels among young people (Aaron, Wold, Kannas, & Rimpola, 1986; Boddewyn, 1986).

An area of concern is tobacco manufacturers sponsorship of televised events (see chap. 2). According to some critics, such sponsorship can function as advertising by enhancing brand awareness and by making smoking seem more attractive through its association with exciting events (Hastings & MacFadyen, 2000). A handful of studies have investigated this issue, and so far little supportive evidence has been produced. Researchers have found that sponsored sports events on television increased cigarette brand awareness among teenagers and created a firm association in teenagers' minds between the brand and the event being sponsored (Ledwith, 1984; Piepe, et al., 1986)—see chapter two. But neither of these studies was able to demonstrate that such enhanced brand awareness encouraged children to take up smoking.

Advertising and Underage Drinking

Controversy has surrounded the marketing of alcoholic products for many years, and manufacturers' policy on alcohol advertising has changed over time. For example, in the United States, manufacturers of liquor products (or spirits) adopted a voluntary code not to advertise on radio or subsequently on television. The television ban, in particular, was designed to avoid exposing children to such advertising. But later, the manufacturers dropped their voluntary ban on television advertising—in 1996, the House of Seagram announced that it would air television advertisements for its liquor brands (Ross & McDowell, 1996). Regulators responded to this more aggressive marketing position, and even the White House joined in the debate with a public appeal to the industry to reinstate its self-imposed advertising ban. The Federal Communications Commission (FCC) was also asked to investigate possible restrictions on liquor advertising on television. Although no federal U.S. regulations have been introduced, some local governments have begun to take action against liquor advertising, though such actions have not yet touched television advertising (Teinowitz, 1997).

The antialcohol advertising lobby has had more influence in cases in which advertisers have been accused of deliberately targeting young (underage) consumers. In one such case about advertising on MTV, featuring Anheuser Busch, and later the Miller Brewing Company, both withdrew their advertising on that station. On another occasion, the U.S. Federal

Trade Commission (FTC) launched an investigation into the airing of an advertisement for Schlitz Malt Liquor on television programs aimed at teenagers. That airing was judged to be in direct violation of the beer industry's own nonmarketing code that stated that beer advertisements should not be placed in programs whose audiences consist mostly of underage viewers (Ross, 1996).

The content of beer advertisements on television has frequently been criticized because they regularly feature young drinkers enjoying a lifestyle clearly designed to appeal to young consumers (Strasburger, 1995). Evidence for possible effects of television advertising for alcoholic drinks on children's and teenagers' interest in alcohol consumption has derived mainly from surveys. Researchers have investigated the extent to which alcohol advertising effects young consumers' level of consumption and how their attitudes toward advertising shapes the influence of that advertising. The evidence, however, has not been conclusive.

American research with teenagers aged 13 to 17 years found no relationship between reported exposure to television advertising for alcoholic drinks and level of consumption. This finding was not consistent for all the teenagers surveyed, however. Those teenagers who were motivated to pay careful attention to such advertisements because they thought they might learn something from them about how to behave in social situations were more susceptible to advertising influences. Advertising for alcoholic drinks was also found to be more influential among teenagers who turned to such advertising to fantasize about certain desired lifestyles. Even when motivated to watch advertising the influence of that advertising was still relatively trivial (Strickland, 1982).

Another U.S. study found that drinkers aged 12 to 16 years or those who intended to drink alcohol when older were more likely to have seen beer, wine, and spirits or liquor advertisements on television (Atkin & Block, 1984; Atkin, Hocking, & Block, 1984). The relationship between reported exposure to television advertising for alcoholic drinks' products and current or intended consumption of these products, however, was relatively strong in respect of liquor consumption, more modest in the case of beer, and weak in relation to wine consumption. One limitation of this study was that the direction of causality was never clearly established. Thus, the relationship found might indicate that exposure to advertising led to their drinking more, or it may indicate that teenagers who were heavier drinkers were more interested in watching alcohol advertisements.

Other evidence suggests that the impact of advertising on children's or teenagers' propensities to drink may operate in more subtle ways. Greenberg et al. (1986) asked 10- to 16-year-olds in the United Kingdom which advertisements they liked or disliked. Advertisements for alcoholic drinks become increasingly salient and attractive as young consumers moved into their teenage years. Although 10-year-olds show little interest in advertisements for beer, for example, by midteens, these advertisements were among the most popular. By midteens, young consumers were demonstrating more complex reasons for liking particular advertisements that represented values and aspirational lifestyles that were important to them. These more subtle reactions to advertisements suggest ways in which advertisements on television may exert influences over young consumers in indirect ways. Alcoholic drinks may be associated with specific role models, social situations, and attractive attributes that teenagers hope to emulate, enjoy, or display themselves. Such advertising conveys messages about a world associated with drinking that is a world to which teenagers aspire and that may be relevant to their developing self-identity.

The importance of the role model factor was underscored by other research that indicated that alcohol advertising combined with other television alcohol consumption portrayals in programs projected drinking as a largely problem-free activity (Grube, 1993). In other words, it was enjoyable and rarely associated with harmful consequences even when indulged in to excess. Grube found that the depiction of drinking by well-off, successful, and attractive people created an ambience around drinking that rendered alcohol consumption an appealing activity. Advertisements often associated alcohol consumption with people who had highly desirable personal attributes and lifestyles. Not surprising, given these associations, young impressionable consumers might develop a taste for alcohol themselves.

The more aware young consumers become of advertisements for alcoholic drinks, the greater the likely influence of these messages (Gentile, Walsh, Bloomgren, Atti, & Norman, 2001). It is not simply a matter of mere exposure but more especially the appeal of such commercial messages. Grube & Wallack (1994) found that 10- to 13-year-olds who had the greatest awareness of television beer advertising had the most favorable opinions about beer, had the greatest knowledge of beer brands and slogans, and had the strongest intentions to drink beer as an adult.

The potential influence of televised alcoholic drinks advertising on children can be affected by advertising-specific factors such as the attractiveness of the characters who drink on screen or promote advertised brands and by the rewards supposedly associated with brand consumption. But the degree to which alcohol is consumed in a child's home is another influential factor. Children make selective use of information from home and from television (advertisements and programs) in formulating their own ideas about alcohol and its consumption (Austin & Meill, 1994).

In one experimental study of the influence of alcohol advertising children (aged 10–11 years) were exposed to beer advertising, and this exposure resulted in positive expectancies about alcohol consumption (Dunn & Yniguez, 1999). Hence, television advertising may cultivate a positive mindset toward alcohol by encouraging children to associate appealing attributes with its consumption.

ADVERTISING AND SOCIAL STEREOTYPING

Another incidental effect of television advertising is related to social perception. Much of the research on this subject has focused on the role advertising plays in influencing gender stereotyping among young people (see chap. 4). Advertisements depict men and women, boys and girls, in different scenarios in relation to different products and services. Quite apart from the product-related information the consumer acquires from these messages, are there other "social" lessons to be learned from them? Does seeing women or men depicted in particular situations with particular products lead children to associate each gender with those situations and products? Might this, in turn, lead to stereotyping such that some products are believed to be most appropriate for females, whereas others are most appropriate for males?

Much research suggests that the mass media can exert powerful influences at the level of social conceptions and perceptions (see Durkin, 1985a, 1985c; Gunter, 1995). In particular, such effects have been demonstrated in relation to gender-related social perceptions. Content analysis has been used to examine the way that the sexes are depicted in advertising, and surveys and experiments have been used to find out whether advertising representations influence audience perceptions (Durkin, 1985b, 1985d).

Content analyses have shown that, over many years, men tend to outnumber women in televised advertising, especially in relation to authority roles speaking on behalf of a product (Courtney & Whipple, 1974; Ferrante, Haynes, & Kingsley, 1988; Lovdal, 1989; McArthur & Resko, 1975; Schneider, 1979). In the 1970s, women were depicted disproportionately in domestic roles compared to men in advertisements (Courtney & Whipple, 1974). By the mid- to late-1980s, it was found that women were portrayed in a wider range of occupations and appeared in more settings outside the home (Ferrante et al., 1988). Although women were still most often portrayed in the role of wife or mother figure, men were increasingly seen in the role of husband or father.

Gender roles vary with the time of day when advertisements are broadcast, with implicit assumptions about the varying gender profile of the audience throughout the day. Previous researchers have shown that products represented by females were far more prominent and numerous during daytime advertisements (Krill, Peach, Pursey, Gilpin, & Perloff, 1981). During the day, when the audience comprised a larger proportion of women, women were more often portrayed in knowledgeable and controlling roles. But during peak-time, when the audience included an equal mix of men and women, men occupied the great majority of authoritative roles within television advertisements (Rak & McMullen, 1987).

A number of content analyses have focused on advertisements aimed at children and found frequent evidence of gender stereotyping (Doolittle & Pepper, 1975; Riff, Goldson, Sexton, & Yang-Chou, 1989). Early studies found that boys tended to outnumber girls, especially in lead roles (Macklin & Kolbe, 1984; McArthur & Eisen, 1976; Winick, Williamson, Chuzmir, & Winick, 1973). Nonetheless, the profile of gender-role representations in advertisements changed during the 1970s and 1980s. The proportion of females, in both on-screen roles and voice-overs, increased in children's advertisements, and although boys still outnumbered girls at the end of the 1980s, the gap between the sexes had narrowed (Kolbe, 1990).

Content analysis is an effective methodology for describing the contents of advertisements and for identifying patterns of objects, situations, and behaviors that are portrayed in advertisements, but such analyses cannot measure the incidental effects of advertising on the audience. It does, nonetheless, serve a useful purpose of generating hypotheses about the potential side-effects of advertisements. If women are depicted more often than men in domestic roles and less often than men in professional and occupational roles, do such depictions teach children incidental lessons about the social roles for each gender?

According to cultivation theory, the more time individuals spend watching television, the more likely they are to develop a view of the real world that reflects the world as displayed on the screen. For example, heavy viewers of a world of television that depicts women primarily in domestic roles may develop the idea that such roles are most appropriate for women (see Gerbner & Gross, 1976).

Although much research has accumulated about the cultivation effects of television on adults, little research has been conducted among children in relation to television advertising. Some researchers have claimed that television advertising can affect children's gender-role stereotypes, much as exposure to gender-stereotyping in programs can (Kimball, 1986). For example, in a survey of 12- to 18-year-olds designed to assess various aspects of consumer socialization, Moschis and Moore (1982) found that exposure to television advertising was associated with a traditional view of sex roles in those adolescents whose parents did not discuss consumer matters with their children. But this research is far from conclusive because it is difficult to assess the influence of stereotyped gender-role portrayals in advertisements as so many other media sources and real-life experiences also provide gender-role models.

Another sign of stereotyping in children's television advertisements has been found in the way that the advertisements have been produced (Welch, Huston-Stein, Wright, & Plehal, 1979). Male-oriented advertisements contained more cuts, loud music, and boisterous activity. According to Welch et al., symbolic messages about what is distinctively "masculine" were conveyed through the high rate of action, aggression, variation, and quick shifts from one scene to another. Female-oriented advertisements, in contrast, featured frequent fades and background music and conveyed images of softness, gentleness, and predictability. These images conveyed the message that females are quiet, soft, gentle, and less active than males. Even young children may believe that certain production treatments are better suited to products for males or to products for females. For example, Huston, Greer, Wright, Welch, and Ross (1984) found that loud music, fast-pacing, and editing were perceived as "masculine," whereas soft music and slower pacing were judged to be "feminine" by children aged five to 12 years.

ADVERTISING AND SELF-IMAGE

Physical attractiveness is an important issue for many people. The way we perceive ourselves and others is critically bound up with physical attractiveness, and judgements about attractiveness begin to emerge very early in life. Two-year-olds exhibit preferences for physically attractive people (Langlois et al., 1987) and preschoolers exhibit stereotyping based on facial attractiveness (Dion, 1973). In storytelling, whether in fiction books or on film, evil is often frequently associated with ugliness and good is often associated with beauty (Eagly et al., 1991).

Physical attractiveness features prominently in advertising. Endorsements for products are often given by attractive actors or models (Downs & Harrison, 1985), and some authors have argued that advertisers have gone too far in promoting standards of attractiveness and beauty that are far beyond the reach of most consumers (Wolf, 1992). But such criticisms have not discouraged advertisers from promoting idealized images of beauty to endorse their products (Richins, 1991) because attractive endorsers are more effective at selling products (Belch, Belch, & Villarreal, 1987; Benoy, 1982).

The use of attractiveness is especially pronounced in advertising aimed at young consumers. During adolescence, young people begin to establish their self-identity, and the conception of self at this time is closely linked to perceptions of attractiveness—and especially physical appearance. Young people are therefore inclined to identify with attractive media role models, including ones in advertisements (Martin & Gentry, 1997; Martin & Kennedy, 1993). There is evidence that adolescents are more susceptible to persuasion by advertisements anyway (Linn, de Benedictis, & Delucchi,

1982; Moschis & Churchill, 1979; Ross et al., 1984) and may be particularly susceptible to persuasion by reference groups to which they aspire (e.g., attractive models in advertisements).

Much attention has been devoted to the susceptibility of teenage girls to the incidental influences of role models in advertising. In particular, there has been concern about the influence of advertisements containing physically attractive actors and models with very slender body shapes. Teenage girls tend to view their bodies critically and may hold negative self-perceptions about their physical appearance (Franzoi, 1995). Teenage girls are much more likely than teenage boys to question their attractiveness (Harter, 1993; Rosenberg, 1986). This negative self-concept is especially likely to be manifest as dissatisfaction with body shape. Girls in their early teens, or even among those who are younger if they achieve puberty early, frequently express dissatisfaction with their body size and appearance (Collins, 1990; Williams & Currie, 2000).

The emergence of body image concerns is important because it may be associated with the appearance of disordered eating patterns. This is especially worrying when it occurs in early teen years that are an crucial period for physical growth. The more dissatisfied young girls are with their bodies, the more likely they are to undereat, with implications for their health and well-being (Griffiths & McCabe, 2000).

Males, in contrast, usually take a different view of their bodies. That is not to say that boys and young men are unconcerned about their body image, but rather than wanting to be thinner and more attractive, many males want to be more muscular with greater bulk. For males, this represents greater power. Whereas girls' self-concepts of attractiveness stem primarily from physical attractiveness, boys' self-concepts are linked to perceptions of physical effectiveness (Lerner, Orlos, & Knapp, 1976). Adolescent girls tend to be preoccupied with their weight, and adolescent boys are generally not (Franzoi & Herzog, 1987; Wadden, Brown, Foster, & Liowitz, 1991).

Analyses of advertising content in the media have shown a preoccupation with thin female body shapes (Guillen & Barr, 1994). Women's magazines frequently contain feature articles that discuss dieting issues, thus reinforcing the subject and raising its place in female consciousness (Anderson & DiDomenico, 1992). Boys and men do not face the same types of attractiveness-related messages. Idealized images of men in advertising differ from those of women, and men's and women's reactions to these images are not the same (Fischer & Halfpenny, 1993).

Franzoi (1995) suggested that, given the differences in body orientation, there is a greater likelihood that females will be influenced by a mediated feminine ideal than men will be influenced by a mediated male ideal. In particular, females with low self-esteem and/or who have poor body images may be especially susceptible to depictions of physically attractive (and slender-shaped) models in advertising (Martin & Kennedy, 1993; Stephens, Hill, & Hanson, 1994). The tendency of female preadolescents and adolescents to compare themselves with models in advertisements is greater for those who hold less flattering self-perceptions of their physical attractiveness. Stephens et al. (1994) also proposed that women who are more dissatisfied with their bodies are also less able to resist peer pressure. Thus, they are more likely to be persuaded by physically attractive endorsers and to evaluate advertisements containing such endorsers and associated products more positively than do those women who have more positive body images.

One explanation for this effect is that consumers make positive inferences about physically attractive endorsers. They attribute socially desirable traits to such individuals that may, in turn, become associated with the products they are endorsing (Brumbaugh, 1993; Maddux & Rogers, 1980). This notion is consistent with the "what is beautiful is good" stereotype (Dion, 1986; Dion, Berscheid, & Walster, 1972). Some researchers have found support for this hypothesis and that a physically attractive endorser does enhance positive attitudes toward the advertised brand (Brumbaugh, 1993). But other researchers have found that the transference of positive feelings does not always occur, nor does an attractive endorser guarantee acceptance of the advertising message by consumers (Maddux & Rogers, 1980).

Martin et al. (1999) showed magazine advertisements to 11- and 15-year-old female and male adolescents. Some of the advertisements contained same-sex attractive models, but others did not. The adolescents were also categorized as those with high body self-esteem and those with low body self-esteem. Boys generally did not react differently to the advertisements as a function of the presence of an attractive same-sex role model nor in relation to their own body self-perceptions. This was not true of girls. Girls with low body self-esteem liked the advertisements with attractive role models better than advertisements without such models, whereas for girls with high body self-esteem, this finding was reversed. The same result occurred for liking the advertised products, with low body-self-esteem girls being more susceptible to the presence of an attractive same-sex endorser. Such findings suggest that the nature of the endorser in an advertisement has an influential effect on certain sectors of the audience.

To turn to evidence for the influence of advertising on body image perceptions and related behavior patterns (e.g., disordered eating), some researchers have investigated associations between self-reported media exposure and self-perceptions. A number of surveys have found a correlation between self-reported media exposure and measures such as body dissatisfaction, disordered eating, and the desire for thinness among young adult females. Such studies have asked respondents in fairly broad terms to report on their recent history of magazine and television exposure (Harrison, 1997; Harrison & Cantor, 1997; Stice, Schupak-Neuberg, Shaw, & Stein, 1994). Further research with similar results has been conducted among adolescent girls (Harrison, 2000a) and preadolescent girls (Harrison, 2000b). Although such research is indicative, it does not reveal anything exclusively about the effects of exposure to advertising given all the other factors that can influence body image perceptions.

Experimental research has focused more directly on the influence of exposure to specified images, though many researchers have focused on magazine advertising rather than television advertising. Exposure to photographic images of thin models produces short-term changes in body shape perceptions and body shape ideal among adolescent and young adult females (Cash, Cash, & Butters, 1983; Champion & Furnham, 1999; Irving, 1990; Ogden & Mundray, 1996; Richins, 1991). Evidence has also emerged that television stimuli—much of it advertising related—can have similar effects (e.g., Cattarin, Williams, Thomas, & Thompson, 1999; Heinberg & Thompson, 1995; Myers & Biocca, 1992; Strauss, Doyle, & Kriepe, 1994). The latter research was mostly conducted among women in their late teens and twenties, and though it does not include young females, it is worth reviewing because some of the effects that have been found might also occur among younger populations than those studied so far.

One study examined the effects of television advertisements on dietary restraint level (Strauss, et al., 1994). Participants were initially divided into those who exhibited high and low restraint in their eating patterns. They were then given a high calorie, nutritionally balanced banana drink. Next they viewed a film interrupted by advertisements that in different conditions promoted either diet-related or nondiet-related products. Both high and low restraint groups watched this material and were provided with nuts and confectionery to eat during the movie. A third group saw the movie without any advertisements. Strauss et al. found that it was the participants with a high restraint level who viewed the movie with diet-related advertisements who ate the most.

Most of these studies focused on the impact of televised advertising images on self-perceptions. For example, Heinberg and Thompson (1995) found that exposure to a sequence of advertisements that promoted the importance of thinness and attractiveness produced increased concerns about weight and body image among young women who already had low self-esteem. But the same effects did not occur among young women with high self-esteem.

In another experiment that combined television programs and advertisements with body-image-related messages, college-age women adjusted their self-perceptions in a less positive direction after exposure to advertisements that emphasized thinness. These young women perceived their waist and hips to be larger following exposure to television advertisements with thin role models (Myers & Biocca, 1992).

In another study, the presentation of television advertisements that portrayed women as sex objects caused increased body dissatisfaction among young women and young men (Lavine, Sweeney, & Wagner, 1999). The sample used here ranged in age from 18 to 35 years. Participants saw either 15 sexist and five nonsexist advertisements or 20 nonsexist advertisements. Female participants exposed to the sexist advertisements judged their current body size as larger and had a larger discrepancy between their actual and ideal body sizes (preferring a thinner body) than did women exposed only to nonsexist advertisements or to no advertisements at all.

Lavine et al (1999) also examined what effects exposure to advertisements with female sex object depictions would have on male viewers. Their reasoning was as follows: "If the female sex object subtype heightens men's beliefs that women are flirtatious and seductive, this may increase the salience of their perceived characteristics of men (e.g., a muscular physique) to which women are attracted. Thus, such ads may increase men's awareness of and concerns about their own bodies and thus increase body dissatisfaction among men" (p. 151). When such advertisements also depict muscular men, then there might be an even more direct effect on men who compare themselves to such models unfavorably. Levine et al. found that men exposed to the sexist advertisements judged their own body size as thinner and revealed a larger discrepancy between their actual and ideal body size (preferring a larger body). They also had a larger discrepancy between their own ideal body size and their perceptions of others' body size preferences (believing that other males preferred a larger ideal) than did men exposed only to nonsexist advertisements or to no advertisements at all.

CONCLUSIONS

This chapter has reviewed evidence on the effects of television advertising that were not originally intended, that is, they were not directly linked to the purpose of the advertisement to promote a specific brand. Most research has focused on incidental and potentially harmful (rather than beneficial) effects of advertising. These effects may shape young consumers' perceptions of themselves or others and their attitudes about food consumption and drinks products that carry health implications. Much advertising targeted at young consumers is for food products, and many of these tend to include foods with high sugar and high salt content (Dibb, 1996). Because advertised products are among the most attractive to youngsters, it follows that there is a likelihood that, through their regular exposure to televised advertising, children will be cultivated to adopt unhealthy eating habits. Research evidence has accumulated to indicate that such effects can and do occur. Children and teenagers may have their food preferences shaped by food-related advertisements with longer-term effects on their dietary behavior.

Although advertisements for tobacco products and alcoholic drinks products are not directly targeted at young people, they have been found to hold strong appeal for young consumers. Part of the reason for this is concerned with the skillful use of humor in advertisements, especially in those for beer. Other alcohol advertisements may associated drinking certain brands with affluent and successful lifestyles to enhance the brand's appeal to young people. Advertisements for smoking may also convey positive images of looking more grown up that have an appeal for adolescents. But one concern is that exposure to such advertising on television may encourage teenagers to take up smoking or drinking while still under age.

The research on the impact of tobacco and alcoholic drinks advertising is not conclusive, but there are clear indications that, for example, beer advertisements feature among children's favorites (Greenberg et al., 1986) and that the humor in them causes them to be thought about (Hanley, Hayward, Sims, and Jones, 2000). It is also apparent that young smokers are knowledgeable about brands and establish clear-cut preferences (Aitken, Leathar, & Squair, 1986a, 1986b). Furthermore, preferred tobacco brands tend to be those that are most heavily advertised (Aitken, Leathar, Scott, & Squair, 1988).

While underage drinkers and smokers tend to know more about brands than do youngsters with little or no interest in alcohol or smoking (Aitken et al., 1986a, 1988; Atkin, Leathar, & O'Hagan, 1985), such data do not represent unambiguous evidence of an advertising effect. Young people may start smoking or drinking alcohol early for many other reasons such as their personal circumstances, parental behavior, and peer pressure. They may therefore know more about brands because they are already active consumers and know about the market. Separating the relative mediating effects of these different social factors and the effects of advertising can be a difficult undertaking in any research project.

On a social level, advertisements contain representations of different aspects of social reality. Repeated patterns of depictions of social groups and social behaviors could shape youngsters' social perceptions and social attitudes especially if they are exposed to these messages on a regular basis. These effects could operate on youngsters' perceptions of their own and others' social groups. There is a significant degree of gender-role stereotyping in television advertising, with men and women being presented in distinct roles or associated primarily with particular types of products or services (Durkin, 1985a; Gunter, 1995). Such stereotyping occurs in advertisements aimed at children as well as in those aimed at adults. Furthermore, advertisements display stereotyped representations of physical beauty and attractiveness (Richins, 1991; Wolf, 1992).

The effects of these stereotypes may be especially profound among teenagers who are struggling to establish a coherent self-identity. Both boys and girls may be susceptible to the influences of gender-role stereotyping in advertisements (Huston et al., 1984; Moschis & Moore, 1982), and teenage girls have been identified as being most vulnerable to depictions of body shape and physical appearance norms in advertisements (Harter, 1993). Even boys may be influenced in their body self-perceptions by male advertising icons (Lerner, et al., 1976), though they do not respond to the same attractiveness messages as girls (Fischer & Halfpenny, 1993). While many girls seek to be thinner, many boys want to become more muscular.

Once again, though, the evidence about the specific effects of advertising is limited because of the other factors that influence children and young people. Teenagers are bombarded with information about how to behave or how to appear from a plethora of sources. Advertisements are only one part of this much bigger mix of social messages. Distinguishing the relative importance of different influences during this period of development is a challenging task and one that still requires much research.

9

Advertising Regulation and Research

This chapter examines the regulation of television advertising with special reference to children. We consider the extent to which advertising regulations are consistent with and supported by research evidence concerning children and advertising, the degree to which regulations have kept pace with research evidence, and whether there are issues raised by the regulations on which further research is needed. We also review the contribution that research might play in further informing current guidelines and codes of practice for television advertisers. In doing this, we consider whether the research evidence presented to regulators has been effectively utilized. In addition, we examine the pressures upon British advertising regulators to conform to European regulations and the feasibility of achieving Europe-wide standardization or harmonization of advertising regulations.

ORIGINS OF CONCERN ABOUT ADVERTISING AND CHILDREN

The most significant sources of criticism and concern about advertising aimed at children have been national and international consumer organizations. According to these bodies, children require special consideration because they are less able than adults to understand fully the intent of advertising or its persuasion techniques and are therefore less able to judge advertising critically (see chaps. 3 and 4).

The extent to which such considerations are contained within regulations or codes of practice, whether internationally or nationally, varies greatly. Some countries, such as Norway and Sweden, do not permit any television advertising to be directed toward children under 12 years of age, and no advertisements at all are allowed during children's programs. In Australia, advertisements are not allowed during programs for preschool children. In the Flemish region of Belgium, no advertising is permitted within five minutes of the beginning or end of any children's program. In contrast, Spain allows advertising of children's products around children's programs. In the United Kingdom, advertising can be aimed at children, but within parameters defined by a detailed code of practice. Although some countries do not have an all-out ban on advertising directed toward children, they may have selective bans on advertising for particular types of product. For example, in Greece, toy advertising is banned.

Consumer organizations' concerns center on several distinct aspects of televised advertising, most especially (a) the amount of advertising to children, (b) the types of advertising that predominate in children's programming, (c) the marketing techniques used to entice children within advertisements, (d) the lack of adequate enforcement of advertising regulations, and (e) the impact of cross-border advertising where advertisers transmit their content from another country to circumvent compliance with the regulations of the receiving country.

Quite apart from the nonspecific concern that children may be exposed to too much advertising anyway, there are special concerns about the predominance of certain types of advertising. Research into advertising output on television has found that food advertising predominates in children's programs (see chaps. 2 and 8). However, the foods most frequently advertised are for products high in fat, sugar, and salt. This may have important implications for children's dietary habits and the status of their nutrition and health. This is true of most major television nations (Dibb, 1996).

In consequence, consumer organizations have made a number of recommendations concerning advertising and children. The Consumers International Survey in 1996 called for high international standards of protection for children and that advertising regulations should protect children from misleading, unfair, or excessive amounts of advertising. This would mean the need for greater cooperation among national regulatory bodies particularly in relation to the issue of cross-border advertising. It would also mean that advertisers should take responsibility for ensuring that their marketing activities take account of the concerns of consumer organizations and parents. The Consumers International Survey drew particular attention to the advertising of certain types of foods that may encourage unhealthy eating habits. Regulators were warned to take account of the age of the children, with younger children requiring greater protection. It suggested there should be a clear break between programs and advertisements through the use of visual and auditory signals and that presentation techniques that might cause confusion between programs and advertisements should be avoided. It also called for more research into the ways that children respond to advertising, especially into the long-term and cumulative effects of exposure to food advertisements.

These are important issues and the concerns of consumer organizations are well meant. Whether such objectives are all necessary or achievable is another matter. Frameworks of regulation already exist at regional, national, and international levels. Some of these regulatory frameworks are underpinned by statute whereas others are voluntary codes of practice adopted by media industries or advertisers, but reaching international agreements about the regulation of television advertising has proven problematic. While common frames of reference have been accepted at the supranational level, they are usually accompanied by opt-out clauses that allow individual nations to adopt unilateral codes of practice. This has been amply illustrated within Europe.

THE POSITION IN EUROPE

Television advertising to children has been the focus of increasing debate across Europe during the past decade. To safeguard children from the effects of television advertising, many countries in the European Union (EU) have taken measures, though these vary in their extent. But within the framework of the Single European Market, there have been attempts to establish standard regulations or, at least, to harmonize regulations concerning advertising that traverses national boundaries.

In spite of a shared concern about advertising when it is directed toward children, the restrictions that have been placed on advertising have varied from one country to the next. One reason for this is that value systems vary among European nations (Young et al., 2003). With regard to television, in particular, advertising practices that are considered false, deceptive, or misleading in one country may be regarded as appropriate in another. Advertising treatments that are accepted in one part of the EU may be regarded as offensive elsewhere (Rijens & Miracle, 1986). Consumers in Germany and Norway may place more literal interpretations on certain promotional statements that do those in Italy or Spain. Although nudity in television advertising may be commonplace and no cause for alarm in France, in the United Kingdom, even a glimpse of a female nipple can cause a widespread public debate.

The scope for regulation also varies from one European country to the next because media and advertising systems vary across the EU. In most EU countries, media institutions retain a firm national orientation and are strongly influenced by internal regulatory regimes that reflect their country's dominant political philosophies. Such differences play a crucial part in determining how the media operate economically as well as culturally (Schlesinger, 1995).

European recognition of children as potentially vulnerable viewers presumes the validity of three related values: (a) respect for children's developing educational needs; (b) fairness, or not exposing children to sophisticated advertising messages before they develop awareness of persuasion; and (c) avoidance of exposure to adult content (Blumler, 1992). Although there may be broad agreement on these points, the steps taken by individual nations to protect children from television advertising vary substantially. For instance, restrictions on advertising aimed at children include all-out bans (e.g., Sweden), partial bans on advertising in or around children's programs (Netherlands), or limits placed on what may be advertised before certain times, when children might be watching (U.K.).

Broadly, two types of regulations are found in Europe: rules and guidelines about (a) the scheduling of advertising and (b) the content of advertising. Scheduling restrictions relate to the timing, frequency, and the amount of advertising aimed at children. These restrictions may also apply to specific types of advertising presented at certain times when children are known to be viewing in large numbers. Restrictions on the content of advertising aimed at children place prohibitions on advertising specified products or prohibit the inclusion of certain behaviors within commercial messages. There are differences across European countries in both the detail of provisions and the way they are implemented. At the national level, the regulation of television advertising aimed at children is a combination of provisions emanating from both regulatory and self-regulatory bodies that are responsible for statutory rules and self-regulatory guidelines. The weight of enforcement of regulations depends upon the degree of authority those bodies have within their respective industries. In addition, consumer lobby groups and organizations have varying degrees of influence, often through the research they produce about advertising and children.

Difficulties in reaching agreement on the implementation of codes of practice about the scheduling, content, and treatments of advertisements often emerge because of different national definitions for key concepts like "the child" or "children's advertising."

WHAT IS A CHILD?

One complicating factor in relation to defining regulations for advertising aimed at children is the definition of a child. This is an area where there is a lack of consistency across European states and regulatory bodies. In countries such as the Netherlands, Spain, and Sweden, the upper age limit for a child is 12 years. In the United Kingdom, children are classed as individuals aged 15 and under. The *International Chamber of Commerce* Code of Advertising Practice considers children as persons under 14 years of age or under whatever age is considered appropriate at the national level (Gonzalez del Valle, 1999).

WHAT IS CHILDREN'S ADVERTISING?

Another issue is how to define children's advertising. Is this type of advertising to be defined, for example, by product category or by the kind of treatment used within the advertising message? At national and pan-European levels, there has been a tendency to define children's television advertising in terms of product category, with food and toys being the types of products most closely associated with advertising aimed at children. But in recent years, other prominent child-oriented product categories have emerged such as computer games, music, films, and clothing.

Detailed codes have been produced, within wider advertising regulations, concerned specifically with television advertising for food and toys. With food advertising, there is special concern about advertising for sugared foods such as breakfast cereals and confectionery because of their health implications for teeth and weight. With toy advertising, the focus of codes of practice is placed more squarely on the use of misleading messages about the product (such as its size and versatility) and the possibility that antisocial conduct may be encouraged through the way that toys are presented (e.g., war toys and violent behavior). More recently, mobile telephones have emerged as another product of great interest to children, with both health and financial implications (Crook & Davison, 2001) as well as providing new opportunities for marketing to children (Jones, 2002) that, in turn, may need regulation.

Television advertising aimed at children is not restricted to spot advertising between or within programs. Children are targeted through sponsorship, children's clubs (tagged to certain child or family-oriented programs), teleshopping, and telepromotions or special competitions. In many countries, and in particular in the United States (e.g., Kunkel, 1988a, 1988b), there have been concerns about program-length advertising, as well as concerns about the tie-in of spot advertising for products when those products are principal features in children's programs.

REGULATORY FRAMEWORKS

Consumer organizations have voiced doubts about the comprehensiveness of regulatory frameworks and the effectiveness of their implementation. But are these criticisms justified? To answer this question, it is necessary to examine the regulatory systems that are already in place. A convenient way to do this is to divide those systems into national, European, and international regulatory systems.

This analysis of regulation of television advertising will focus primarily on the arrangements in the United Kingdom. It will, nevertheless, examine the wider picture across Europe because this also provides an important context for U.K. regulation. We will also take into account even wider international regulatory codes for advertising, as they provide a backdrop for U.K. regulation.

National Regulation—United Kingdom

Between 1991 and 2003, the Independent Television Commission (ITC) was the regulatory body responsible for licensing and regulating commercial television channels in the United Kingdom, whether transmitted terrestrially or via cable or satellite systems. The ITC also licensed and regulated new digital terrestrial television services. The BBC is governed by a Royal Charter and applies a set of internal rules for its public service television services, none of which carry any commercial product advertising or sponsorship. In July 2003, a new Communication Act legally underpinned the introduction of a new regulator, the Office of Communication (Ofcom), which would be responsible for all broadcasting and Internet-related regulation. Under the terms of the 2003 Act, Ofcom was required to draw up its own codes of practice for televised advertising and for program sponsorship.

The lynchpin of U.K. advertising regulation had been the 1988 Consumer Protection Act that is concerned with misleading advertising. The Broadcasting Act 1990 was the key statutory instrument for the regulation of commercial television that followed on from the earlier act. It required the ITC to draw up and enforce, after appropriate consultation, a code setting out standards for television advertising and sponsorship. In response to this statutory duty, the ITC produced a Code of Advertising Standards and Practice (CASP) and a Code of Programme Sponsorship. Section 9(7) and (8) of the 1990 Broadcasting Act empowered the ITC to give directions on the amount, distribution and presentation of advertising, and the ITC's Rules on Advertising Breaks (RAB) set the basic rules for the duration of advertising breaks. These codes evolved through a number of iterations and revisions during the 1990s and into the new millennium (see ITC, 1991a, 1991b, 1991c, 1993, 1995, 1997, 2003).

The ITC required all of the television companies it licenses to comply with the Codes. Broadcasters had to demonstrate to the ITC that they had satisfactory arrangements in place to ensure that any television advertising they transmitted was prevetted and complied with the ITC Codes, though there was some variation in the rules for terrestrial, cable, and satellite transmission systems. The ITC worked within a statutory framework and the rules reflected the conclusions of formal consultations rather than empirical research. Nevertheless, certain parts of these Codes made assumptions about audiences' responses to advertising and the potential effects of certain forms of advertising that were supported by research evidence.

Although the BBC's public service channels do not carry advertising, BBC World-Wide Television, which is commercially funded, is permitted to take advertising and sponsorship for some programs. In this case, the service, up to 2003, had to comply with ITC codes of practice for advertising (and then subsequently with those of the new regulator, Ofcom). The BBC also has its own internal code covering program sponsorship.

In the commercial sphere, broadcasters are responsible for the advertising they transmit and the ITC had control over the broadcaster, not the advertiser. If any licensed broadcaster failed to comply with the conditions set out in the 1990 Broadcasting Act or the ITC codes, the latter could impose penalties, which ranged from warnings, through fines, to the shortening or revocation of the broadcast licence. From January 1993, the legal responsibility for controlling television output was shifted from the regulator to the broadcasters. Broadcasters elected to use the organization that already existed, the ITVA Copy Clearance department. It was then transformed into the Broadcast Advertising Clearance Centre (BACC). It was this industry body that was responsible for the pretransmission examination and clearance of television advertisements. At the time of writing, new codes and practices were not in place, but it seemed likely that this same system would continue under Ofcom.

The BACC is a self-regulatory body that applies a statutory code, not their own self-regulatory code. However, the BACC Notes of Guidance further interpret the codes. The BACC rules have their origin in cases submitted to the Copy Committee, the ITC Code, and agreements reached with the ITC. The Copy Committee consists of six television broadcasters and meets once a month and is responsible for decisions taken on the acceptability of television advertisements. It also acts as a policymaker and court of appeal.

Broadcasters can choose not to join the BACC and must then make their own arrangements for copy control, either individually or collectively, but they were under the same obligations to comply with the ITC rules. Some broadcasters, for example, MTV, or certain local services in Northern Ireland, do not use the BACC services. They clear advertising in-house. In these cases, they might transmit an advertisement that the BACC would not have approved. The ITC could have required amendment or withdrawal of those advertisements that did not comply with the rules. Any decision to withdraw the advertisement had a mandatory and immediate effect.

The ITC handled complaints from the public. If addressed to the ITC, ITC staff analyzed them and, where appropriate, requested a response from the advertiser and from the BACC. Complaints could be upheld or not upheld. If upheld, the advertisement in question was normally required to be withdrawn or amended though it had been given clearance by the BACC. If the advertising was found misleading, it would be immediately removed. If it was considered harmful to children, it could be restricted to showings only after certain times. Although the BACC were involved in the complaint resolution process, the final decision rested with the ITC.

Provisions for Children

The rules and regulations governing advertising to children were covered by the ITC's codes. Children were defined as individuals aged 15 years or under, and children's programs were defined as those designed primarily for that audience. The Code of Advertising Standards and Practice (CASP) stated that advertisers should take particular care over advertisements that were likely to be seen by large numbers of children or in which children were employed. Appendix 1 of the CASP comprises a special section on *Advertising and Children* and offered more detailed guidance (ITC, 1991a, 1993, 1995, 1997). Specific sets of rules pertained to misleadingness in advertisements, advertising treatments and potential harm, product category restrictions, and scheduling.

Misleadingness. These rules drew attention to the vulnerability of children, their lack of maturity, and their inability to make adult-like judgements about advertisements. Many of the clauses in this section referred to toy advertising. Advertisers were warned not to give any unreasonable expectation of performance of a toy through the use of special effects or imaginary backgrounds. Advertisements should include scale reference points so that the true size of the product can be readily determined. In any demonstration, it must be made clear whether the toy can move independently or only through manual operation. Toys that result from construction from a kit must be readily attainable by the average child. Advertisements for expensive products must carry a clear indication of the price, though when a range of products from the same range was shown, only the most expensive item in the series needs to be priced. Advertisers were also required to take care in advertising premium offers in which the premium items were not supplied with the product. For any competitions, the rules had to be supplied in advance to the regulator for inspection.

Advertising Treatments and Potential Harm. The ITC regulations stipulated that advertisements should not contain anything that might be copied and cause harm to children. The CASP emphasized the importance of safety in advertisements in which children are shown. Children must not be shown in dangerous situations, for example, leaning out of windows, climbing, or tunneling dangerously. Children must not be shown playing unsupervised near water, in a bath, or on a staircase. Children must not be shown using matches or any gas, petrol, mechanical- or mains-powered appliance, nor can they be shown driving or riding agricultural machines. Open fires must always have a fireguard clearly visible. There were road safety provisions guided by the UK's Highway Code that must be followed in advertisements featuring children. Advertisements must not portray children in a sexually provocative manner. Children must not be shown in distress. They were not allowed to present products or services they could not buy themselves or endorse products they could not be expected to know anything about. The appearance of children in advertisements for alcoholic drinks was also outlawed. Children must not be shown entering strange places or conversing with strangers. Advertisements should not imply that children who fail to use a product are in any way inferior to others. Finally, children must not be shown asking their parents, friends, or relatives to buy them things.

Product Category Restrictions.   These restrictions applied especially to toys, food, and medicines. Advertisements for toy replicas of tools or household appliances must avoid scenes that might encourage children to play with the real thing in the home. Potentially dangerous toys such as air guns, sharp knives, or other guns firing projectiles capable of causing injury could not be advertised.

Appendix 3 of the Code of Advertising Standards and Practice laid down rules regarding advertising food and medicine. The food-related regulations were especially influenced by the 1991 White paper *The Health of the Nation* and are mindful of some of the issues raised by consumer organizations about the need for advertising to promote healthy rather than unhealthy dietary behavior. There were a number of specific food-related advertising regulations. Advertisements must not condone excessive consumption of food. Thus, advertisements should not show someone taking second and third helpings of chocolate or consuming a whole box of chocolates.

Advertisements must not damage good dietary habits or discourage the consumption of food that is generally accepted as a good dietary option, such as fruit and vegetables. Confectionery and snacks products should only be presented as an occasional pleasure. Particular attention must be paid to advertisements of snacks and confectionery addressed to children in respect to oral health. They must not include frequent consumption of sugar throughout the day or after meals, for example, or depict situations where teeth were unlikely to be cleaned, such as consuming food in bed.

Specific nutrition claims or health claims such as "full of the goodness of vitamin C" or "aids a healthy digestion" had to be supported by sound scientific evidence and must not give a misleading impression of the nutritional or health benefits of the food as a whole. Claims such as "wholesome" were acceptable without stating the basis for them explicitly in the commercial but only if that basis could be supported by sound scientific evidence.

Advertisements for medicines had to comply with other relevant regulations, such as the Medicines Act 1968 or the Medicines (Advertising) Regulations 1994, which implemented the provisions of EC Council Directive 92/28/EEC concerning the advertising of medicinal products for human use. Medicines were defined as products that carry a product licence. Dietary supplements were defined as isolated, highly purified or concentrated products sold in forms similar to medicines, for example, vitamins or minerals.

Advertising for a medicinal product could not be directed at people under the age of 16 and should not show medicines being administered to children unless the product is suitable for them. The correct children's dose must be stated. In addition, BACC Notes of Guidance advise advertisers to take special care that medicines or vitamins are not confused with sweets.

Medicines, disinfectants, antiseptics, and caustic or poisonous substances must not be shown within reach of children without parental supervision. References to pain or symptoms that could indicate a serious condition should be avoided, such as abdominal pain. No claims that medicinal preparations enhance physical or mental performance in children are permitted. In the case of growing children, advertisements for dietary supplements could not suggest that it was necessary or therapeutic for children to augment their intake or that such supplements could enhance normal, good physical or mental function. Advertisements for slimming products could not be addressed to people under 18.

Scheduling Restrictions.   This category of restrictions concerned material that was potentially distressing or frightening to children or sexually explicit. This category also included rules about the placement of certain types of advertisement adjacent to children's programs. Advertising was not permitted in a program for children of less than half an hour of scheduled transmission, and this rule accorded with European legislation. There were a number of products that may not be advertised adjacent to children's programs. These products included medicines, matches, liqueur chocolates, trailers of films with 15 and 18 certificates, premium rate telephone services, lotteries or other forms of gambling, religious advertising, advertising of merchandise based on children's programs, advertising that is potentially frightening or distressing to very young children or which contains references to sexual behavior or to alcoholic drinks.

A number of types of advertisements could not be transmitted before the 9:00 pm watershed. These included advertisements that contained images that were unsuitable for children to see, ones for medicines specially formulated for children, ones containing personalities or characters who regularly appeared in children's programs endorsing products aimed at children, ones for branded contraceptives, and advertisements for sanitary protection products.

European Regulations

Formal European regulations concerning advertising have been founded in three principal EC Directives, (a) the Misleading Advertising Directive, (b) the Television Without Frontiers Directive, and (c) the Directive on Advertising of Medicinal Products for Human use. A number of further EC Green Papers and Resolutions have recommendations for consumer safeguards linked to advertising, though these do not have the same force as the Directives.

Misleading Advertising Directive

The general framework for advertising in the EU was set in 1984 by the Directive 84/450/EEC about misleading and comparative advertising. The purpose of this Directive is to protect consumers and the interests of the public against misleading advertising and its unfair consequences. As a result of an amendment in 1996, it also lays down the criteria for comparative advertising. Misleading advertising is defined in Article 3 as:

> Any advertising, which in any way, including its presentation, deceives or is likely to deceive the persons to whom it is addressed or whom it reaches and which, by reason of its deceptive nature, is likely to affect their economic behavior or which injures or is likely to injure a competitor.

To determine whether advertising is misleading in nature, Article 3 also lays down some of the factors to be taken into account: (a) the characteristics of goods or services; (b) the price; (c) the conditions governing the supply of the goods or the provision of services; and (d) the nature, qualities, and rights of the advertiser.

Article 4 requires that Member States provide effective means to combat misleading advertising and ensure compliance with the provisions on comparative advertising. To control misleading advertising, the Member States have to ensure that those persons or organizations can bring a court action against misleading advertising and unfair comparative advertising and/or bring the advertising before a competent administrative body to rule on the complaints or institute the appropriate legal proceedings. The courts or administrative bodies should have the powers to order the withdrawal of misleading advertising or unfair comparative advertising. The courts should also have the powers to forbid misleading or unfair comparative advertising.

Article 5 recognizes the voluntary control of misleading advertising by self-regulatory bodies. Article 6 states that advertisers may be required, in civil or administrative proceedings, to provide evidence, establishing the accuracy of factual claims in advertising. Factual claims can be considered inaccurate if the evidence is not furnished or is insufficient. Article 7 allows member States to adopt more restrictive provisions to protect consumers from misleading advertising. Finally, the Directive does not exclude voluntary control of misleading advertising by self-regulatory bodies if these are in addition to existing administrative bodies.

In 1984, when the Directive was agreed, harmonized rules for regulating misleading advertising were considered necessary to improve consumer protection and to end distortions of competition arising from divergences among the Member States' laws against misleading advertising. The Directive was adopted before the Single European Act of 1986: it recognized the power of member States to provide for the necessary means to ensure that misleading advertising does not occur.

Television Without Frontiers Directive

The Directive 97/36/EC of 30 July 1997 that amended the previous Directive 89/552/EEC of 3 December 1989 (TWF Directive) is perhaps the most significant legislation concerning children's advertising on television. However, the enforcement of the TWF Directive and the systems of control and legal proceedings differ according to the implementation taken by the Member States, whether by law, regulation or administrative action.

Chapter IV of the TWF Directive lays down the provisions for advertising and teleshopping. On the content of advertisements, Article 12 (d) establishes that advertising and teleshopping shall not "encourage behaviour prejudicial to health or safety." Overall bans in Articles 13 and 14 also affect children. All forms of television and teleshopping for cigarettes and other tobacco products are prohibited. Advertising for medicines available under prescription, teleshopping for medicines that are subject to market authorization, and teleshopping for medical treatments are prohibited. Article 15 requires that television advertising and teleshopping for alcoholic beverages comply with set criteria; for example, that they may not be aimed at minors or depict minors consuming such beverages.

Finally, Article 16 establishes the rule that advertising must protect minors, thus:

1. Television advertising shall not cause moral or physical detriment to minors, and shall therefore comply with the following criteria for their protection:
   a. it shall not directly exhort minors to buy a product or service by exploiting their inexperience or credulity;
   b. it shall not directly encourage minors to persuade their parents or others to purchase the goods or services being advertised;
   c. it shall not exploit the special trust minors place in parents, teachers or other persons;
   d. it shall not unreasonably show minors in dangerous situations.
2. Teleshopping shall comply with the requirements referred to in paragraph 1 and, in addition, shall not exhort minors to contract for the sale or rental of goods and services.

The TWF Directive also lays down some rules for the frequency and amount of advertising and teleshopping allowed in children's programs. Article 11(5) states that advertising or teleshopping shall not interrupt children's programs, when their scheduled duration is less than 30 minutes. If their scheduled duration is 30 minutes or longer, they can include advertising breaks. If the programs consist of autonomous parts, center breaks are allowed between the autonomous parts or at intervals. A 20-minute period should elapse in between center breaks.

Article 3 lays down the possibility for member states to apply stricter rules to broadcasters under their jurisdiction. Article 20 complements these provisions by allowing Member States to lay down different conditions on the frequency and scheduling of commercial breaks, as well as for time limits for spot advertising and teleshopping.

Article 2(a) stipulates that if a broadcaster established in a Member State is subject to the laws of that State, other Member States cannot restrict the reception of its broadcasts within their territory, except in respect of the protection of minors. Other parts of the TWF legislation cover broadcasting in general, but in doing so, have implications for advertising. Article 22 requires Member States to take steps to ensure that programs broadcast within their areas of jurisdiction do not impair the physical, mental, or moral development of minors and makes special reference to pornography and violence. But although the TWF Directive requires special care in the treatment of "sensitive" products from a health and consumer protection viewpoint, it does not identify "children's advertising" as a separate category nor does it define the age-group covered by "minors" in relation to harmful content.

Directive on Advertising of Medicinal Products for Human Use

This Directive (92/28/EEC) states that advertising of a medicinal product shall not be misleading. The Directive bans advertising for prescription medicines. In relation to children, it bans all advertising of a medicinal product directed exclusively or principally at children.

International Codes

In addition to the statutes laid down with the United Kingdom and Europe, a number of other codes of practice have been produced at an international level that have also influenced national-level regulation of advertising aimed at children. Such codes have tended to emanate from international trade associations, some of which have been attached to specific industries such as advertising or manufacturing.

The ICC Code

At the international level, the International Chamber of Commerce (ICC) *International Code of Advertising Practice* (the ICC Code) provides a widely accepted framework for self-regulation and also regulatory procedures in many countries. The aim of the ICC Code is to promote high standards of ethics in marketing against a background of international and national law. The ICC Code applies to all advertisements for the promotion of any form of goods and services. It sets standards of ethical conduct to be followed by marketers, advertisers, advertising practitioners or agencies, and media. The Code includes Guidelines for Advertising Addressed to Children that applies to children or young people who are minors under the laws of their own countries. A number of specific guidelines are laid down that require advertisers to avoid harm to young viewers and any exploitation of their inexperience and credulity and to promote social values. The guidelines state:

- Because of the particular vulnerability of children, if there is any likelihood of advertisements being confused with editorial or program material, they should be clearly labeled "advertisement" or identified in an equally effective manner.
- Advertisements should not exploit the inexperience or credulity of children or young people.
- Advertisements should not understate the degree of skill or age level required to enjoy the product.
- Special care should be taken to ensure that advertisements do not mislead children as to the true size, value, nature, durability and performance of the product.
- If extra items are needed to use a product or to create the result shown (e.g., batteries or paint) this should be made clear.

- A product that is part of a series should be clearly indicated, as should the method of acquiring the series.
- The advertisement should represent the result that is reasonably attainable by the average child in the age range for which the product is intended.
- Price indication should not lead children to an unreal perception of the true value of the product, for instance, by using the word "only." No advertisement should imply that the advertised product is within reach of the family budget.
- Advertisements should not contain any statement or visual representation that could have the effect of harming children mentally, morally or physically or of bringing them into unsafe situations or activities seriously threatening their health or security, or encouraging them to go with strangers or enter strange places.
- Advertisements should not suggest that possession or use of a product alone will give the child social or physical advantages over other children, or that the non-possession of the product would have the opposite effect.
- Advertisements should not undermine the authority, responsibility, judgement or tastes of parents, taking into account the current social values. Advertisements should not include any direct appeal to children to persuade their parents or other adults to buy advertised products for them.

Code of Toy Advertising

The Toy Industries of Europe (TIE) have developed a code for advertising toys to children that applies to all their members. This Code has modeled national self-regulation codes on toy advertising which are followed by the toy industry. The Code recognizes the impressionable nature and vulnerability of children. The principles on which its Code is founded are consistent with European Community and national law. There are six key principles:

1. Advertisers have a special responsibility to protect children from their own susceptibilities, because younger children have a limited capacity for the evaluation of the information they receive.
2. Because of the imitative nature of young children, advertisers should take extreme care not to exult violence, or present it as being an acceptable method of achieving social or interpersonal aims.
3. Advertisers should communicate information in a truthful and accurate manner and be aware that a child may learn practices from advertising that can affect his or her health and well being.

4. Advertisers should use advertising that displays good taste, and which addresses positive, beneficial and pro-social behavior, such as friendship, kindness, honesty, justice, generosity, the protection of the environment and respect for other people and for animals. Advertising should not portray children in a sexually provocative manner.
5. Advertisers should take care neither to mislead children, nor to exploit the imaginative quality of children. Advertising should not stimulate unreasonable expectations of product quality or performance.
6. Advertisers should contribute to the parent–child relationship in a constructive manner.

These principles are elaborated on and operationally defined via a set of guidelines that provide more detailed recommendations to advertisers about their dealings with children. The guidelines address a number of important issues: the use of treatments that may mislead children; the need to provide clear separation between programs and advertisements; avoidance of placing undue sales pressure on children; the clarity and comprehensibility of disclaimers and qualifiers; the provision of clear factual information to reinforce comparative claims; the use of celebrity or TV characters as product endorsers; the use of premium offers, sweepstakes, and children's clubs; and safety issues.

KEY ISSUES AND RESEARCH

Concern about advertising aimed at children on television represents part of a wider public debate about how much protection children need in a society where sources of information and entertainment are expanding and new communications technologies have facilitated greater access to content through a variety of platforms. In this environment, it may become increasingly difficult for parents to control their children's media consumption, despite their willingness to continue to assume such responsibility wherever possible. Hence, there remains a need for centralized regulation and control over media content of all kinds. But what degree of regulation is needed to offer children effective protection against misleading commercial messages and advertising that might encourage potentially harmful behavior? Within this context, how relevant is research into children and advertising? Has it yielded useful findings to inform policy, regulation, codes of practice, and control implementation strategies?

How Do Regulations Map Onto Knowledge About Advertising Influences?

A key question is whether the regulations that cover television advertising correspond with evidence from audience research about the impact or influences of advertising—intended and unintended—on children. Regulations that derive from national and international regulators, industry, and trade associations and consumer groups are extensive. They can be reduced to a small number of categories of concern about advertising. The main headings under which these issues can be conveniently divided are: (a) scheduling restrictions; (b) product category restrictions; (c) advertising treatments; and (d) misleadingness. Regulations pertaining to each of these issues are designed to protect all consumers to some degree but have a special part to play in the protection of young consumers whose cognitive immaturity is believed to render them more vulnerable to the effects of advertising.

The next section discusses each of the four issues about regulation (listed earlier) and their relationship to what we know about the effects of advertising on children. The discussion is brief because the background and the research evidence related to most of these issues have already been discussed in previous chapters, and we will refer back to those chapters as necessary.

Scheduling Restrictions

There are two main reasons for the imposition of scheduling restrictions. The first is to reduce the likelihood that children will see advertising that is deemed unsuitable for them. This type of restriction derives from regulatory practices for programs. Such restrictions apply to advertising products or the use of production treatments that are not deemed inappropriate for broadcast in general but are regarded as unsuitable for young viewers. The second reason for scheduling restrictions is to make it easier for children to recognize an advertisement as distinct from a program.

The imposition of scheduling restrictions on certain kinds of advertising is grounded in some sense of when children watch television. For example, by restricting advertisements for alcoholic drinks to the post-9 pm period, it is believed that there is less likelihood that children will see such advertisements. Moreover, in the United Kingdom, there is a principle that broadcasters will take primary responsibility for safeguarding children up to 9 pm, but that parents assume that responsibility increasingly after that time. In reality, children (i.e., individuals up to 12 and certainly up to 15 years of age) may be watching at any time of the day. Television viewing figures may indicate that child audiences peak consistently at particular times and that these are therefore times to be avoided, but they may also show that children are still present in the audience at times when broadcast regulators presume many have gone to bed. Achieving scheduling standards, across Europe is therefore difficult given different lifestyles and diurnal patterns in different member states.

The need to help children distinguish between advertising and programs has led to regulations that impose restrictions on certain types of advertisements. Any features of advertisements that might weaken children's ability to make such a distinction are regarded as placing children at a disadvantage. For this reason, characters from children's programs cannot appear in advertisements embedded within the programs that include those characters, and merchandise that derives from a program cannot be advertised in close proximity to those programs. How serious is this issue?

Researchers have shown that advertisements are the earliest category to emerge in a child's understanding of television (Jaglom & Gardner, 1981). But as we discussed in chapter three, different researchers have suggested different ages for when children can distinguish advertisements from programs. Estimates of when children understand the distinction between advertisements and programs vary from three years of age to six years of age. As explained in chapter three, the varying estimates may derive from the different ways that children's ability has been tested. Researchers who have used nonverbal methods have suggested that children may be able to discriminate between advertisements and programs from three or four years of age. But researchers who have used other methods of testing have suggested slightly older ages. A conservative estimate of when most children can consistently distinguish advertisements and programs might be five years of age. Before that age children may need as much support as possible to distinguish between advertisements and programs, and regulations that help to emphasize the distinction between the two are important.

The need for caution in the placing of advertisements in programs has been reinforced by research that has revealed powerful influences of the surrounding program environment on adults' memory for television advertising (see chap. 6). As discussed in that chapter, the nature of the surrounding programming has also been found to affect children's recall of television advertising. Such evidence supports the point made in the previous paragraph—that regulations about the placement of advertisements can help young children distinguish the content of an advertisement from the content of the surrounding program.

Product Category Restrictions

Rules relating to advertising content are frequently linked to laws that place prohibitions on children's consumption of specified products, such as tobacco, alcohol, and prescription medicines. Some critics argue that advertising such products may encourage young consumers to adopt behaviors that are damaging to them. For instance, advertisements for tobacco products are believed to encourage teenage smoking, and advertisements for alcoholic drinks may encourage underage drinking (see Pollay, 1995). Social statistics show that both of these behaviors have increased and have heightened concerns among consumer and health lobbyists that advertising such products should remain tightly controlled.

Chapter eight discussed the effects of advertising on young people's consumption of products like tobacco and alcohol. As we pointed out in that chapter, tobacco and alcohol have rarely been directly advertised to young people, but children and young people may see advertisements for such products, and this is one aspect of the "incidental" effects of advertising. From such incidental exposure children may well develop an awareness of brands and a desire to consume such products in the future (see chap. 8). For this reason, regulations that just control the scheduling of advertisements for certain products may not be sufficient, and there may be a need for more extensive bans on advertising products that a society considers harmful for children. Having said that, the points made in earlier chapters should be repeated—that television advertising for such products (such as alcohol) is only one of the influences on young people's desire to consume those products. There are also opposing viewpoints in terms of interpretation of empirical data on the role of advertising and marketing, for example, in relation to the initiation of behavior such as smoking among teenagers (Pollay, 1995; van Raaij, 1990).

Another aspect of product category restrictions is the advertising of food products on television. Advertising for such products can legally be directed at children. The concern, voiced usually by health consumer lobby groups, is that there is a disproportionate, even excessive, amount of advertising for food products of questionable nutritional value. In chapter eight, we discussed the research showing that the amount of television children watched was correlated with their consumption of foods advertised on television and with their attempts to influences their mothers' food purchases. Heavily advertised foods often have high status even though they may not be the most nutritious food to consume. As with alcohol and other products, television advertising is only one factor in influencing children's diet and eating habits (see chap. 8), but it is one that has generated a great deal of concern. This is one of the reasons why the ITC Code of Advertising Standards and Practice states that: advertisements must not encourage children to eat frequently throughout the day, or encourage them to consume food or drink (especially sweet, sticky foods) near bedtime or suggest that confectionery and snack foods can be substituted for balanced meals (ITC, 1991a, 1993, 1995, 1997).

Advertising Treatments

Three broad categories of treatment apply here: on-screen behaviors that (a) put children at risk, (b) encourage antisocial behavior, or (c) promote excessive purchase demands. In addition, there is the more general concern about children's awareness of the tactics used by advertisers to persuade consumers to prefer the advertised brand above others. While six-year-olds may exhibit no understanding of advertisers' motives, older children slowly develop an awareness of the purpose of advertising (see chaps. 3 and 4). By their early teens, young consumers display an understanding of advertisers' use of tactics such as humor, celebrity endorsement, and product comparisons to establish a persuasive appeal (Boush, Friestad, & Rose, 1994). Skepticism about advertising is especially likely to emerge among children brought up in homes where their parents encourage them to think for themselves, who are less susceptible to peer group influences, and who watch more (rather than less) television (Mangleburg & Bristol, 1999).

At Risk Behaviors.   As discussed earlier in this chapter advertising treatment regulations focus on the depiction of children in advertisements and restrict the portrayal of on-screen behaviors that might be copied and might put children at risk. Although no research has examined whether advertising that depicts prohibited behaviors would result in harm to children, research with television programs shows that displays of physical risk-taking behavior can lead to an increased willingness on the part of children to take physical risks themselves (Potts, Doppler, & Hernandez, 1994).

Antisocial Conduct.   Advertisements must not encourage children to be impolite or ill-mannered or to behave in an antisocial manner. These restrictions are based on concerns about children copying antisocial behaviors, especially if they see those behaviors carried out by child actors. Laboratory research evidence over many years has indicated that children will copy the actions of attractive screen role models (Young, 1998). For example, research in the United States has indicated that children display increased aggressiveness in a play context after watching an episode from a popular television series for children, *The Mighty Morphin Power Rangers*, and this was especially true of boys in the audience (Boyatzis, Matillo, & Nesbitt, 1995). However, whether children respond in an antisocial way to antisocial conduct may also depend on their preexisting personalities. Children who already exhibit aggressive dispositions are more likely to display enhanced antisocial conduct after viewing screen violence than are children with nonaggressive personalities (Wiegman, Kuttschreuter, & Baarda, 1992).

Research into the possible antisocial or physically damaging effects of advertising portrayals has been rare and has tended to take the form of qualitative investigations rather than experimental methodologies. For example, Hanley et al. (2000) interviewed children and teenagers, aged nine to 16 years, in focus groups. The participants were also shown television advertisements that exemplified the specific concerns of adult audiences about advertising, in some cases as registered through viewers' complaints to the television advertising regulator. We have mentioned one particular advertisement for a fizzy drink product—Tango Orange—in chapter seven. This advertisement depicted a youth taking a sip of Tango, on which a strange looking, partly naked man with all-over orange make-up rushes up and slaps the youth simultaneously on both cheeks. The youth's shock is supposed to illustrate the sharp bite of the drink. The Independent Television Commission received reports of playground emulation of this behavior and cases of children suffering ear damage as a result. Children and teenagers found this advertisement familiar and appealing. They liked the product and thought the treatment was funny and entertaining, especially the slapping and the expression of the slapped man. They imagined that other children would be quite likely to copy the behavior, though generally they projected this belief on to an age group slightly younger than themselves. Although such research cannot demonstrate specific cause-effect relationship between the behavior of children and exposure to this advertisement, the unusual and readily imitative behavior in the advertisement did attract children's attention and stuck in their minds.

Excessive Purchase Demands.   There is much evidence that children pester their parents to buy them products and the kinds of items most frequently requested are breakfast cereals, snacks, or confectionery, or toys (see chap. 7). Not all pestering stems from television advertising because there will be other influences on children (e.g., from peer groups), nonetheless advertising does lead to parents being pestered to buy products (see chap. 7). The most significant period for parental pestering is the pre-Christmas spell when there are large numbers of television advertisements for toys and other gifts aimed at children. Indeed, it has been observed that children may increase their viewing at this time in pursuit of ideas for Christmas gifts (Buckingham, 1993; Pine & Nash, in press).

There are restrictions on advertising treatments that center on consumer behavior, including pestering parents. For example, advertisements should not show children pestering their parents or other adults to buy them things. Nor should advertisements give the impression that by not buying something a child will be placed at a social or physical disadvantage.

Misleadingness

Perhaps the primary concern about advertising, and one of the key areas of regulation in the United Kingdom, Europe, and other parts of the world, is that it should not mislead consumers. Most commentators believe that advertisers have a special responsibility not to mislead children about products (Young, 1990, 1998). Essentially, the demand placed on advertisers is to be truthful.

Specific requirements related to misleadingness have emerged in the context of advertising toys. Toy advertising should not give children the impression that a toy is bigger, better, and more versatile than it really is. Advertising treatments should enable a child in the audience to determine the scale and size of the toy, to realize whether it is self-propelled or manually operated, and to know whether some degree of self-construction is needed once the product has been acquired. Such requirements along with others have not only been integrated into official codes of advertising practice but also endorsed by the toy manufacturers in Europe.

As far as truthfulness is concerned, some advertisements for toys and foods have been reportedly misleading for younger children because the special visual and auditory techniques used require certain cognitive skills for evaluating the reliability of the message (Condry, 1989). For example, advertising can make toys appear bigger than they really are or capable of feats that they cannot possibly achieve.

Moreover, special efforts should be made to ensure that the commercial information is presented in a form that is comprehensible to young children. Disclaimer messages can be effective, provided the messages are understood by children. For example, very young children under the age of five years may be unable to understand the nature and intent of disclaimers in advertising (Stutts & Hunnicutt, 1987). Of fundamental importance to children's understanding of disclaimers, however, is the language they use. Toy advertisements that use a standard disclaimer such as "some assembly required" do not invariably lead to a better understanding that the toy has to be put together than do similar advertisements without a disclaimer. But if the disclaimer is reworded to the child's level of comprehension, it can be understood by nearly all children, even as young as four or five years. Advertisements that include statements like, "you have to put it together," or "it must be put together before you can play with it" have been found to be quite effective at telling a child what is required (Faber, Meyer, & Miller, 1984).

In 1996, the Independent Television Commission in the United Kingdom conducted research to examine whether rules in its *Code of Advertising Standards and Practice* were sufficient to prevent children being misled by toy advertising (Hanley, 1996). Focus group interviews were carried out with children aged four to nine years and with their mothers. Copies of American toy advertisements were obtained that had not been shown on television in the United Kingdom and that were therefore unfamiliar to the children. These advertisements were placed between two cartoon program segments and presented as if forming a commercial break. Families were given a copy of the tape with this material before being interviewed to give them the opportunity to become familiar with the advertisements.

The study found that the children, particularly the older ones, were quick to assimilate and interpret what they were shown. For instance, the older children (eight–nine-year-olds) accepted and understood a range of special effects and devices within the advertisements, but younger children were less experienced in recognizing and interpreting advertisements. The younger children also had exhibited more literal interpretations of advertising and had heightened expectations about the products they saw compared with the older children. When the children could equate an unfamiliar toy with a toy or category of toys they already knew about, they were able to make sense of the advertisement and the product more readily. But danger of being misled about a toy increased when the product defied classification or did not conform to the expected category.

CONCLUSIONS

Television advertising regulation in Britain and Europe recognizes the need for special consideration to be given to children, and the national and transnational codes of advertising practice accord children additional protection over and above the standard regulations that cover advertising to consumers in general. The nature and stringency of advertising regulation varies from one country to another, with some countries employing more restrictive codes than others. A few countries observe an all-out ban on advertising directed at children, but others place selective restrictions on certain categories of advertising or on the times when particular types of advertisement may be transmitted.

The core principle for advertising that is reflected in all codes of practice, whether observed on an international or national scale, endorsed by statutory legislation, or voluntary industry codes, is the need for advertising to be truthful in its claims and the way it represents the product being promoted. This principle is never disputed, although the degree of detail in which misleadingness is defined can vary from code to code.

Criticism of television advertising and its regulation has predominantly derived from consumer organizations. One of the chief areas of complaint has centered on the advertising of foods directed at children and advertising has been accused of focusing on promotion of foods of dubious nutritional value. Current regulations and codes of practice in countries such as the United Kingdom do advise advertisers against reinforcing unhealthy eating habits, but critics feel that such codes, although helpful, do not go far enough (Dibb, 1996). One limitation of the codes is that they focus on individual advertisements and do not address the volume and intensity of such advertising in its totality. In any case, it is unlikely that any code could address advertising in its totality (e.g. by introducing restrictive quotas for advertising of particular categories of product).

Codes of practice for television advertising are comprehensive in scope and generally effective. But perhaps the weakest area of regulation in the United Kingdom, when judging the codes against research evidence, is that of scheduling restrictions. Such restrictions are designed to minimize the chances that children will be exposed to advertising that is inappropriate for them. In other words, they should not be exposed to advertisements for products they are legally unable to buy or to consume (e.g., alcoholic drinks,). They should not experience advertising treatments deemed inappropriate for them (e.g., advertisements featuring nudity or potentially frightening images). And they should not be exposed to advertising that bears a close resemblance to programs that they might normally watch (e.g., products that are endorsed by children's TV presenters).

But the reality of children's television viewing habits means that such restrictive scheduling practices are unlikely to be totally successful because children often watch television long after dedicated children's programs have finished. The implicit "deal" between broadcasters and parents that after an agreed watershed parents will assume greater responsibility for their children's viewing (e.g., after 9 pm), removes the responsibility from the broadcasters. But it does not necessarily get round the problem of children seeing advertisements that have a content that is inappropriate for them.

The debate about children and the regulation of advertising could be broadened out to consider the wider implications of tighter regulation or alternative modes of protecting children's interests as consumers. However, tighter regulation of advertising could be interpreted as an infringement of the right to freedom of speech, and this is certainly true in the United States. In Europe, case law of the European Court of Human Rights has established that "information of a commercial nature" falls under the protection of article 10 of the European Convention on Human Rights. In practice, however, commercial speech has not received as much legal protection as other forms of public speech (Voorhoof, 1993).

An alternative to tighter regulation might be better consumer literacy training. In chapter three, we discussed media training programs for children, and some of these programs include raising children's awareness about the nature of advertising. The assumption behind advertising literacy programs is that if young children can be taught about advertising they will develop better "cognitive defences" to protect themselves from the claims of advertisements and, therefore, like adults, they will be in less need of protective regulation. In chapter five, however, we argued that very young children may simply not have the available cognitive processes to develop a full understanding of advertisements. If this is the case, then advertising regulations will always be an important way to protect children until they reach an age when they can develop their own full appreciation of the form, nature, and content of advertising.

10

Concluding Comments

Increased merchandising to young consumers has placed consumerism center stage in the lives of children and teenagers. This phenomenon has been accompanied by growing concerns about the ability of youngsters to make mature judgements about commercial messages. The psychological immaturity of children may render them more susceptible to the temptations of promotional messages and campaigns. While this fact is not inherently or necessarily a bad thing, it may mean that youngsters may be particularly vulnerable to misleading commercial messages that make claims about products or brands that do not represent the truth. Before accusing advertisers and marketers of unscrupulous behavior and of deliberate attempts to lead child consumers astray, it is important to study the evidence about the ways children engage with advertising and the significance it may have in relation to their brand preferences, purchase behavior and consumer socialization.

Over the years, research into advertising has accumulated giving rise to a body of knowledge about the part it plays in shaping consumers' desires, beliefs, values, and choices. Television has emerged as a particularly salient advertising medium, which is not surprising given its ubiquity and prominence as a source of entertainment and information. This book represents one attempt to review research evidence about children and advertising on television, examining the nature of advertising on the small screen, children's awareness and understanding of televised advertising, and the different ways in which advertising messages can influence youngsters.

Much of the research reported in this book has derived from academic studies into children and television advertising. While much research is conducted by advertisers and advertising agencies, this tends to be proprietary and therefore not in the public domain. Nonetheless, such research has also been drawn upon as well where available. We have examined a number of research themes across the foregoing chapters and drawn conclusions in relation to these in each case. In this final chapter, we will summarize some of the key issues raised by the academic research, make some general comments that cut across the more specific topics that have been discussed in each chapter, and suggest areas where further, or new, research would be appropriate.

As pointed out in chapter one, advertising to children generates strong feelings, and in recent years, there have been major debates about the ethics of advertising to children. On the one hand, marketers stress the right to advertise their products, emphasizing their right to free speech and the importance of a free economic environment. One frequent argument is that advertising makes the consumer aware of the available products, but it is consumers themselves who choose what to buy, and no amount of advertising will persuade consumers to buy products that they do not like. Put this way, advertising is seen more in terms of competition between brands and for supporting the sale of new products. Advertisers point out that increasing the sales of any product supports economic growth in general, with positive implications for employment, investment, and development. In particular, advertising directly supports the media, and marketers have often pointed out that without the revenue from advertisements the quality of television programming for children would be poorer, or children's programs might not exist at all.

On the other hand, consumer groups and parents have often voiced their concerns about advertising to children who might not have a full critical awareness of the nature of advertising. As we have pointed out, these concerns are related to several issues. The effects of food advertising on children's health has been a major concern (Dalmeny et al., 2003), but so has the influence of alcohol advertising on young people, and in some countries, the effects of tobacco advertising (see chap. 8). There may be more general concerns about the presentation of products and the incidental effects of that presentation for implying social and gender stereotypes. Parents have also expressed concerns that, in recent years, new markets have been developed to target ever younger children with programs and products aimed specifically at very young children (e.g., the BBC program, *Teletubbies*). At the same time, a number of new products have become available (from computer games to mobile telephones) and are now marketed to children. The increasing children's market may lead to more family conflicts as children want or expect a larger number of possessions, including products that are often more expensive to buy and update than traditional toys and games.

The research described in this book can be, very broadly, divided into two parts. The research that has focused on children's understanding of advertising messages (in chaps. 2 through 5) and the research that has examined the effects of advertising on children (chaps. 6 through 8). Both these areas have been extensively researched, and therefore, we have some idea of when children are aware of advertising and some idea of the effects that advertising can have. Nonetheless, both areas of research have some limitations.

As pointed out in chapter five, most research into children's understanding of television advertising has been carried out in the absence of any strong theoretical framework. For this reason, much of the evidence about children's understanding remains descriptive, and although the results of the research have indicated when children can (and cannot) understand various concepts associated with advertising, we do not know very much about the factors that contribute to the development of that understanding. Or indeed, why young children who may have watched many thousands of advertisements do not have greater insights into advertising. We have suggested that children's understanding of concepts (such as the nature of persuasion in advertisements) may be directly related to their understanding of the same concepts in other contexts. However, as yet we know comparatively little about the development of children's notions of persuasion, honesty, truthfulness, misleadingness, exaggeration, self-presentation, or any of the other factors that might be associated with advertising messages. Even when those factors have been researched by developmental psychologists, they have been researched in contexts far removed from television advertising.

Children may need to achieve certain levels of cognitive development before they have an understanding of the factors related to advertising. For example, we suggest that once children understand the nature of persuasion in social contexts, they may then be able to apply that concept to other areas, such as advertising messages. Research into children's understanding of advertising cannot therefore be separated from research into the development of their cognitive abilities in general. However, researchers have not yet compared children's understanding of advertising concepts with their understanding of the same concepts in other domains. For this reason, the studies into children and advertising tend to be an island of research. Although informative in themselves, this work has hardly ever, and with any degree of sophistication, been joined to the wider research into, and the contemporary theories of, children's development.

In future research, it will be important to make stronger links between children's understanding of advertisements and children's cognitive development, for several reasons. First, although what has been said earlier implies a causal relationship, with developing cognitive abilities leading to a better understanding of advertisements, there may well be an effect in the opposite direction, with children's growing awareness of advertising influencing their understanding of concepts like persuasion, presentation, and misleadingness. After all, as pointed out in chapter four, children's awareness, and occasional cynicism, about advertising may stem from their disappointment between expectations about a product and the actual experience of the product. Given the role that advertising plays in children's lives it would not be surprising if children learn some concepts as much from the media as from other areas of their experience.

Second, young children's understanding of advertising may be informed by other factors. It is possible that parents' comments or specific teaching (e.g., in media skills courses—see chap. 4) could play an important part in enhancing their consumer literacy. More recently, it has become possible that some young children may even develop their own advertising skills through using advertisements to swap items over the Web. To do this successfully, they need to find ways to describe items effectively and attractively, and they must also do so with some accuracy and fairness if they want to be recognized as reliable "traders" (Attwood & Elton, 2003). The relative importance of all these factors in contributing to children's understanding of advertisements still needs to be researched. In particular, training programs (e.g. MediaSmart, 2003—see chap. 4) that have been specifically designed to help children understand the nature of advertising and demonstrate how advertisements are created, need to be critically evaluated to find out how effective they are in increasing children's awareness.

The second broad area of research into children and advertising considered the effects of advertising on children. This includes both the deliberate effects, such as whether children are more likely to want or buy products that they have seen advertised (see chaps. 6 and 7), and the incidental or unintended effects of advertising (see chap. 8). Advertising does work, and chapter seven included examples of experimental work in which children saw a product advertised and were then more likely to choose that product soon afterward. However, this research is limited in that it is difficult to design experiments to investigate the effects of advertising when there is a delay between viewing an advertisement and making a product choice. This is especially the case in real life contexts when there will usually be a long delay between an advertising message and a purchase and where there will also be many other influences on children's choices.

Two of the most important influences upon children's consumer socialization are parents and peer groups (see chap. 7; also Gunter & Furnham, 1998), although there has been little research into the relative importance of advertising influences, parental influence, and peer influence. In fact, it might be difficult ever to establish exactly how these influences interact as the precise balance of influence from advertising and from other sources varies depending on many factors. These factors will include the age of the child, the child's perception of the importance of parents' or peers' comments at the time, and the attractiveness of a particular product. The relationship between such factors is likely to be fluid, and the relative importance of any one factor at any one time may be hard to determine.

Most of the research has considered the effects of advertising on children in the context of mediating factors like the influence of parents and peers (where peers usually means face-to-face friendship groups). With the advent of contemporary communication technology (the Internet and mobile telephones), however, children now have access to friends, peers, and chat rooms, well beyond their immediate family or a friendship group. For this reason, the influences on contemporary children are much broader and more complex than the influences on children in previous generations. More important, access to the Internet not only provides ideas and influences but can also be a source of information so that children can actively search out details about products. They can locate reviews of those products and can obtain information to check out the claims of any advertisement before deciding whether or not to purchase the product (Thomson & Laing, 2003). Children's role as searchers of information, rather than simply being recipients of views from family or immediate friends, is a major change in the independence of children as consumers. Children now have the ability to compare advertising claims about a product with a range of sources providing other information about that product from different Web sites. How this ability will affect children's purchase behavior is unknown but will be an important area of research in the future.

The majority of academic research studies into children and advertising has been carried out in North America, and most of the rest has been conducted in Western Europe. This bias may not have serious implications for our knowledge of children's understanding of advertisements. If we assume that understanding follows in the wake of cognitive development and that all children do develop in similar ways in different cultures, then children's ability to recognize, and later to interpret advertisements, should be a similar achievement irrespective of the culture in which they are brought up.

The concentration of research in just a few countries, however, might affect our interpretation of the research into the effects of advertising. The influence of advertising is likely to be mediated by the culture and the social traditions in which children are reared. Children in different cultures may be more or less materialistic than children in other cultures (Chan, 2003), and the effects of advertising may also differ, but there has been little research comparing children from different countries. In a world with global markets and global advertising, there is a need to increase the number of studies from different countries to establish similarities and differences in the effects of advertising on children.

One of the most important changes in contemporary children's lives is the rapid increase in all forms of electronic communication (see Livingstone, 2002). Not only does such communication connect children instantly to other children across the globe, but as these forms of communication become both cheaper and more portable, they are accessible to all. A generation of children with constant access to the Internet, wherever they are and whatever they are doing, represent a new market access opportunity for advertisers who target children. As Internet advertising, including text and video messaging, increases with the growth of electronic communication, then the context of television advertising will change. At present, television advertising is the predominant form of marketing to children, but this may well change as other forms of advertising become more common.

The relative influence of television advertising in the context of all the new ways that children will experience advertising will be an important research area in the near future. Most of the current academic studies into children and advertising have considered only children's understanding of television or the effects of that advertising. This focus has been appropriate while television advertising has dominated all advertising to children, but in the future, children's awareness of television advertising will need to be considered in a wider context because television advertising is likely to become only one of many marketing channels to children.

The advance of home entertainment technology and the merging of currently distinct technologies, such as the television and home computer, will also empower consumers in ways that may render traditional forms of advertising redundant or no longer effective. Television will become an interactive medium and technologically enhanced to enable media consumers to control reception of content to a far greater extent than today. New reception technologies may enable viewers to screen out advertisements in traditional "natural breaks" within and between programs. Advertisers will need to become more inventive and subtle in the ways they get their messages through. Program sponsorship could become more significant along with product placement. While most countries deploy regulatory restrictions of these forms of advertising, there may be financial pressures upon the media and communications sectors that encourage regulators or governments to relax these restrictions.

Interactive television opens up other new marketing and promotional possibilities for advertisers. Advertisers such as Coca Cola have already begun to experiment with interactive advertising campaigns in which viewers are encouraged to connect with competitions and free offers through the interactive facility of interactive digital television (Wray, 2003). In this way, advertisements become intimately linked to entertainment activities via television that tempt consumers to pay attention to the advertising and present the advertisers with subtle opportunities to reinforce brand awareness by grabbing and maintaining consumers' attention beyond the advertising itself. Such developments will undoubtedly raise significant questions about the effects such schemes may have on young consumers. It will be important that researchers are equipped theoretically and methodologically to investigate these new advertising phenomena.

References

Aaron, L. E., Wold, B., Kannas, L., & Rimpola, M. (1986). Health behaviour in school children: A WHO cross-national survey. *Health Promotion, 1,* 17–23.

Adler, R. P., Lesser, G. S., Meringoff, L. K., Robertson, T. S., Rossiter, J. R., & Ward, S. (1980). *The effects of television advertising on children: Review and recommendations.* Lexington, MA: Lexington.

Aitken, P. P., & Eadie, D. R. (1990). Reinforcing effects of cigarette advertising on under-age smoking. *British Journal of Addiction, 85,* 399–412.

Aitken, P. P., Eadie, D. R., Hastings, G. B., & Haywood, A. J. (1991). Predisposing effects of cigarette advertising on children's intentions to smoke when older. *British Journal of Addiction, 86,* 383–390.

Aitken, P. P., Leathar, D. S., & O'Hagan, F. J. (1985). Children's perceptions of advertisements for cigarettes. *Social Science and Medicine, 21*(7), 785–797.

Aitken, P. P., Leathar, D. S., O'Hagan, F. J., & Squair, S. I. (1987). Children's awareness of cigarette advertisements and brand imagery. *British Journal of Addiction, 82,* 615–622.

Aitken, P. P., Leathar, D. S., Scott, A. L., & Squair, S. I. (1988). Cigarette brand preferences of teenagers and adults. *Health Promotion, 2,* 219–226.

Aitken, P. P., Leathar, D. S., & Squair, S. I. (1986a). Children's awareness of cigarette brand sponsorship of sports and games in the U.K. *Health Education Research, Theory and Practice, 1*(3), 203–211.

Aitken, P. P., Leathar, D. S., & Squair, S. I. (1986b). Children's opinions on whether or not cigarette advertising should be banned. *Health Education Journal, 45*(4), 204–207.

Ajzen, I., & Fishbein, M. (1980). *Understanding attitudes and predicting behavior.* Englewood Cliffs, NJ: Prentice-Hall.

Alexander, A., Benjamin, L. M., Hoerrner, K. L., & Roe, D. (1999). We'll be back in a moment. In M. C. Macklin & L. Carlson (Eds.), *Advertising to children: Concepts and controversies* (pp. 97–116). Thousand Oaks, CA: Sage.

Anderson, A. E., & DiDomenico, L. (1992). Diet vs. shape content of popular male and female magazines: A dose-response relationship to the incidence of eating disorders? *International Journal of Eating Disorders, 11*, 283–287.

Anderson, J. R. (1976). *Language, memory and thought*. Hillsdale, NJ: Lawrence Erlbaum Associates.

Anderson, W. K. (1929, December 18). Will they force us to it? Inexcusable cigarette advertising. *Christian Century, 46*, 1576–1577.

Atkin, C. K. (1975). Effects of television advertising on children: Second year experimental evidence. Report 2. Ann Arbor, MI: Michigan State University.

Atkin, C. K. (1978). Observation of parent-child interaction in supermarket decision making. *Journal of Marketing, 42*, 41–45.

Atkin, C. K. (1980). Effects of television advertising on children. In E. L. Palmer & A. Dorr (Eds.), *Children and the faces of television, teaching, violence, selling* (pp. 287–306). New York: Academic Press.

Atkin, C. K. (1982). Television advertising and socialisation to consumer roles. In D. Pearl, L. Bouthilet, & J. Lazar (Eds.), *Television and behaviour: Ten years of scientific progress and implications for the eighties: Vol. 2. Technical review* (pp. 199–209). Rockville, MD: National Institutes for Mental Health.

Atkin, C. K., & Block, M. (1984). *Content and effects of alcohol advertising.* Report presented for the Bureau of Alcohol, Tobacco and Firearms, NO. PB82-123142, Springfield, VA: National Technical Information Service.

Atkin, C. K., & Gibson, W. (1978). *Children's responses to cereal commercials.* Report to Public Advocates, Inc. East Lansing, MI: Michigan State University.

Atkin, C. K., Hocking, J., & Block, M. (1984). Teenage drinking: Does advertising make a difference? *Journal of Communication, 34*(2), 157–167.

Atkin, C. K., Reeves, B., & Gibson, W. (1979, August). *Effects of televised food advertising on children.* Paper presented at the Association for Education in Journalism, Baltimore.

Attwood, J., & Elton, E. (2003). Taking kids and teens seriously as influencers and consumers. *International Journal of Advertising and Marketing to Children, 4*(4), 47–61.

Austin, E. W., & Meill, H. K. (1994). Effects of interpretation of televised alcohol portrayals on children's alcohol beliefs. *Journal of Broadcasting and Electronic Media, 38*, 417–435.

Axelrod, J. (1963). Induced moods and attitudes towards products. *Journal of Advertising Research, 3*, 19–24.

Bahn, K. D. (1986). How and when do brand perceptions and preferences first form? A cognitive developmental investigation. *Journal of Consumer Research, 13*, 382–393.

Bandyopadhyay, S., Kindra, G., & Sharp, L. (2001). Is television advertising good for children? Areas of concern and policy implications. *International Journal of Advertising, 20*(1), 89–116.

Barcus, F. E. (1980). The nature of television advertising to children. In E. L. Palmer & A. Dorr (Eds.), *Children and the faces of television: Teaching, violence, selling* (pp. 273–286). New York: Academic Press.

Baron-Cohen, S., Leslie, A. M., & Frith, U. (1985). Does the autistic child have a "theory of mind"? *Cognition, 21*, 37–46.

Barry, T. E., & Gunst, R. F. (1982). Children's advertising: The differential impact of appeal strategy. In J. H. Leigh & C. R. Martin, Jr. (Eds.), *Current issues and research in advertising* (pp. 113–125). Ann Arbor: Graduate School of Business Administration, University of Michigan.

Barry, T. E., & Sheikh, A. A. (1977). Race as a dimension in children's TV advertising: The need for more research. *Journal of Advertising, 6*(3), 5–10.

Bartholomew, A., & O'Donohoe, S. (2003). Everything under control: A child's eye view of advertising. *Journal of Marketing Management, 19*(4), 433–457.

Bartsch, K., & London, K. (2000). Children's use of mental state information in selecting persuasive arguments. *Developmental Psychology, 36*, 352–365.

Baumrind, D. (1980). New directions in socialisation research. *American Psychologist, 35*, 639–652.

Bechtel, R., Achelpol, C., & Akers, R. (1972). Correlations between observed behaviour and questionnaire responses on television viewing. In E. A. Rubinstein, G. A. Comstock, & J. P. Murray (Eds.), *Television and social behaviour*, Vol. 4. Washington, DC: U.S. Government Printing Office.

Belch, G. E., Belch, M. A., & Villarreal, A. (1987). Effects of advertising communications: Review of research. *Research in Marketing, 9*, 59–117.

Benoy, W. J. (1982). The credibility of physically attractive communicators: A review. *Journal of Advertising, 11*, 15–24.

Bergler, R. (1999). The effects of commercial advertising on children. *International Journal of Advertising, 18*(4), 411–25.

Berti, A., & Bombi, A. (1979). Where does money come from? *Archivio di Psicologia, 40*, 53–77.

Berti, A., & Bombi, A. (1981). The development of the concept of money and its value: A longitudinal study. *Child Development, 52*, 1179–1182.

Berti, A., Bombi, A., & de Bens, R. (1986). Acquiring economic notions: Profit. *International Journal of Behavioural Development, 9*, 15–29.

Bever, T. G., Smith, M. L., Bengen, B., & Johnson, T. G. (1975, Nov/Dec). Young viewers' troubling response to TV ads. *Harvard Business Review*, 155–66.

Bijmolt, T. H. A., Claassen, W., & Brus, B. (1998). Children's understanding of TV advertising: Effects of age, gender and parental influence. *Journal of Consumer Policy, 21*, 171–194.

Bjurström, E. (1994). *Children and television advertising*. Vallingby, Sweden: Konsumentverket.

Blumler, J. (1992). *Television and the public interest: Vulnerable values in Western Europe*. London: Sage.

Boddewyn, J. J. (1986). *Why do juveniles start smoking?* New York: International Advertising Association.

Bolton, R. N. (1983). Modeling the impact of television food advertising on children's diets. In J. H. Leigh & C. R. Martin, Jr. (Eds.), *Current issues and research in advertising*. Ann Arbor Press, Chicago: Graduate School of Business Administration.

Boush, D. M., Friestad, M., & Rose, G. M. (1994). Adolescent skepticism toward TV advertising and knowledge of advertiser tactics. *Journal of Consumer Research, 21*, 165–175.

Bowen, M. (2000). Kids culture. *International Journal of Advertising and Marketing to Children, 2*(1), 19–23.

Boyatzis, C. J., Matillo, G. M., & Nesbitt, K. M. (1995). Effects of the "Mighty Morphin Power Rangers" on children's aggression with peers. *Child Study Journal, 25*(1), 45–55.

Brittain, C. V. (1963). Adolescent choices and parent-peer cross pressures. *American Sociological Review, 28*, 385–391.

Brody, J. E. (1991, December 11). Smoking among children is linked to cartoon Camel. *New York Times*, D22.

Bronson, W. C. (1972). The role of enduring orientations to the environment of personality development. *Genetic Psychology Monographs, 86*, 3–80.

Brown, J. (1977). Graduate students examine TV ads for food. *Journal of Nutrition Education, 9*(3), 120–122.

Brown, J. A. (2001). Media literacy and critical television viewing in education. In D. G. Singer & J. L. Singer (Eds.), *Handbook of children and the media* (pp. 681–698). Thousand Oaks, CA: Sage.

Brucks, M., Armstrong, G. M., & Goldberg, M. E. (1988). Children's use of cognitive defenses against television advertising: A cognitive response approach. *Journal of Consumer Research, 14*, 471–482.

Brumbaugh, A. M. (1993). Physical attractiveness and personality in advertising: More than just a pretty face. In L. McAlister & M. L. Rothschild (Eds.), *Advances in consumer research* (Vol. 20, pp. 159–163). Provo, UT: Association for Consumer Research.

Bryant, J., & Comisky, P. W. (1978). The effect of positioning a message within differentially cognitively involving portions of a television segment on recall of the message. *Human Communication Research, 5*, 63–75.

Bryant, J., & Zillmann, D. (1994). *Media effects: Advances in theory and research.* Hillsdale, NJ: Lawrence Erlbaum Associates.

Buckingham, D. (1993). *Children talking television: The making of television literacy.* London: The Falmer Press.

Buckingham, D. (2000). *After the death of childhood: Growing up in the age of electronic media.* Cambridge, UK: Polity Press.

Burr, P. L., & Burr, R. M. (1976). Television advertising to children: What parents are saying about government control. *Journal of Advertising, 5*, 37–41.

Bushman, B. J. (1998). Effects of television violence on memory for commercial messages. *Journal of Experimental Psychology: Applied, 4*(4), 291–307.

Butter, E. J., Popovich, P. M., Stackhouse, R. H., & Garner, R. K. (1981). Discrimination of television programmes and commercials by preschool children. *Journal of Advertising Research, 21*, 53–56.

Butter, E. J., Weikel, K. B., Otto, V., & Wright, K. P. (1991). TV advertising of OTC medicines and its effects on child viewers. *Psychology and Marketing, 8*, 117–128.

Byfield. S. (2002). Snapshots of youth: The lives of teens across the world. *International Journal of Advertising and Marketing to Children, 3*(4), 15–20.

Cantor, J. (1981). Modifying children's eating habits through television ads: Effects of humorous appeals in a field setting. *Journal of Broadcasting, 25*, 37–47.

Carlens, D. (1990). *Kinderen, Televisie en de Vlaamse media-markt. Een terreinverkennend onderzoek naar het kijkgedrag van 9– tot 12-jarigen en hun houding t. o. v. BRT en VTM: Een klassikale schriftelijke enquete.* Brussels: Licentiaatsverhandeling V. U. B.

Carlson, L., & Grossbart, S. (1988). Parental style and consumer socialisation. *Journal of Consumer Research, 15*, 77–94.

Caron, A., & Ward, S. (1975). Gift decisions by kids and parents. *Journal of Advertising Research, 15*(4), 15–20.

Case, R. (1985). *Intellectual development: Birth to adulthood.* New York: Academic Press.

Cash, T. F., Cash, D. W., & Butters, J. W. (1983). Mirror, mirror on the wall … ? Contrast effects and self-evaluations of physical attractiveness. *Personality and Social Psychology, 9*, 359–364.

Cattarin, J., Williams, R., Thomas, C. M., & Thompson, J. K. (2000). The impact of televised images of thinness and attractiveness on body image: The role of social comparison. *Journal of Social & Clinical Psychology, 19*(2), 220–239.

Chaffee, S., McLeod, J. M., & Wackman, D. (1973). Family communication patterns and adolescent political participation. In J. Dennis (Ed.), *Socialisation to politics.* New York: Wiley.

Champion, H., & Furnham, A. (1999). The effect of the media on body satisfaction in adolescent girls. *European Eating Disorders Review, 7*, 213–228.

Chan, K. (2000). Hong Kong children's understanding of television advertising. *Journal of Marketing Communications, 6*, 37–52.

Chan, K. (2003). Materialism among Chinese children in Hong Kong. *International Journal of Advertising and Marketing to Children, 4*(4), 17–24.

Chan, K., & McNeal, J. (2002). Children's perceptions of television advertising in urban China. *International Journal of Advertising and Marketing to Children, 3*(3), 69–79.

Chapman, S., & Fitzgerald, B. (1982). Brand preference and advertising recall in adolescent smokers: Some implications for health promotion. *American Journal of Public Health, 72*(5), 491–494.

Charlton, A. (1986). Children's advertisement-awareness related to their views on smoking. *Health Education Journal, 45*, 75–79.

Chi, M. T. H. (1978). Knowledge structures and memory development. In R. S. Siegler (Ed.), *Children's thinking: What develops?* Hillsdale, NJ: Lawrence Erlbaum Associates.

Christenson, P. G. (1982). Children's perceptions of TV commercials and products: The effects of PSAs. *Communication Research, 9*(4), 491–524.

Clark, C. D. (1999). Youth, advertising and symbolic meaning. In M. C. Macklin & L. Carlson (Eds.), *Advertising to children. Concepts and controversies.* Thousand Oaks, CA: Sage.

Clark, R. A., & Delia, J. G. (1976). The development of functional persuasive skills in childhood and early adolescence. *Child Development, 47*, 1008–1014.

Clarke, J. (2002). The internet according to kids. *International Journal of Advertising and Marketing to Children, 3*(2), 45–52.

Cohen, M., & Cahill, E. (1999). Getting older younger: Developmental differences in children and the challenge of developmental compression. *International Journal of Advertising and Marketing to Children, 1*(4), 271–278.

Collins, J. (1990). Television and primary school children in Northern Ireland: The impact of advertising. *Journal of Educational Television, 16*, 31–39.

Comstock, G., Chaffee, S., Katzman, N., McCombs, M., & Roberts, D. (1978). *Television and human behavior.* New York: Columbia University Press.

Condry, J. (1989). *The psychology of television.* Hillsdale, NJ: Lawrence Erlbaum Associates.

Conner, M., & Armitage, C. J. (2002). *The social psychology of food.* Buckingham, UK: Open University Press.

Cooke, R. (2002). Kids and media. *International Journal of Advertising and Marketing to Children, 3*(4), 29–36.

Cotugna, N. (1988). TV ads on Saturday morning children's programming—what's new. *Journal of Nutrition Education, 20*(3), 125–127.

Courtney, A. E., & Whipple, T. W. (1974). Women in TV commercials. *Journal of Communication, 24*(2), 110–118.

Craggs, C. E. (1992). *Media education in the primary school.* London: Routledge.

Crook, C., & Davison, K. (2001, September). *Mobile phones: Themes of social development.* Paper presented to the British Psychological Society, Developmental Section Conference, Worcester, UK.

Crosby, L. A., & Grossbart, S. L. (1984). Parental style segments and concern about children's food advertising. In J. H. Leigh & C. R. Martin (Eds.), *Current issues and research in advertising, 1984.* Ann Arbor: Graduate School of Business Administration, University of Michigan.

Crouch, C. (1999). Case study—GMTV competing for children. *International Journal of Advertising and Marketing to Children, 1*(1), 37–42.

Culley, J. A., & Bennett, R. (1976). Selling women, selling blacks. *Journal of Communication, 26,* 168–178.

Curran, C. M., & Richards, J. I. (2000). The regulation of children's advertising in the U.S. *International Journal of Advertising and Marketing to Children, 2*(2), 139–154.

Dalmeny, K., Hanna, H., & Lobstein, T. (2003). *Broadcasting bad health. Why food marketing to children needs to be controlled.* A Report for the World Health Organization consultation on a global strategy for diet and health. London: International Association of Consumer Food Organization.

Dammler, A., & Middelmann-Motz, A. (2002). I want one with Harry Potter on it. *International Journal of Advertising and Marketing to Children, 3*(2), 3–8.

Dawson, B., Jeffrey, D. B., Peterson, P. E., Sommers, J., & Wilson, G. (1985). Television commercials as a symbolic representation of reward in the delay of gratification paradigm. *Cognitive Therapy and Research, 9,* 217–224.

De Bens, E., & Vandenbruane, P. (1992). *TV Advertising and children, Part IV, Effects of TV advertising on children.* Ghent: University of Ghent, Belgium: Centre for Media, Opinion and Advertising Research.

De Bruin, A., & Eagle, L. (2002, April). Regulating the medium and the message: Parental perceptions of television advertising directed at children. Proceedings of the 7th Annual Conference on Corporate and Marketing Communications, University of Antwerp.

De Chenecey, S. P. (1999). The cellular family at the millennium. *International Journal of Advertising and Marketing to Children, 1*(4), 333–337.

Desmond, R. J., Singer, J. L., & Singer, D. G. (1990). Family mediation: Parental communication patterns and the influences of television on children. In J. Bryant (Ed.), *Television and the American family* (pp. 293–310). Hillsdale, NJ: Lawrence Erlbaum Associates.

Dibb, S. (1996). *A Spoonful of sugar: Television food advertising aimed at children: An international comparative survey.* Brussels: Consumers International.

Dibb, S., & Castell, A. (1995). *Easy to swallow, hard to stomach: The results of a survey of food advertising on television.* London: National Food Alliance.

Dickinson, R. (1997). *Television and food choice.* London: Ministry of Agriculture, Fisheries and Food, MAFF R & D and surveillance report 267.

Dickinson, R. (2000, November 21). Young people, food and television. Proceedings of the "With the Eyes of a Child" Food Advertising Unit/Children's Programme Conference, London.

Dickinson, R., & Leader, S. (1996, September 10). The role of television in the food choices of 11–18-year-olds. *Nutrition & Food Science, 5*, 9–14.

Dion, K. K. (1973). Young children's stereotyping of facial attractiveness. *Developmental Psychology, 9*(2), 183–188.

Dion, K. K. (1986). Stereotyping based on physical attractiveness: Issues and conceptual perspectives. In C. P. Herman, M. P. Zanna, & E. T. Higgins (Eds.), *Physical appearance, stigma and social behavior: The Ontario Symposium* (Vol. 3, pp. 7–21). Hillsdale, NJ: Lawrence Erlbaum Associates.

Dion, K. K., Berscheid, E., & Walster, E. (1972). What is beautiful is good. *Journal of Personality and Social Psychology, 24*, 285–290.

Donaldson, M. (1978). *Children's minds.* London: Fontana.

Donkin, A. J., Neale, R. S., & Tilson, C. (1993). Children's food purchase requests. *Appetite, 21*(3), 291–294.

Donohue, T. R., Henke, L. L., & Donohue, W. A. (1980). Do kids know what TV commercials intend? *Journal of Advertising Research, 20*(5), 51–57.

Donohue, T. R., & Meyer, T. P. (1984). Children's understanding of television commercials: The acquisition of competence. In R. N. Bostrum (Ed.), *Competence in communication.* Beverly Hills, CA: Sage.

Doolittle, J., & Pepper, R. (1975). Children's TV ad content: 1974. *Journal of Broadcasting, 19*, 131–142.

Dorr, A. (1986). *Television and children: A Special medium for a special audience.* Beverly Hills, CA: Sage.

Dorr, A., Graves, S. B., & Phelps, E. (1980). Television literacy for young children. *Journal of Communication, 30*(3), 71–83.

Dorr, A., Kovaric, P., & Doubleday, C. (1989). Parent-child co-viewing of television. *Journal of Broadcasting & Electronic Media, 33*, 35–51.

Downs, C. A., & Harrison, S. K. (1985). Embarrassing age spots or just plain ugly? Physical attractiveness stereotyping as an instrument of sexism on American television commercials. *Sex Roles, 13*, 9–19.

Dunlap, O. E., Jr. (1931). Cigarette sales hit 295 billion. *Advertising Agency and Advertising & Selling, 44*(1), 67.

Dunn, J. (1999). Mind reading and social relationships. In M. Bennett (Ed.), *Developmental psychology: Achievements and prospects.* Philadelphia: Psychology Press.

Dunn, M. E., & Yniguez, R. M. (1999). Experimental demonstration of the influence of alcohol advertising on the activation of alcohol expectancies in memory among fourth- and fifth-grade children. *Experimental & Clinical Psychopharmacology, 7*(4), 473–483.

Durkin, K. (1985a). Television and sex role acquisition 1: Content. *British Journal of Social Psychology, 24*, 101–113.

Durkin, K. (1985b). Television and sex role acquisition 2: Effects. *British Journal of Social Psychology, 24*, 221–222.

Durkin, K. (1985c). *Television, sex roles and children.* Milton Keynes, UK: Open University Press.

Durkin, K. (1985d). Television and sex role acquisition 3: Counter-stereotyping. *British Journal of Social Psychology, 24*, 211–222.

Eagle, L., & de Bruin, A. (2001). Advertising restrictions: Protection of the young and vulnerable. *International Journal of Advertising and Marketing to Children, 2*(4), 259–271.

Eagly, A. H., Ashmore, R. D., Makhaijani, M. G., & Longo, L. C. (1991). What is beautiful is good, but … A meta-analytic review of research on the physical attractiveness stereotype. *Psychological Bulletin, 110*(1), 109–128.

Eden, K. (2000). Let's go Euro. *International Journal of Advertising and Marketing to Children, 2*(1), 83–93.

Edling, A. (1999, November 23). *Ethics and public policy.* TV Advertising and Children: Ethics and Public Policy Conference, London.

Ellyatt, J. (1999a, November 1). *Marketing to kids.* Chartered Institute of Marketing lecture, Sheffield Hallam University, UK.

Ellyatt, J. (1999b). McVitie's Penguin—How role reversal led to a reversal of fortune. *International Journal of Advertising and Marketing to Children, 1*(1), 43–53.

Elmer-Dewitt, P. (1995, January 16). Fat times. *Time*, 58–65.

"Embattled tobacco's new strategy." (1963). *Fortune, 48*(6), 100–102.

Enis, B. M., Spencer, D. R., & Webb, D. R. (1980). Television advertising and children: Regulatory vs. competitive perspectives. *Journal of Advertising, 9*, 19–26.

Erftmier, T., & Dyson, A. H. (1986). "Oh, ppbbt!": Differences between oral and written persuasive strategies of school-aged children. *Discourse Processes, 9*, 91–114.

Esserman, J. (Ed.). (1981). *Television advertising and children: Issues, research and findings.* New York: Child Research Services.

Faber, R. J., Meyer, T. P., & Miller, M. M. (1984). The effectiveness of health disclosures within children's television commercials. *Journal of Broadcasting, 4*, 463–476.

Fabricant, F. (1994, October 19). Today's foods may be lower in fat, but big bottoms still make big people. *New York Times*, B1, B6.

Ferrante, C. L., Haynes, A. M., & Kingsley, S. M. (1988). Images of women in television advertising. *Journal of Broadcasting & Electronic Media, 32*(2), 231–237.

Finholn, V. (1997, May 7). Experts worry about overweight kids. *Ann Arbor News*, p. C3.

Fishbein, M., & Ajzen, L. (1975). *Belief, attitude, intention and behaviour: An introduction to theory and research.* Reading, MA: Addison-Wesley.

Fischer, M. A. (1985). A developmental study of preference for advertised toys. *Psychology and Marketing, 2*(1), 3–12.

Fischer, E., & Halfpenny, K. (1993). The nature of influence of idealised images of men in advertising. In J. A. Costa (Ed.), *Gender and consumer behavior, proceedings of the second conference* (p. 196). Salt Lake City, UT: University of Utah Printing Services.

Fisher, D. A., & Magnus, P. (1981). Out of the mouths of babes: The opinions of 10 and 11 year old children regarding the advertising of cigarettes. *Community Health Studies, 5,* 22–26.

Fox, R. F. (1996). *Harvesting minds: How TV commercials control kids.* Westport, CT: Praeger.

Fox, R. J., Krugman, D. M., Fletcher, J. E., & Fischer, P. M. (1999). Adolescents' attention to beer and cigarette print ads and associated product warnings. In M. C. Macklin & L. Carlson (Eds.), *Advertising to children: Concepts and controversies* (pp. 251–272). Thousand Oaks, CA: Sage.

Franzoi, S. L. (1995). The body-as-object versus the body-as-process: Gender differences and gender considerations. *Sex Roles, 33*(5/6), 417–437.

Franzoi, S. L., & Herzog, M. E. (1987). Judging physical attractiveness: What body aspects do we use? *Personality and Social Psychology Bulletin, 13,* 19–33.

Furnham, A. (2000). *Children and advertising: The allegations and the evidence.* London: Social Affairs Unit.

Furnham, A., Abramsky, S., & Gunter, B. (1997). A cross-cultural content analysis of children's television advertisements. *Sex Roles, 37,* 91–99.

Furnham, A., Bergland, J., & Gunter, B. (2002). Memory for television advertisements as a function of advertisement-programme congruity. *Applied Cognitive Psychology, 16,* 525–545.

Furnham A., & Cleare, A. (1988). School children's conceptions of economics: Prices, wages, investments and strikes. *Journal of Economic Psychology, 9,* 467–479.

Furnham, A., Gunter, B., & Richardson, F. (2001). The effects of programme-product congruity and viewer involvement on memory for television advertisements. *Journal of Applied Social Psychology, 32*(1), 124–141.

Furnham, A., Gunter, B., & Walsh, D. (1998). Effects of programme context on memory of humorous television commercials. *Applied Cognitive Psychology, 12,* 555–567.

Furth, H. (1980). *The world of grown-ups.* New York: Elsevier.

Gaines, L., & Esserman, J. (1981). A quantitative study of young children's comprehension of TV programmes and commercials. *Television Advertising & Children.* New York: Child Research Service.

Galst, J. P. (1980). Television food commercials and pro-nutritional public service announcements as determinants of young people's snack choices. *Child Development, 51,* 935–938.

Galst, J. P., & White, M. A. (1976). The unhealthy persuader: The reinforcing value of television and children's purchase-influencing attempts at the supermarket. *Child Development, 47,* 1089–1096.

Gamble, M., & Cotugna, N. (1999). A quarter century of TV food advertising targeted at children. *American Journal of Health Behaviour, 23*(4), 261–267.

Gentile, D. A., Walsh, D. A., Bloomgren, B. W., Atti, J. A., & Norman, J. A. (2001, April). *Frogs sell beer: The effects of beer advertisements on adolescent drinking knowledge, attitudes and behaviour.* Paper presented to the Society for Research in Child Development Conference, Minneapolis.

Gerbner, G., & Gross, L. (1976). Living with television: The violence profile. *Journal of Communication, 26,* 173–199.

Gerbner, G., Gross, L., Morgan, M., & Signorielli, N. (1981). Special report: Health and medicine on television. *New England Journal of Medicine, 305,* 901–904.

Geuens, V., De Pelsmacker, P., & Mast, G. (2002). Attitudes of school directors towards in-school marketing: An exploratory study. *International Journal of Advertising and Marketing to Children, 3*(3), 57–67.

Goldberg, M. E. (1990). A quasi-experiment assessing the effectiveness of TV advertising directed to children. *Journal of Marketing Research, 27,* 445–454.

Goldberg, M. E., & Gorn, G. J. (1987). Happy and sad TV programs: How they affect reactions to commercial. *Journal of Consumer Research, 14,* 387–403.

Goldberg, M. E., Gorn, G. J., & Gibson, W. (1987). TV messages for snacks and breakfast foods: Do they influence children's preferences? *Journal of Consumer Research, 5,* 73–81.

Goldstein, A. O., Fischer, P. M., Richards, J. W., & Creten, D. (1987). Relationship between high school student smoking and recognition of cigarette advertisements. *Journal of Pediatrics, 110*(3), 488–491.

Goldstein, J. (1999). Children and advertising—the research. *International Journal of Advertising and Marketing to Children, 1*(2), 113–118.

Gonzalez del Valle, A. (1999). *An overview and comparison of rules, regulations and policies affecting advertising to children in the Netherlands, UK, Spain and Sweden.* London: The Advertising Association.

Gorn, G. J. (1982). The effects of music in advertising on choice behavior: A classical conditioning approach. *Journal of Marketing, 46,* 94–101.

Gorn, G. J., & Goldberg, M. E. (1978). The impact of television advertising on children from low income families. *Journal of Consumer Research, 4,* 86–88.

Gorn, G. J., & Goldberg, M. E. (1980). Children's responses to repetitive television commercials. *Journal of Consumer Research, 6,* 421–424.

Gorn, G. J., & Goldberg, M. E. (1982a). Some unintended consequences of TV advertising to children. *Journal of Consumer Research, 8,* 86–88.

Gorn, G. J., & Goldberg, M. E. (1982b). Behavioral evidence of the effects of televised food messages on children. *Journal of Consumer Research, 9,* 200–205.

Greenberg, B. S., Fazal, S., & Wober, M. (1986). *Children's views on advertising.* London: Research Department, Independent Broadcasting Authority.

Griffiths, J. A., & McCabe, M. P. (2000). The influence of significant others on distorted eating and body dissatisfaction among early adolescent girls. *European Eating Disorders Review, 8*(4), 301–314.

Grossbart, S. L., Carlson, L., & Walsh, A. (1988). Consumer socialisation and frequency of shopping with children. *Journal of the Academy of Marketing Science, 19,* 155–163.

Grossbart, S. L., & Crosby, L. A. (1984). Understanding the basis of parental concern and reaction to children's food advertising. *Journal of Marketing, 48,* 79–92.

Grube, J. W. (1993). Alcohol portrayals and alcohol advertising on television: Content and effects on children and adolescents. *Alcohol Health & Research World, 17*(1), 54–60.

Grube, J. W., & Wallack, L. (1994). Television beer advertising and drinking knowledge, beliefs and intentions among school children. *American Journal of Public Health, 84*(2), 254–259.

Guillen, E. O., & Barr, S. I. (1994). Nutrition, dieting and fitness messages in a magazine for adolescent women, 1970–1990. *Journal of Adolescent Health, 15,* 464–472.

Gunter, B. (1995). *Television and Gender Representation*. Luton, UK: John Libbey.

Gunter, B., Baluch, B., Duffy, L., & Furnham, A. (2002). Children's memory for television advertising: Effects of programme-advertising congruency. *Applied Cognitive Psychology, 16*, 171–190.

Gunter, B., & Furnham, A. (1998). *Children as consumers: A psychological analysis of the young people's market*. London: Routledge.

Gunter, B., Furnham, A., & Beeson, C. (1997). Recall for television advertisements as a function of program evaluation. *Journal of Psychology, 131*, 541–553.

Gunter, B., Furnham A., & Frost, C. (1994). Recall by young people of television advertisements as a function of programme type and audience evaluation. *Psychological Reports, 75*, 1107–1120.

Gunter, B., & McAleer, J. (1997). *Children and television* (2nd ed.). London: Routledge.

Gunter, B., McAleer, J., & Clifford, B. R. (1992a, March 11–13). Children and television advertising: A developmental perspective. In *Children and young people: Are they the new consumers?* (pp. 187–209). Amsterdam, The Netherlands: European Society for Opinion and Marketing Research, Conference proceedings, Milan, Italy.

Gunter, B., McAleer, J., & Clifford, B. R. (1992b). *Children's views about television*. Aldershot, UK: Avebury.

Gunter, B., Tohala, T., & Furnham, A. (2001). Television violence and memory for television advertisements. *Communication, 26*(2), 109–127.

Gussow, J. (1972). Counternutritional messages of TV ads aimed at children. *Journal of Nutrition Education, 4*, 48–52.

Haedrich, G., Adam, M., Kreilkamp, E., & Kuss, A. (1984). Zur verhaltenswirking der fernehwerbung bei kindern. *Marketing, 6*, 129–133.

Hahlo, G. (1999). Millennium kids and the post-modern family. *International Journal of Advertising and Marketing to Children, 1*(3), 229–237.

Hanley, P. (1996). *Children's perceptions of toy advertising*. London: Independent Television Commission.

Hanley, P., Hayward, W., Sims, L., & Jones, J. (2000). *Copycat kids? The influence of television advertising on children and teenagers*. London: Independent Television Commission.

Hansen, L. (1997). Television advertising directed at children. *Commercial Communications Newsletter of the European Commission*, July. Retrieved June 1, 2002 from http://europa.eu.int/comm/dg15/comcom/newsletter/edition09/page30_en.htm

Hanson, M. (2000). Banning ads for kids stops open communication. *Marketing*, April 22, p. 10.

Harrison, K. (1997). Does interpersonal attraction to thin media personalities promote eating disorders? *Journal of Broadcasting & Electronic Media, 41*, 478–500.

Harrison, K. (2000a). The body electric: Thin-ideal media and eating disorders in adolescents. *Journal of Communication, 50*(3), 119–143.

Harrison, K. (2000b). Television viewing, fat stereotyping, body shape standards, and eating disorder symptomatology in grade school children. *Communication Research, 27*(5), 617–640.

Harrison, K., & Cantor, J. (1997). The relationship between media consumption and eating disorders. *Journal of Communication, 47*(1), 40–67.

Harter, S. (1993). *Visions of self: Beyond the me in the mirror: The importance of looks in everyday life*. Albany: State University of New York Press.

Harvey, H., & Blades, M. (2002). *Do four, five, and six year old children understand the selling intent of television advertising?* Unpublished manuscript, Department of Psychology, University of Sheffield.

Hasting, G., & MacFadyen, L. (2000, August 5). A day in the life of an advertising man: Review of internal documents from the UK tobacco industry's principal advertising agencies. *British Medical Journal, 321*, 366–371.

Hastings, R. (2000). International differences among kids and age compression. *International Journal of Advertising and Marketing to Children, 2*(3), 187–189.

Heinberg, L. J., & Thompson, J. K. (1995). Body image and televised images of thinness and attractiveness: A controlled laboratory investigation. *Journal of Social and Clinical Psychology, 14*, 325–338.

Herr, P. M. (1986). Consequences of priming: Judgment and behaviour. *Journal of Personality and Social Psychology, 51*, 1106–1115.

Higgins, E. T., & King, G. (1981). Accessibility of social constructs: Information-processing consequences of individual and contextual variability. In N. Cantor & J. F. Kihlstrom (Eds.), *Personality, cognition and social interaction* (pp. 69–121). Hillsdale, NJ: Lawrence Erlbaum Associates.

Hill, A. J., Oliver, S., & Rogers P. J. (1992). Eating in the adult world: The rise of dieting in childhood and adolescence. *British Journal of Clinical Psychology, 31*, 95–105.

Hind, A. (2003). Brands for the under-3s: Teletubbies, a case study. *International Journal of Advertising and Marketing to Children, 4*(2), 25–33.

Hitchings, E., & Moynihan, P. J. (1998). The relationship between television food advertisements recalled and actual foods consumed by children. *Journal of Human Nutrition and Dietetics, 11*, 511–517.

Hite, C. F., & Hite, R. E. (1995). Reliance on brand by young children. *Journal of the Market Research Society, 37*(2), 185–193.

Hoek, J., Gendall, P., & Stockdale, M. (1993). Some effects of tobacco sponsorship advertisements on young males. *International Journal of Advertising, 12*, 25–35.

Howard, J. A., Hulbert, J. M., & Lehman, D. A. (1973). An exploratory analysis of the effect of television advertising on children. *Proceedings of the American Marketing Association*. Washington, DC: American Marketing Association.

Huston, A. C., Greer, D., Wright, J. C., Welch, R., & Ross, R. (1984). Children's comprehension of televised formal features with masculine and feminine connotations. *Developmental Psychology, 20*, 707–716.

Irving, L. (1990). Mirror images: Effects of the standard of beauty on the self and body esteem of women exhibiting varying levels of bulimic symptoms. *Journal of Social and Clinical Psychology, 9*, 230–242.

Isler, L., Popper, E., & Ward, S. (1987). Children's purchase requests and parental responses. *Journal of Advertising Research, 27*, 54–59.

IBA. (1990). *Television sponsorship survey*. London: IBA.

ITC. (1991a, January). *The ITC code of advertising standards and practice*. London: Independent Television Commission.

ITC. (1991b, March). *The ITC code of programme sponsorship*. London: Independent Television Commission.

ITC. (1991c, January). *ITC rules on advertising breaks*. London: Independent Television Commission.

ITC. (1993, May). *The ITC code of advertising standards and practice*. London: Independent Television Commission.

ITC. (1995, Autumn). *The ITC code of advertising standards and practice*. London: Independent Television Commission.

ITC. (1997, Summer). *The ITC code of advertising standards and practice*. London: Independent Television Commission.

ITC. (2000, Autumn). *The ITC code of programme sponsorship*. London: ITC.

ITC. (2003). *The ITC code of advertising standards and practice*. London: Independent Television Commission.

Jaglom, L. M., & Gardner, H. (1981). The preschool television viewer as anthropologist. In H. Kelley & H. Gardner (Eds.), *Viewing children through television*. San Francisco, CA: Jossey-Bass.

John, D. R. (1999a). Consumer socialization of children: A retrospective look at twenty-five years of research. *Journal of Consumer Research, 26*(3), 183–213.

John, D. R. (1999b). Through the eyes of a child: Children's knowledge and understanding of advertising. In M. C. Macklin & L. Carlson (Eds.), *Advertising to children: Concepts and controversies* (pp. 3–26). Thousand Oaks, CA: Sage.

Johnson, H. (1992, January 17). Attention seekers. *Media Week*, pp. 14–15.

Jones, A. (2002). Wireless marketing: The linking value of text messaging. *International Journal of Advertising and Marketing to Children, 3*(2), 39–44.

Joossens, L. (1984). Het effect van cumulatieve blootstelling aan reclamescpots op kinderen: Een experimenteel onderzoek. *Communicatie, 3*, 8–12.

Kamins, M. A., Marks, L. J., & Skinner, D. (1991). Television commercial evaluation in the context of program-induced mood: Congruity versus consistency effects. *Journal of Advertising, 20*, 1–14.

Kapferer, J. N. (1985). *L'Enfant et las publicite: Les chemins de la seduction*. Paris: Dunod.

Kemp, G. (1999, September). Commercial break: Should kids' TV ads be banned? *Marketing Business*, pp. 16–18.

Kimball, M. (1986). Television and sex-role attitudes. In T. M. Williams (Ed.), *The impact of television* (pp. 265–301). London: Academic Press.

Kinsey, J. (1987). The use of children in advertising and the impact of advertising aimed at children. *International Journal of Advertising, 6*, 169–177.

Kline, S. (1993). *Out of the garden*. London: Verso.

Kolbe, R. H. (1990). Gender roles in children's television advertising: A longitudinal content analysis. *Current Issues and Research in Advertising, 13*, 197–206.

Kotz, K., & Story, M. (1994). Food advertisements during children's Saturday morning television programming: Are they consistent with dietary recommendations? *Journal of the American Dietetic Association, 94*(11), 1296–1300.

Krill, B. J., Peach, M., Pursey, G., Gilpin, P., & Perloff, R. M. (1981). Still typecast after all these years: Sex role portrayals in television advertising. *International Journal of Women's Studies, 4*, 497–506.

Krugman, H. E. (1965). The impact of television advertising: Learning without involvement. *Public Opinion Quarterly, 29*, 349–356.

Kunkel, D. (1988a). Children and host-selling television commercials. *Communication Research, 15*(1), 71–92.

Kunkel, D. (1988b). From a raised eyebrow to a turned back: The FCC and children's product-related programming. *Journal of Communication, 38*(4), 90–108.

Kunkel, D. (2001). Children and television advertising. In D. G. Singer and J. L. Singer (Eds.), *Handbook of children and the media* (pp. 375–394). Thousand Oaks, California: Sage.

Kunkel, D., & Gantz, W. (1992). Children's televison advertising in the multi-channel environment. *Journal of Communication, 42*, 134–152.

Kunkel, D., & Roberts, D. (1991). Young minds and marketplace values: Issues in children's television advertising. *Journal of Social Issues, 57*, 57–72.

Lambo, A. M. (1981). Children's ability to evaluate television commercial messages for sugared products. *American Journal of Public Health, 71*(9), 1060–1062.

Langlois, J. H., Roggman, L. A., Casey, R. J., Ritter, J. M., Rieser-Danner, L. A., & Jenkins, V. Y. (1987). Infant preferences for attractive faces: Rudiments of a stereotype? *Developmental Psychology, 23*, 363–369.

Lastovicka, J. L., & Gardner, D. M. (1979). Components of involvement. In J. C. Maloney & B. Silverman (Eds.), *Attitudes play for high stakes*. Chicago: American Marketing Association.

Lavine, H., Sweeney, D., & Wagner, S. H. (1999). Depicting women as sex objects in television advertising: Effects on body dissatisfaction. *Personality and Social Psychology Bulletin, 25*(8), 1049–1058.

Lavidge, R., & Steiner, G. A. (1961). A model for predictive measurements of advertising effectiveness. *Journal of Marketing, 25*, 59–62.

Lawlor, M-A., & Prothero, A. (2002). The established and potential mediating variables in the child's understanding of advertising intent: Towards a research agenda. *Journal of Marketing Management, 18*, 481–499.

Lawlor, M.-A., & Prothero, A. (2003). Children's understanding of advertising intent—towards and beyond the advertiser's perspective. *Journal of Marketing Management, 19*(4), 411–431.

Ledwith, F. (1984). Does tobacco sports sponsorship on television act as advertising to children? *Health Education Journal, 43*(4), 85–88.

Lee, E. B., & Browne, L. A. (1995). Effects of television advertising on African American teenagers. *Journal of Black Studies, 25*(5), 523–536.

Lemin, B. (1966). A study of the smoking habits of 14-year-old pupils in six schools in Aberdeen. *Medical Officer, 116*, 82–85.

Lerner, R. M., Orlos, J. B., & Knapp, J. A. (1976). Physical attractiveness, physical effectiveness, and self-concept in late adolescents. *Adolescence, 11*, 313–326.

Levin, S. R., & Anderson, D. R. (1976). The development of attention. *Journal of Communication, 26*(2), 126–135.

Levin, S. R., Petros, T. V., & Petrella, F. W. (1982). Preschoolers' awareness of television advertising. *Child Development, 53*, 933–937.

Levitt, E. E., & Edwards, J. A. (1970). A multivariate study of correlative factors in youthful cigarette smoking. *Developmental Psychology, 2*, 5–11.

Lewis, C., Freeman, N. H., Kyriakidou, C., Maridaki-Kassotaki, K., & Berridge, D. M. (1996). Social influences on false belief access: Specific sibling influences or general apprenticeship? *Child Development, 67*, 2930–2947.

Lewis, M. K., & Hill, A. J. (1998). Food advertising on British children's television: A content analysis and experimental study with nine-year-olds. *International Journal of Obesity, 22*, 206–214.

Liebert, D. E., Sprafkin, J. N., Liebert, R. M., & Rubinstein, E. A. (1977). Effects of television commercial disclaimers on the product expectations of children. *Journal of Communication, 27*, 1–15.

Linn, M. C., de Benedictis, T., & Delucchi, K. (1982). Adolescent reasoning about advertisements: Preliminary investigations. *Child Development, 53*, 1599–1613.

Livingstone, S. (2002). *Young People New Media*. London: Sage.

Lloyd, D. W., & Clancy, K. J. (1991). CPMs versus CPMIs: Implications for media planning. *Journal of Advertising Research, 31*, 34–44.

Loughlin, M., & Desmond, R. J. (1981). Social interaction in advertising directed to children. *Journal of Broadcasting, 25*, 303–307.

Lovdal, L. T. (1989). Sex role messages in television commercials: An update. *Sex Roles, 21*(11/12), 715–724.

Lury, C. (1996). *Consumer Culture*. Cambridge: Polity.

Lvovich, S. (2003). Advertising and obesity: The research evidence. *International Journal of Advertising and Marketing to Children, 4*(2), 35–40.

Lynn, M. (2002, April). I'm Britney, buy me. *Business Life*, 38–43.

MacIndoe, G. (1999). A case study of "Schoolcards": Innovative communication with teenagers in secondary schools. *International Journal of Advertising and Marketing to Children, 1*(3), 219–228.

MacKenzie, S. B., Lutz, R. J., & Belch, G. E. (1986). The role of attitude toward the ad as a mediation of advertising effectiveness: A test of competing explanations. *Journal of Marketing Research, 23*, 130–143.

Macklin, M. C. (1983). Do children understand TV ads? Measures make a difference. *Journal of Advertising Research, 23*(1), 63–70.

Macklin, M. C. (1987). Preschoolers' understanding of the informational function of advertising. *Journal of Consumer Research, 14*, 229–239.

Macklin, M. C. (1996). Preschoolers' learning of brand names from visual cues. *Journal of Consumer Research, 23*, 251–261.

Macklin, M. C., & Kolbe, R. H. (1984). Sex role stereotyping in children's advertising: Current and past trends. *Journal of Advertising, 13*, 34–42.

Maddux, J. E., & Rogers, R. W. (1980). Effects of source expertness, physical attractiveness and supporting arguments on persuasion: A case of brains over beauty. *Journal of Personality and Social Psychology, 39*(2), 235–244.

Mangleburg, T. F., & Bristol, T. (1999). Socialisation and adolescents' skepticism toward advertising. In M. C. Macklin & L. Carlson (Eds.), *Advertising to children: Concepts and controversies* (pp. 27–47). Thousand Oaks, CA: Sage.

Marin, A. (1980). *50 Years on advertising: 1930–1980*. Chicago: Crabe.

Marsh, J., & Millard, E. (2000). *Literacy and popular culture*. London: Paul Chapman.

Marshall, D., & Ffelan, S. (1999). To infinity and beyond: Character merchandising and children's toys. *International Journal of Advertising and Marketing to Children, 1*(3), 249–253.

Martensen, A., & Hansen, F. (2001). *Children's knowledge and interpretation of commercial advertising: Intentions, truthfulness and viewing habits* (Research Paper No. 15). Denmark: Copenhagen Business School.

Martin, M. C. (1997). Children's understanding of the intent of advertising: A meta-analysis. *Journal of Public Policy and Marketing, 16*(2), 205–216.

Martin, M. C., & Gentry, J. W. (1997). Stuck in the model trap: The effects of beautiful models in ads on female pre-adolescents and adolescents. *Journal of Advertising, 26*, 19–33.

Martin, M. C., Gentry, J. W., & Hill, R. P. (1999). The beauty myth and the persuasiveness of advertising: A look at adolescent girls and boys. In M. C. Macklin & L. Carlson (Eds.), *Advertising to children: Concepts and controversies* (pp. 165–187). Thousand Oaks, CA: Sage.

Martin, M. C., & Kennedy, P. F. (1993). Advertising and social comparison: Consequences for female pre-adolescents and adolescents. *Psychology and Marketing, 10*, 513–530.

McArthur, L. Z., & Eisen, S. (1976). Achievements of male and female storybook characters as determinants of achievement behaviour in boys and girls. *Journal of Personality and Social Psychology, 33*, 467–473.

McArthur, L. Z., & Resko, B. G. (1975). The portrayal of men and women in American television commercials. *Journal of Social Psychology, 97*, 209–220.

McGuire, W. J. (1969). An information-processing model of advertising effectiveness. In H. L. Davis & A. J. Silk (Eds.), *Behavioural and management sciences in marketing*. New York: Ronald.

McLeod, J., & Brown, J. D. (1976). The family environment and adolescent television use. In R. Brown (Ed.), *Children and television* (pp. 199–233). London: Collier Macmillan.

McNeal, J. U. (1969, Summer). The child as consumer: A new market. *Journal of Retailing*, 15–22.

McNeal, J. U. (1992). *Kids as customers: A handbook of marketing to children*. New York: Lexington.

McNeal, J. U., & Yeh, C. H. (1990). Taiwanese children as consumers. *Asia Pacific Journal of Marketing, 2*, 32–43.

McNeal, J. U., & Zhang, H. (2000). Chinese children's consumer behaviour: A review. *International Journal of Advertising and Marketing to Children, 2*(1), 31–37.

Media Smart. (2003). *Be Adwise. Helping children to watch wisely. A primary teaching resource about advertising*. Media Smart: London. Retrieved March 10, 2003 from www.mediasmart.org.uk

Messaris, P., & Sarett, C. (1982). On the consequences of television-related parent-child interaction. In E. Wartella & G. C. Whitney (Eds.), *Mass Communication Review Yearbook* (Vol. 3, pp. 365–383). Beverly Hills: Sage.

Milavsky, R., Pekowsky, B., & Stipp, H. (1975). TV drug advertising and proprietary and illicit drug use among teenage boys. *Public Opinion Quarterly, 39*, 457–481.

Mitchell, A. A. (1981). The dimensions of advertising involvement. In K. Monroe (Ed.), *Advances in Consumer Research* (Vol. 8, pp. 25–30). Ann Arbor, MI: Association for Consumer Research.

Mitchell, A. A. (1983). The effects of visual and emotional advertising: An information-processing approach. In L. Percy & A. G. Woodside (Eds.), *Advertising and consumer psychology* (pp. 197–218). Lexington, MA: Lexington.

Mitchell, A. A., & Olson, J. C. (1981). Are product attribute beliefs the only mediator of advertising effects on brand attitudes? *Journal of Marketing Research, 18,* 318–332.

Moore, E. S., & Lutz, R. J. (2000). Children, advertising, and product experiences: A multimethod inquiry. *Journal of Consumer Research, 27,* 31–48.

Moore, R. L. (1990). Effects of television on family consumer behavior. In J. Bryant (Ed.), *Television and the American family* (pp. 275–290). Hillsdale, NJ: Lawrence Erlbaum Associates.

Moore, R. L., & Moschis, G. P. (1978). Teenagers' reactions to advertising. *Journal of Advertising, 7,* 24–30.

Moore, R. L., & Moschis, G. P. (1981). The role of family communication in consumer learning. *Journal of Communication, 31,* 42–51.

Morton, H. (1990). A survey of the television viewing habits, food behaviours and perception of food advertisements among South Australian year 8 high school students. *Journal of the Home Economics Association of Australia, 22*(2), 34–36.

Moschis, G. P., & Churchill, G. A. (1978). Consumer socialisation: A theoretical and empirical analysis. *Journal of Marketing Research, 15,* 599–609.

Moschis, G. P., & Churchill, G. A. (1979). An analysis of the adolescent consumer. *Journal of Marketing, 43,* 40–48.

Moschis, G. P., & Moore, R. L. (1979a). Decision making among the young: A socialization perspective. *Journal of Consumer Research, 6,* 101–112.

Moschis, G. P., & Moore, R. L. (1979b). Family communication and consumer socialization. In W. L. Wilkie (Ed.), *Advances in Consumer Research* (Vol. 6, pp. 359–363). Ann Arbor, MI: Association for Consumer Research.

Moschis, G. P., & Moore, R. L. (1979c). Mass media and personal influences on adolescent consumer learning. *Developments in Marketing Science, 2,* 12–20.

Moschis, G. P., & Moore, R. L. (1982). A longitudinal study of television advertising effects. *Journal of Consumer Research, 9*(3), 279–286.

Muehling, D. D., & Kolbe, R. H. (1999). A comparison of children's and prime-time fine print advertising disclosure practices. In M. C. Macklin & L. Carlson (Eds.), *Advertising to children: Concepts and controversies* (pp. 143–164). Thousand Oaks, California: Sage.

Munoz, K. A., Krebs-Smith, S. M., Ballard-Barbash, R., & Cleveland, G. E. (1997). Food intakes of U.S. children and adolescents compared with recommendations. *Pediatrics, 100*(3), 323–329.

Myers, P. N., & Biocca, F. A. (1992). The elastic body image: The effect of television advertising and programming on body image distortion in young women. *Journal of Communication, 42*(3), 108–133.

National Heart Forum. (1996). *Eat your words: Understanding healthy eating and food messages.* London: National Heart Forum.

Norris, C. E., & Colman, A. M. (1992). Context effects on recall and recognition of magazine advertisements. *Journal of Advertising, 21,* 37–46.

Norris, C. E., & Colman, A. M. (1993). Context effects on memory for television advertisements. *Social Behavior and Personality, 21,* 279–296.

Norris, C. E., & Colman, A. M. (1994). Effects of entertainment and enjoyment of television programs on perception and memory of advertisements. *Social Behavior and Personality, 22,* 365–376.

Oates, C., Blades, M., & Gunter, B. (2002). Children and television advertising. When do they understand persuasive intent? *Journal of Consumer Behaviour, 1,* 238–245.

Oates, C., Blades, M., Gunter, B., & Don, J. (2003). Children's understanding of television advertising: A qualitative approach. *Journal of Marketing Communications, 9,* 59–71.

O'Cass, A., & Clarke, P. (2002). Dear Santa, do you have my brand? A study of the brand requests, awareness and request styles at Christmas time. *Journal of Consumer Behaviour, 2*(1), 37–53.

O'Connell, D. L., Lloyd, D. M., Alexander, H. M., Hardes, G. R., Dobsob, A. J., & Springthorpe, H. J. (1981). Cigarette smoking and drug use in school children: II, Factors associated with smoking. *International Journal of Epidemiology, 10,* 223–231.

O'Donohoe, S. (1994). Advertising uses and gratifications. *European Journal of Marketing, 28*(8/9), 52–75.

Ogden, J., & Mundray, K. (1996). The effect of the media on body satisfaction: The role of gender and size. *European Eating Disorders Review, 4,* 171–181.

O'Hanlan, T. (2000). Building a "kid contract" with Chinese children: Truths and trends. *International Journal of Advertising and Marketing to Children, 2*(2), 123–127.

Paget, K. P., Kritt, D., & Bergemann, L. (1984). Understanding strategic interactions in television commercials: A developmental study. *Journal of Applied Developmental Psychology, 5,* 145–161.

Palmer, E. L., & McDowell, C. N. (1979). Program/commercial separators in children's television programming. *Journal of Communication, 29,* 197–201.

Park, C. W., & McLung, G. W. (1986). The effect of TV program involvement on involvement with commercials. *Advances in Consumer Research, 13,* 544–548.

Parker, C. (2001). More than just play dough: Children, money and marketing. *International Journal of Advertising and Marketing to Children, 3*(1), 47–51.

Parkin, A. J. (1993). *Memory phenomena, experiment and theory.* Oxford: Blackwell.

Pawlowski, D. R., Badzinski, D. M., & Mitchell, N. (1998). Effects of metaphors on children's comprehension and perception of print advertisements. *Journal of Advertising, 27*(2), 83–98.

Pecora, N. O. (1998). *The Business of Children's Entertainment.* New York: Guilford.

Pereira, J. (1990, April 30). Kids' advertisers play hide-and-seek, concealing commercials in every cranny. *Wall Street Journal,* pp. 131–136.

Peskin, J. (1992). Ruse and representations: On children's ability to conceal information. *Developmental Psychology, 28,* 84–87.

Petty, R. E., & Cacioppo, J. T. (1979). Issue involvement can increase or decrease persuasion by enhancing message-relevant cognitive responses. *Journal of Personality and Social Psychology, 37,* 1915–1926.

Petty, R. E., Cacioppo, J. T., & Kasmer, J. A. (1987). The role of affect in the elaboration likelihood model of persuasion. In L. Donohew, H. Sypher, & E. T. Higgins (Eds.), *Communication, social cognition, and affect* (pp. 177–243). Hillsdale, NJ: Lawrence Erlbaum Associates.

Piachaud, D. (1998, December 19). Present dangers. *The Guardian,* pp. 1–2.

Piaget, J., & Inhelder, B. (1956). *The child's conception of space.* London: Routledge & Kegan Paul.

Piepe, A., Charlton, P., Morey, J., Yerrel, P., & Ledwith, F. (1986). Does sponsored sport lead to smoking among children? *Health Education Journal, 45*(3), 145–148.

Pilgrim, L., & Lawrence, D. (2001). Pester power is a destructive concept. *International Journal of Advertising and Marketing to Children*, 3(1), 11–21.

Pine, K., & Nash, A. (in press). Dear Santa: The effects of television advertising on young children. *International Journal of Behavioral Development*.

Pine, K., & Veasey, T. (2003). Conceptualising and assessing young children's knowledge of television advertising. *Journal of Marketing Management*, 19(4), 459–473.

Pollay, R. W. (1988, January). *Promotion and policy for a pandemic product: Notes of the history of cigarette advertising*. Vancouver, B.C.: History of Advertising Archives (Working Paper).

Pollay, R. W. (1994). Exposure of U.S. youth to cigarette television advertising in the 1960s. *Tobacco Control*, 3(2), 130–133.

Pollay, R. W. (1995). Targeting tactics in selling smoke: Youthful aspects of 20th century cigarette advertising. *Journal of Marketing Theory and Practice*, 59, 1–21.

Pollay, R. W., Carter-Whitney, D., & Lee, J. S. (1992). Separate, but not equal: Racial segmentation in cigarette advertising. *Journal of Advertising*, 16(1), 45–57.

Potts, R., Doppler, M., & Hernandez, M. (1994). Effects of television content on physical risk-taking in children. *Journal of Experimental Child Psychology*, 58(3), 321–331.

Prasad, V. K., Rao, T. R., & Sheikh, A. A. (1978). Mother vs commercial. *Journal of Communication*, 28, 91–96.

Prasad, V. K., & Smith, L. J. (1994). Television commercials in violent programming: An experimental evaluation of their effects on children. *Journal of the Academy of Marketing Sciences*, 22(4), 340–351.

Preston, C. (2000). Are children seeing through ITC advertising regulations? *International Journal of Advertising*, 19(1), 117–136.

Preston, L. (1982). The Association Model of the advertising communication process. *Journal of Advertising*, 11, 3–15.

Proctor, J., & Richards, M. (2002). Word-of-mouth marketing: Beyond pester power. *International Journal of Advertising and Marketing to Children*, 3(3), 3–11.

Rajecki, D. W., McTavish, D. G., Rasmussen, J. L., Schreuders, M., Byers, D. C., & Jessup, K. S. (1994). Violence, conflict, trickery, and other story themes in TV ads for food for children. *Journal of Applied Social Psychology*, 24(19), 1685–1700.

Rak, D. S., & McMullen, L. M. (1987). Sex-role stereotyping in television commercials: A verbal response mode and content analysis. *Canadian Journal of Behavioral Science*, 19(1), 25–29.

Randrup, L., & Lac, K. T. (2000). *Children and TV commercials*. Research Paper No. 1, Dept of Marketing, Copenhagen Business School, Denmark.

Ray, M. (1973). Marketing communication and the hierarchy-of-effects. In P. Clarke (Ed.), *New models for mass communication research* (pp. 147–176). Beverly Hills, CA: Sage.

Reece, B. B., Rifon, N. J., & Rodriguez, K. (1999). Selling food to children. In M. C. Macklin & L. Carlson (Eds.), *Advertising to children: Concepts and controversies*. Thousand Oaks, CA: Sage.

Resnik, A. J., & Stern, B. L. (1977). Children's television advertising and brand choice: A laboratory experiment. *Journal of Advertising*, 6(3), 11–17.

Revill, J. (2002, November 3). NHS wakes up to child obesity crisis. *The Observer*, 5.

Reynolds, F. D., & Wells, W. D. (1977). *Consumer behavior*. New York: McGraw Hill.

Richins, M. (1991). Social comparison and the idealised images of advertising. *Journal of Consumer Research, 18*, 71–83.

Riecken, G., & Yavas, U. (1990). Children's general, product, and brand-specific attitudes towards television commercials. *International Journal of Advertising, 9*(2), 136–148.

Riem, H. (1987). *Recalme en het Kind: De Invloed van TV-Reclame op Kinderen*. Antwerp, Belgium: University of Antwerp.

Riff, D., Goldson, H., Saxton, K., & Yang-Chou, Y. (1988). Females and minorities in TV ads in 1987 Saturday children's programs. *Journalism Quarterly, 65*, 129–136.

Rijens, R., & Miracle, G. (1986). *European regulation of advertising*. Amsterdam: North-Holland.

Ritson, M., & Elliott, R. (1998). *The social contextualisation of the lonely viewer: An ethnographic study of advertising interpretation* (working paper). University of Minnesota, Minneapolis.

Ritson, M., & Elliott, R. (1999). The social uses of advertising: An ethnographic study of adolescent advertising audiences. *Journal of Consumer Research, 26*(3), 260–277.

Robertson, T. S. (1979). Parental mediation of television advertising effects. *Journal of Communication, 29*, 12–25.

Robertson, T. S., & Rossiter, J. R. (1974). Children and commercial persuasion: An attribution theory analysis. *Journal of Consumer Research, 1*, 13–20.

Robertson, T. S., Ward, S., Gatignon, H., & Klees, D. M. (1989). Advertising and children: A cross-cultural study. *Communication Research, 16*, 459–485.

Roedder, D. L. (1981). Age differences in children's responses to television advertising: An information-processing approach. *Journal of Consumer Research, 8*, 144–153.

Roedder, D. L., Sternthal, B., & Calder, B. J. (1983). Attitude-behavior consistency in children's responses to television advertising. *Journal of Marketing Research, 20*, 337–349.

Rogers, D. (2002, November 14). Media Smart tells kids "be sceptics." *Marketing*, p. 4.

Rosenberg, M. (1986). Self-concept from middle childhood through adolescence. In J. Suls & A. G. Greenwald (Eds.), *Psychological perspectives on the self* (Vol. 3, pp. 107–136). Hillsdale, NJ: Lawrence Erlbaum Associates.

Ross, C. (1996, January 6). Anheuser-Busch pulls beer ads off MTV network. *Advertising Age, 4*, 36.

Ross, C., & McDowell, B. (1996, September 23). Seagram prepares barrage of TV ads. *Advertising Age, 1*, 60.

Ross, R. P., Campbell, T., Huston-Stein, A., & Wright, J. C. (1981). Nutritional misinformation of children: A developmental and experimental analysis of the effects of televised food commercials. *Journal of Applied Developmental Psychology, 1*, 329–347.

Ross, R. P., Campbell, T., Wright, J. C., Huston, A. C., Rice, M. L., & Turk, P. (1984). When celebrities talk, children listen: An experimental analysis of children's response to TV ads with celebrity endorsement. *Journal of Applied Developmental Psychology, 5*, 185–202.

Rossano, M. J., & Butter, E. J. (1987). Television advertising and children's attitudes towards proprietary medicine. *Psychology and Marketing, 4*, 213–224.

Rossiter, J. R., & Robertson, T. S. (1974). Children's TV commercials: Testing the defenses. *Journal of Communication, 24,* 137–144.

Rothschild, M. L. (1987). *Advertising: From fundamentals to strategy.* Lexington, MA: D. C. Heath.

Ryan, M. S. (1965, May). *Factors related to satisfaction with girls' blouses and slips: A comparison of mothers' and adolescent daughters' opinions.* New York: Cornell University, Agricultural Experiment Station Bulletin 1003.

Sanbonmatsu, D. M., & Fazio, R. H. (1991). Construct accessibility: Determinants, consequences, and implications for the media. In J. Bryant & D. Zillmann (Eds.), *Responding to the screen: Reception and reaction processes* (pp. 45–62). Hillsdale, NJ: Lawrence Erlbaum Associates.

Saunders, J. R., Samli, A. C., & Tozier, E. F. (1973). Congruence and conflict in buying decisions of mothers and daughters. *Journal of Retailing, 49,* 3–18.

Scammon, D. C., & Christopher, C. L. (1981). Nutrition education with children via television: A review. *Journal of Advertising, 10*(2), 26–36.

Schlesinger, P. (1995). *Europeanisation and the media: National identity and the public sphere. Arena* (Working paper No. 7).

Schleuder, J., Thorson, E., & Reeves, B. (1988, May). *Effects of time compression and complexity on attention to television commercials.* Paper presented at the International Communication Association annual conference, New Orleans.

Schneider, C. (1987). *Children's Television: The art, the business and how it works.* Chicago: NTC Business Books.

Schneider, K. C. (1979, Fall). Sex roles in television commercials: New dimensions for comparison. *Akron Business and Economic Review,* 20–24.

Schneider, W., & Pressley, M. (1997). *Memory development between two and twenty* (2nd ed.). Second edition. Mahwah, NJ: Lawrence Erlbaum Associates.

Schudson, M. (1986). *Advertising, the uneasy persuasion: Its dubious impact on American society.* New York: Basic Books.

Schumann, D., & Thorson, E. (1990). The influence of viewing context on commercial effectiveness: An intensity-affect response model. In J. H. Leigh & C. R. Martin (Eds.), *Current issues and research in advertising* (Vol. 12, pp. 1–24). Ann Arbor: Division of Research, Graduate School of Business Administration, University of Michigan.

Seiter, E. (1995). Different children, different dreams. In G. Dines & J. M. Humez (Eds.), *Gender, race and class in media.* Thousand Oaks, CA: Sage.

Selman, R. L. (1980). *The growth of interpersonal understanding.* New York: Academic Press.

Shannon, J. (2000). Reassuring an ad-cynical public. *Marketing Week,* August 28.

Sheikh, A. A., & Moleski, L. M. (1977). Conflict perception of the value of an advertised product. *Journal of Broadcasting, 21*(3), 347–354.

Shen, F., & Prinsen, T. (1999). Audience responses to TV commercials embedded in violent programmes. In M. S. Roberts (Ed.), *The proceedings of the 1999 Annual Conference of the American Academy of Advertising* (pp. 100–106). Gainesville: University of Florida.

Sherif, M., & Hovland, C. (1961). *Social Judgment: Assimilation and Contrast Effects in Communications and Attitude Change.* New Haven, CT: Yale University Press.

Shimp, T. A. (1981). Attitude toward the ad as a mediator of consumer brand choice. *Journal of Advertising, 10*, 9–15.

Siegal, M. (1997). *Knowing children. Experiments in conversation and cognition* (2nd ed.). Hove, East Sussex, UK: Psychology Press.

Siegler, R. S. (1998). *Children's thinking* (3rd ed.). Englewood Cliffs, NJ: Prentice-Hall.

Signorielli, N., & Lears, M. (1992). Children, television and conceptions about chores: Attitudes and behaviors. *Sex Roles, 27*(3/4), 157–170.

Singer, D. G., & Singer, J. L. (1981). Television and the developing imagination of the child. *Journal of Broadcasting, 25*(4), 373–387.

Singh, S. N., Churchill, G. A., & Hitchon, J. C. (1987). *The intensifying effects of exciting television programs on the reception of subsequent commercials* (unpublished working paper). Department of marketing, University of Kansas.

Smith, C. (2001). Talking to kids. *International Journal of Advertising and Marketing to Children, 3*(1), 57–69.

Smith, G. (1983). Advertising and children. In J. J. D. Bullmore & M. J. Waterson (Eds.), *The advertising association handbook*. London: Holt, Rinehart & Winston.

Smith, G., & Sweeney, E. (1984). *Children and television advertising: An overview*. London: Children's Research Unit.

Smith, P. K., Cowie, H., & Blades, M. (2003). *Understanding children's development* (4th ed.). Oxford: Blackwell.

Sparks, R. (1999). Youth awareness of tobacco sponsorship as a dimension of brand equity. *International Journal of Advertising and Marketing to Children, 1*(3), 193–218.

Srull, T. K., & Wyer, R. S., Jr. (1979). The role of category accessibility in the interpretation of information about persons: Some determinants and implications. *Journal of Personality and Social Psychology, 37*, 1660–1672.

Stephens, D. L., Hill, R. P., & Hanson, C. (1994). The beauty myth of female consumers: The controversial role of advertising. *Journal of Consumer Affairs, 28*, 137–153.

Stice, E., Schupak-Neuberg, E., Shaw, H. E., & Stein, R. (1994). Relation of media exposure to eating disorder symptomatology: An examination of mediating mechanisms. *Journal of Abnormal Psychology, 103*, 836–840.

Stoneman, Z., & Brody, G. H. (1982). The indirect impact of child-oriented advertisements on mother-child interactions. *Journal of Applied Developmental Psychology, 2*, 369–376.

Strasburger, V. C. (1995). *Adolescents and the media: Medical and psychological impact*. Thousands Oaks, CA: Sage.

Strasburger, V. C. (2001). Children, adolescents, drugs and the media. In D. G. Singer & J. L. Singer (Eds.), *Handbook of children and the media*. Thousand Oaks, CA: Sage.

Strasburger, V. C., & Wilson, B. J. (2002). *Children, adolescents and the media*. Thousand Oaks, CA: Sage.

Strauss, J., Doyle, A. E., & Kriepe, R. E. (1994). The paradoxical effect of diet commercials on reinhibition of dietary restraint. *Journal of Abnormal Psychology, 103*, 441–444.

Strickland, D. E. (1982). Alcohol advertising: Orientations and influence. *Journal of Advertising, 1*, 307–319.

Strong, M. (1999). What are today's children eating? *International Journal of Advertising and Marketing to Children, 1*(1), 73–81.

Stuart, E., Shimp, T., & Engle, R. (1987). Classical conditioning of consumer attitude: Four experiments in an advertising context. *Journal of Consumer Research, 14*(3), 334–349.

Stutts, M. A., & Hunnicutt, G. G. (1987). Can young children understand disclaimers in television commercials? *Journal of Advertising, 16*, 41–46.

Stutts, M. A., Vance, D., & Hudleson, S. (1981). Program-commercial separators in children's television. *Journal of Advertising, 10*, 16–25.

Summerfield, L. (1990). *Childhood obesity.* ERIC Digest, ED 328556.

Swain, G. (2002, December 29). Pester power. *The Sunday Times,* p. 16.

Sylvester, G. P., Achterberg, C., & Williams, J. (1995). Children's television and nutrition: Friends or foes. *Nutrition Today, 30*(1), 6–15.

Szymanski, M. (2002, Jan/March). Marketing toys by developmental stages. *International Journal of Advertising and Marketing to Children,* 25–32.

Teinowitz, I. (1997, January 20). Justice dept backs FDA, sees cig ad/kid linkage. *Advertising Age,* p. 39.

Thorson, E., Reeves, B., & Schleuder, J. (1985). Message complexity and attention to television. *Communication Research, 12*(4), 427–454.

Thorson, E., Reeves, B., & Schleuder, J. (1987). Local and global complexity and attention to television. In M. M. Mclaughlin (Ed.), *Communication Yearbook* (Vol. 10). Beverly Hills, CA: Sage.

Thomas, L. M., & Dillenbeck, M. S. (2002). Legal considerations for advertising to children. *International Journal of Advertising and Marketing to Children, 3*(4), 43–49.

Thomson, E. S., & Laing, A. W. (2003). "The Net Generation": Children and young people, the Internet and online shopping. *Journal of Marketing Management, 19*, 491–512.

Tide. (1995). Dress rehearsal for a press conference. *Tide, 28*(20), p. 31.

Tilley, N. M. (1985). *The R. J. Reynolds Tobacco Company.* Chapel Hill, NC: University of North Carolina Press.

Towler, R. (2003). *The public's view—2002.* London: Independent Television Commission.

Trawick-Smith, J. (1992). A descriptive study of persuasive preschool children: How they get others to do what they want. *Early Childhood Research Quarterly, 7*, 95–114.

Tufte, B. (1999). *Children and TV commercials.* Copenhagen: Royal Danish School of Educational Studies.

Van Evra, J. P. (1995). Advertising's impact on children as a function of viewing purpose. *Psychology & Marketing, 12*(5), 423–432.

van Raaij, W. F. (1990). The effect of marketing communication on the initiation of juvenile smoking. *International Journal of Advertising, 9*, 15–36.

Verhaeren, J. (1991). *Kinderen en Televisiereklame: Een Oondezoek naar de (wan)orde in Rehuleringen met betrekking tot Kinderen, Aanzet tot een bruikbaar Model voor Vlaaderen?* Brussels: Licentiaatsverhaneling, V. U. B.

Voorhoof, D. (1993). Restrictions on television advertising and article 10 of the European Convention on Human Rights. *International Journal of Advertising, 12*, 189–210.

Wadden, B. S., Brown, G., Foster, G. D., & Liowitz, J. R. (1991). Salience of weight-related worries in adolescent males and females. *International Journal of Eating Disorders, 10*(4), 407–414.

Wade, S. E. (1973). Interpersonal discussions: A critical predictor of leisure activity. *Journal of Communication, 23,* 426–445.

Ward, S. (1974). Consumer socialization. *Journal of Consumer Research, 1,* 1–16.

Ward, S. (1978, Nov/Dec). Compromise in commercials for children. *Harvard Business Review,* 167–175.

Ward, S., Popper, E., & Wackman, D. (1977). *Parent under pressure: Influences on mothers' responses to children's purchase requests.* Report No. 77–107. Cambridge, MA: Marketing Science Institute.

Ward, S., Reale, G., & Levinson, D. (1972). Children's perceptions, explanations and judgements of television advertising. In E. A. Rubinstein, G. A. Comstock, & J. P. Murray (Eds.), *Television and Social Behaviour* (Vol. 4). Washington, DC: US Government Printing Office.

Ward, S., Robertson, T. S., Klees, D., Takarada, K., & Young, B. (1984, December). *A cross-cultural analysis of children's commercial television viewing and product requesting behaviour.* Paper presented at American Psychological Association conference, Honolulu, Hawaii.

Ward, S., & Wackman, D. (1972). Television advertising and intra-family influence: Children's purchase influence attempts and parental yielding. *Journal of Marketing Research, 9,* 316–319.

Ward, S., & Wackman, D. (1973). Children's information processing of television advertising. In F. G. Kline and P. Clarke (Eds.), *New models for mass communication research.* Beverley Hills, CA: Sage.

Ward, S., Wackman, D., & Wartella, E. (1977). *How children learn to buy.* Beverly Hills, CA: Sage.

Wartella, E. (1982). Changing conceptual views of children's consumer information processing. In A. A. Mitchell (Ed.), *Advances in consumer research* (Vol. 9, pp. 144–146). Ann Arbor, MI: Association for Consumer Research.

Wartella, E., & Ettema, J. S. (1974). A cognitive developmental study of children's attention to television commercials. *Communication Research, 1,* 46–69.

Wartella, E., Wackman, D., Ward, S., Shamir, J., & Alexander, A. (1979). The young child as consumer. In E. Wartella (Ed.), *Children communicating: Media and development of thought, speech, understanding.* Beverly Hills, CA: Sage.

Weiss, D. M., & Sachs, J. (1991). Persuasive strategies used by pre-school children. *Discourse Processes, 14,* 55–72.

Welch, R. L., Huston-Stein, A., Wright, J. C., & Plehal, R. (1979). Subtle sex-role cues in children's commercials. *Journal of Communication, 29*(3), 202–209.

Weller, D. C. (2002). When is a brand not a brand? *International Journal of Advertising and Marketing to Children, 3*(3), 13–18.

Wiegman, O., Kuttschreuter, M., & Baarda, B. (1992). A longitudinal study of the effects of television viewing on aggressive and prosocial behaviours. *British Journal of Social Psychology, 31,* 147–164.

Williams, J. M., & Currie, C. (2000). Self-esteem and physical development in early adolescence: Pubertal timing and body image. *Journal of Early Adolescence, 20*(2), 129–149.

Wilson, B. J., & Weiss, A. J. (1992). Developmental differences in children's reactions to a toy advertisement linked to a toy-based cartoon. *Journal of Broadcasting & Electronic Media, 36,* 371–394.

Wiman, A. R. (1983). Parental influence and children's responses to television advertising. *Journal of Advertising, 12,* 12–18.

Wiman, A. R., & Newman, L. M. (1989). Television advertising exposure and children's nutritional awareness. *Journal of Academy of Marketing Science, 17*(2), 179–188.

Winick, C., Williamson, L. G., Chuzmir, S. F., & Winick, M. P. (1973). *Children's television commercials: A content analysis.* New York: Praeger.

Wolf, N. (1992). *The beauty myth: How images of beauty are used against women.* Garden City, NY: Anchor.

Wray, R. (2003, March 10). Thinking inside the box. *The Guardian,* New Media, p. 35.

Young, B. (1986). New approaches to old problems: the growth of advertising literacy. In S. Ward & R. Brown (Eds.), *Commercial television and European children* (pp. 67–83). Aldershot: Gower.

Young, B. (1990). *Children and television advertising.* Oxford, UK: Clarendon Press.

Young, B. (1998). *Emulation, fears and understanding: A review of recent research on children and television advertising.* An ITC Research Publication. London: Independent Television Commission.

Young, B. (2000). The child's understanding of promotional communication. *International Journal of Advertising and Marketing to Children, 2*(3), 191–203.

Young, B. (2003). Does food advertising make children obese? *International Journal of Advertising and Marketing to Children, 4*(3), 19–26.

Young, B., De Bruin, A., & Eagle, L. (2003). Attitudes of parents toward advertising to children in the U.K., Sweden, and New Zealand. *Journal of Marketing Management, 19,* 475–490.

Zuckerman, P., & Gianino, L. (1981). Measuring children's response to television advertising. In J. Esserman (Ed.), *Television advertising and children.* New York: Child Research Service.

Zuckerman, P., Ziegler, M. E., & Stevenson, H. W. (1978). Children's viewing of television and recognition memory for commercials. *Child Development, 49,* 96–104.

Author Index

Subject Index